Andrew Marriott was an army officer for over thirty years, seeing service in conflicts in Europe, the Middle East and West Africa. He received a commendation for devotion to duty as a platoon commander in Northern Ireland and was later awarded an MBE. He has since become an archaeologist and, after taking degrees at the University of York, in 2018, he was awarded a doctorate by Newcastle University.

He is married with two daughters and lives in North Yorkshire.

Dedicated to all those who, directly or indirectly, have been victims of Lariam 'friendly fire'.

Andrew Marriott

# IF YOU WAKE
# AT MIDNIGHT

The Lariam Wonder
Drug Scandal

AUSTIN MACAULEY PUBLISHERS™

LONDON • CAMBRIDGE • NEW YORK • SHARJAH

A CIP catalogue record for this title is available from the British Library.

ISBN 9781398454507 (Paperback)
ISBN 9781398454514 (Hardback)
ISBN 9781398454538 (ePub e-book)
ISBN 9781398454521 (Audiobook)

www.austinmacauley.com

First Published 2022
Austin Macauley Publishers Ltd®
1 Canada Square
Canary Wharf
London
E14 5AA

This endeavour could never have been accomplished without the courage and generosity of those people who have valiantly shared their stories for the greater good. I am hugely indebted to them all for the additional sacrifices they have made in offering their personal testimonies for this book.

Particular thanks are due to Dr Jane Quinn, Dr Remington Nevin and Bea Coldwell for reviewing the text and providing much-valued advice and encouragement throughout. And I must also express my gratitude to Dr Ashley Croft, Trixie Foster and David Rimmington for all their work in this field.

Above all, I have to acknowledge the support of family and friends who have come to understand the nature of Lariam injuries. Their patience and kind tolerance over many years has been inspirational.

Mad Larry! Psycho Tuesday! A horror movie in a pill!

---

'When you're wounded and left on Afghanistan's plains…
Jest roll to your rifle and blow out your brains
An' go to your Gawd like a soldier.'

–Rudyard Kipling, The Young British Soldier

# Preface

*11 March 2006, West Linton, the Scottish Borders*

"He told me he had had Lariam dreams during the night. He gave no warning and left no note." (Dr Jane Quinn)

That evening, Cameron Quinn, once a major in The Highlanders, left his wife Jane and two daughters, aged eight and five, to clear away after dinner. He went upstairs to the spare room. That is where Jane found him. He had hanged himself.

*23 November 2015, Somerset*

"Alastair has been let down by the country he served with honour, and he is not alone. I believe there are thousands suffering as he is." (Mrs Ellen Duncan)

Major General Alastair Duncan, CBE, DSO, having been sectioned for a year and a half in a secure psychiatric unit, died in Northampton General Hospital on 24 July 2016. His incarceration, stemming from mental injuries sustained during service, was caused or exacerbated by Lariam.

"Who do I speak to if I think I have taken Lariam? I am having terrible mood swings and panic attacks." (Facebook post by former soldier Chris Small)

On 29 November 2016 Chris committed suicide in his home. He had hanged himself.

These men had several things in common; they had loyally served their country in various conflict zones, and they had also been required to take the antimalarial Lariam as part of their military service. Lariam, also known by its generic name mefloquine hydrochloride, is an anti-malarial drug identified from a secret military drug development programme in the United States, which was subsequently introduced to global markets by the drug company Roche, without the normal safety trials required for pharmaceutical registration.

A third common denominator is that each soldier, and their next of kin, was abandoned by the Ministry of Defence in a shameful cover-up which attempted to hide the institutional negligence and malpractice exhibited by their use of this drug, malpractice that extended over almost two decades and affected many thousands of British soldiers. This sordid story of deceit, cover-up, obfuscation and avoidance has been repeated by military organisations all over the globe, and particularly those of the 'Five-Eyes' military alliance which includes Australia, Canada and the USA.

———

*5 March 2007, The Convention Center, Basel Trade Fair Complex, Switzerland*

"Science had advanced; more effective antimalarials with better side effect profiles were now available, and these were generally used." So said Chairman of the Board, Roche Holding Limited, Dr Franz B. Humer, in the minutes of the Roche Holding Limited AGM, in answer to the question:

*Why Lariam was still being prescribed even though other, less dangerous drugs existed that were just as effective or even more effective and comparable in cost, and whether the profits from the sale of Lariam justified the risks involved?*

———

Why did British government ministers and service chiefs fail to notice that science had advanced and that safer anti-malarials were available for those sent overseas into malarial zones of operation? How did a policy of enforcing one drug, Lariam, over its safer alternatives arise and why did this policy persist for so long? Why did senior military officers, surgeons general and government ministers perpetuate this situation and serially mislead Parliament, next of kin and the public about the safety of this neuro-toxic drug? And how many service personnel or veterans have ultimately succumbed to one of the many known side-effects of Lariam, that of suicide ideation, and completion?

This book cannot answer the last question, not least since the Ministry of Defence has stated that it has no means of collecting such data. The others, however, must be resolved. While reflecting on something of a personal journey, the following pages will attempt to expose this tale of international pharmaceutical and governmental collusion and present plausible theories for what is one of the greatest scandals inflicted on armed forces personnel and their families in modern times. It should make uncomfortable reading for many in Whitehall and beyond, whether they were implicated by negligence, incompetence, conflicts of interest, or all three.

# Chapter 1

## Taken on Trust

*There is no alternative. Lariam is the only drug that works against the sort of malaria we have in West Africa... The Surgeon General has conducted a risk assessment and it's Lariam, with a few harmless side-effects, or a deadly disease.*

*-Senior British Medical Officer, Sierra Leone, 2003*

Northern Ireland, 1978. It's the middle of the afternoon but the city-centre shoppers in Londonderry have all dispersed. I'm a $2^{nd}$ Lieutenant and have just crashed out with my platoon in response to another IRA killing. On the pavement, just outside a shop doorway, I'm looking down at a body: a local member of the security forces. There isn't much blood (it looks like a single shot to the head) and others on the scene have already determined that there is nothing we can do for him.

What I can and must do is to secure the area, prevent more loss of life and locate the abandoned firing point, evidentially a part of the crime scene. It's not my first military encounter with violence but one of the more immediate so far. I don't reflect on it, but I know there are things that duty and responsibility require of me. I issue some quick orders and we get to work. It wasn't so very long ago that I had been an officer cadet at the Royal Military Academy Sandhurst whose motto and cap badge extoled us to "Serve to Lead".

Much later, I was to discover how a drug would poison not just the people we were commanding but the very essence of military service and that most precious ethos of leadership.

———

Fast-forward to mid-November 2003 in Bishkek, the capital of Kyrgyzstan, one of the Central Asian republics that had recently formed part of the Soviet Union. After a year in the West African state of Sierra Leone, I had been posted to a branch of the Ministry of Defence at Shrivenham, in Wiltshire, where we developed the UK's approach to the conduct of military operations. My specialism was to be in Peace Support Operations; essentially all military activities short of full-scale war. Within days I had joined a small team who were to run a three-day symposium in Bishkek on peace intervention operations. Our delegates were drawn from former Soviet states, including Russia and Kazakhstan. We have checked into our hotel and I have a room on one of the upper floors.

The hotel was a typical Soviet-era structure. It was clean enough but suffused with those lingering musty smells that suggest only basic hygiene, while the tired décor and colour schemes might generously be described as retro. My room was reasonably lit, but either the power supply was dodgy or the bulbs had a low wattage. A narrow set of French windows opened onto a shallow balcony and I stepped out to view the late afternoon sky, a vivid deepening orange contrasting with the darkening outline of far-off mountain peaks. I had a presentation to finalise and was also due to meet my colleagues downstairs so I didn't want to linger.

Then it crept on me. It wasn't depression but as I assessed my height from the ground below, I made the calculation that death from the fall would be instantaneous. I had no desire to die but I seemed to be gripped by a sudden fascination with suicide. Why not do it? *Why not?* Oddly, my heart wasn't racing as I slowly came to terms with what I was considering and I cannot recall exactly how long this urge lasted; perhaps less than a minute.

I stepped back from the balcony, closed the windows and made a resolve to suppress any memory of that event. To have declared it to anyone would have cost me my career and it's simply not something you want to admit to your family. Of course, I now know the cause, and I can take some solace in understanding that the problem was not *me*.

Only a couple of weeks before, I had consumed the last of a course of almost fifty Lariam (mefloquine) pills. And while I was one of the luckier ones, it would take years to discover what had actually happened to me. Now almost twenty years on, our government continues to cover up a medical and military scandal. Sadly, it is not just denial; it is deceit.

———

The conical and steeply sloped Leicester Peak sits high above the urban sprawl of Freetown, the capital of Sierra Leone. It dominates the Freetown peninsula and the Atlantic coast rather like a West African Rock of Gibraltar. In 2003 it was still largely undeveloped and thickly forested, while around its lower slopes nestled villages retaining pre-independence names such as Gloucester and Regent, rather like some post-colonial Monopoly board, even if more Old Kent Road than Mayfair. Jumbles of houses of wood, stone, brick or mud, mostly with corrugated iron roofs, seemed to be locked in an eternal struggle, competing with the Peak's vegetation for ownership of the paths and drains which defined each community.

The crushing poverty of the city's slums seemed remote from these semi-rural outposts until closer inspection revealed endemic roadside begging alongside huddles of women and children engaged in breaking stones by hand, materials needed for the site of the planned new United States Embassy near the village of Leicester. Somehow things are never quite what they might seem.

Just a broken stone's throw from Leicester, the UK had located its International Military Advisory and Training Team (IMATT) headquarters, home to around 120 servicemen and women, mostly British, whose job was to assist the reconstruction of the Republic of Sierra Leone Armed Forces (RSLAF) which, like the rest of the country, had been ravaged by years of violence and civil war. Behind a high concrete wall and metal gates was Leicester Square, with its air-conditioned bungalows, offices, medical centre, club and swimming pool. A bit colonial?

Not really. Given the mammoth task facing the IMATT staff, as they each spent up to a year away from home in hazardous and demanding working environments, few should have begrudged them decent and secure living conditions, and especially the expectation that they would be provided with competent medical care. But as I have just said, things are never quite what they might seem.

In January 2003, four days after arriving in Sierra Leone, I set off from Leicester Square with three of the small team I had just taken over from Johnny Aisbitt from another infantry regiment, the Green Howards. In two white Defender Land Rovers, we turned left out of the base and, with Leicester Peak disappearing behind us, embarked on the hot, dusty and rough drive of 200 miles to Kenema in the Eastern Province. Kenema was to be my base for much of 2003 where I led a group of British, Canadian and American military advisers. We were mentoring a newly reconstructed RSLAF formation, 3 Brigade, which was now deployed along the eastern border with Liberia, itself now in the grip of a vicious civil war.

Sierra Leone's own civil war had formally ended a year earlier in January 2002. Up to 50,000 people had died during eleven years of violence and countless thousands injured, many suffering the brutal amputations regularly used by rebels to punish or intimidate men, women and even young children. Driving down from the Freetown peninsula we passed an open-air rehabilitation school where some of the maimed could learn to use handless arms and regain some basic life-supporting skills.

A little further on, brightly clad women were laundering clothes in the fast flowing river, the black rocks covered with a rainbow of fabrics all drying in the baking hot sun. But as a reminder that all was still far from stable, the array of military helicopters at Hastings Airfield gave a hint at the size of the ongoing United Nations mission, with large contingents scattered across the country.

Passing through Devil Hole and Waterloo, we enjoyed the respite of a tarmac surface before turning south and east past Masiaka towards Mile 91. We took advantage of a roadside trader to buy a few bananas while we had a break in the journey. It was safe enough to do so as the gangs that once roamed these areas had surrendered or dispersed after a Special Forces operation just over two years earlier. Rebels known as the Westside Boys had taken a number of British soldiers and their Sierra Leone liaison officer captive and submitted them to brutal and humiliating tortures in a remote village deep in the forest.

Operation Barras, conducted by the SAS and the Parachute Regiment, recovered the hostages from the village of Gberi Bana and destroyed the Westside Boys' encampments at Magbeni and Forodugu. At least twenty five rebels were killed with just one British fatality [1]. The psychological effect of that operation had extended far beyond Sierra Leone and I had personal reasons to be grateful for it.

In 2001, I had served as an unarmed UN observer in the Former Soviet Republic of Georgia. With colleagues from France, Jordan and Poland and a locally employed Georgian interpreter, I had to visit a remote mountain base in the abandoned coalmining settlement of Tkvarcheli in the breakaway region of Abkhazia. Inside the gloomy partial ruin that acted as his HQ, a bear-like, vodka-addled thug in command, aware that we were beyond radio contact and at the mercy of his company, threatened to take us hostage and hold us in the forest. While I couldn't predict how other nations might respond, it really did prove sobering for him to be reminded of the Westside Boys and that he should expect a similar fate from Britain if he carried through his threat. Thus his calculations changed, his temper ameliorated and his Makarov pistol remained holstered. Now, by some quirk of fate, in Sierra Leone we each carried a Makarov, as well as a Soviet Kalashnikov assault rifle.

During our break, the team talked a bit more about Kenema and the country beyond. The roads would be much worse, especially in the rainy season and I already knew that we would face a completely different security environment. In Leicester Square Johnny Aisbitt had explained just how fragile the situation was in the east. Armed incursions by Liberian factions were becoming regular and more violent.

Earlier in January, a cross-border raid on a remote village had routed the Sierra Leone company meant to defend it. Johnny had shown me how 3 Brigade was deployed, implausibly over an area of around 3,000 square miles. Its four battalions, of around 400 men each, were scattered in company or platoon groups along the border and in a few depth positions. It looked fine on a map. But what the military symbols didn't show was the logistical reality confronting the armed forces of one of the world's poorest nations. Delivery of pay and rations was erratic, as was the fuel required for the distressed fleet of vehicles (two trucks and two Land Rovers per battalion).

And while I was to encounter some outstanding soldiers, our units were constantly undermined by ill-discipline, not least from the former rebel combatants who had been incorporated into the new army. Better to have them under control and far from the capital, but the downside was to appear in the form of corruption, disobedience and even mutiny.

I took a short stroll into the forest. The dappled sunlight of the afternoon broke through the tree canopy and among the lush green was a fabulous display of tropical butterflies.

Returning to the others, I climbed into the Land Rover to drive the second leg, one of the team leaving something for a begging child with an old and blind leper.

We made Kenema at dusk. The drive was uneventful except for a sharp swerve to avoid an oncoming truck that, at some speed, had decided that a collision with us was preferable to hitting a family of ducks waddling across the rusty-red laterite road. The ducks scattered before us. One of the team said "Glad you missed them, Sir. They say it's bad juju to kill a duck!" It was a relief to be unloading the Land Rovers as the light failed. I'd driven a lot in Kenya and Uganda where, like Sierra Leone, darkness settles quickly and you simply cannot see what is on the road. Few of the trucks have functioning headlights and, because of their badly distorted chassis, they tend to crab along the road with the back end encroaching beyond the centre of the highway. If the indicators are working, and at the whim of the driver, they might be turned on so that you can avoid a collision. Equally dangerous will be the truck ahead of you showing no lights. Dirt, dust and the almost volcanic exhaust fumes will obscure any reflectors that might advertise the truck's rear.

Our team base was co-located with the Brigade HQ, quartered in the semi-derelict remains of an agricultural school next to an air strip on the edge of the town. Eight of us shared a small bungalow. An enclosure at the back surrounded with a bamboo fence gave the place the feeling of a stockade. Even if it wasn't that secure we did have some privacy for washing. There was a small generator but even when fuel was available it rarely worked. But with torches and hurricane lamps, we didn't really need much electricity. And as the generator pit seemed to be a favoured site for the local snakes it was best avoided in the dark.

It seems that the locals had been made aware that a new team leader had arrived and before I could take up formal occupancy of my room (a small cell of about five feet by eight at the end of the veranda) it was to be purged of evil spirits by a 'Bush Devil'. Adorned mostly in dried grass and wearing a wooden mask, his dance and incantations seemed to variously delight and alarm his spontaneously acquired audience of women and children. The welcome was appreciated but it also served as a salutary reminder that we were working in a culture deeply embedded in ancient traditional beliefs, not all of which were benign. The influence of witch doctors and native medicines was strong, Female Genital Mutilation was commonplace and many people, even in Freetown, adhered to beliefs in the powers of 'human baboons', men that at night could assume the form of these creatures and visit terror and death at random.

That night we had supper in our kitchen by torchlight. It had been prepared by our Canadian warrant officer who quickly became unwell and soon departed to throw up. Over dinner, and with the edge taken off my appetite, I got to know the other members of the team. We discussed plans for the next two days which were to be spent visiting brigade units to the north and having a first sight of the Liberian border. Our meal was then interrupted by a visit from the team cat, Zorro, a characteristically independent animal with a remarkably healthy black and white coat. Clenched in his jaws, he was proudly sporting the trophy of a rat which he deposited on the floor. At least there was some form of pest control. The team medic, a corporal from the Royal Army Medical Corps, donned a protective rubber glove and disposed of the corpse.

My diary notes for the next day say "Up at about 6.30 for shower. Didn't sleep well—mixture of Lariam [dreams] and noisy signallers." After breakfast I had a quick tour of the camp. As it was a Saturday things were fairly quiet and it didn't take too long to take in a general air of dilapidation and the very basic living conditions of the soldiers and their families. Improving housing, hygiene and regular access to clean water were high among our priorities. I also noted, a little beyond the living quarters and the Brigade HQ, a pair of newly constructed timber-framed buildings with plastic sheet walls and roofs. This was the brigade's Lassa fever hospital. I knew little of this illness although it is endemic in Sierra Leone, and Kenema was one of its hot spots. Apparently, local treatment regimens were both limited and rudimentary. I was soon to learn that the disease, which attacks organs such as the liver and kidneys, is passed to humans through food or household items contaminated with rat urine. It also, apparently, defies easy diagnosis as many of those infected do not display visible symptoms.

The rest of the weekend was to be spent visiting some of our forward positions and was fairly typical of the work that lay ahead. We usually deployed in two Land Rovers, each equipped with recovery tools and two spare wheels. After checking radios, rations and medical kit, and with the thickly forested Kumbui Hills to our left and the sun scorching the road, we headed north and then east towards the small town of Daru. There we checked out work on the reconstruction of a rifle range and a battle school due to become operational later in the year. We then pressed on northwards as I was keen to see some of our remote outposts, especially the position at the village of Manduvulahun which, as Johnny had said, had been routed by the recent Liberian raid. Even in the dry season, the drive would prove challenging for our Land Rovers. When the rains came, some parts were all but inaccessible.

The hills and thick tropical forests of the border region with Liberia are stunning, almost magical, but they also provide ideal cover for any hostile armed group. It was easy to see how the company defending Manduvulahun had been surprised when they were attacked by Liberian rebel insurgents known as 'Liberians United for Reconciliation and Democracy' (LURD). Engaged in a civil war against the then Liberian President, Charles Taylor, the LURD cross-border raids were essentially looting missions foraging for food or supplies from isolated border settlements. Even if surprised, our company should have been equal to the task they had been given. Or so I thought until I arrived at Manduvulahun.

The village was protected by about sixty men, some deployed forward in yet more isolated settlements still closer to the border which was both unmarked and entirely porous. Morale was not high and the RSLAF soldiers were concerned about rations and pay while their commander was worried about how long his company was to be deployed and an absence of medical supplies. The first machine-gunner I spoke to was clearly unwell, possibly suffering from malaria, and was also being troubled by an old shrapnel wound in his skull. Another was obviously suffering pain from a leg injury and it appeared that his kneecap was swimming loose under the skin. A third had significant swelling of his arm clearly caused by a poorly treated wound to his hand. We suspected septicaemia and made arrangements for the three to be evacuated for medical treatment. That night we made camp with our Sierra Leone colleagues. Again, my diary recorded disturbed sleep but I put much of that down to the intermittent gunfire in the forest just across the border.

Back in Kenema a few days later, I reviewed our mission tasks. We had a busy year ahead, working in a very fluid and unstable political environment. That, along with border incursions and, later, an influx of Liberian refugees and ex-combatants, meant that the physical security of the team was always my primary concern. The next priority was probably basic hygiene. Of course, we were all professionals but there was a risk of complacency and, for some of the team, this was their first experience of truly Third-World living conditions. Sundays in Kenema would include deep cleaning and disinfecting of our accommodation. And while we always had our vehicles overhauled when back in Freetown, Sunday mornings also allowed time to give the Land Rovers a regular field check. Driving-sense and vehicle maintenance were essential to mission success and safety. At that time, I had confidence in our medical support. It would be helpful to ascertain which snakes were venomous, but otherwise we had all been fully inoculated before deployment and we had our weekly Lariam anti-malarial tablets. But then, as if to reinforce my concerns about complacency, I received a rather disturbing report from Freetown.

Two of the team, a sergeant major and our medic, were in Leicester Square about to fly home for some leave. The IMATT Chief of Staff phoned me to say that the medic had contracted malaria. It was unlikely that he would ever be returning to us and in due course we would get a replacement.

How on earth had the medic got malaria? We immediately had a team meeting and it was then that I discovered that few were complying with the Lariam regime. The general consensus was that the risk of malaria was preferable to enduring the side-effects of Lariam, especially the dreams, irritability, memory lapses and effects on coordination. The pills were simply being thrown away.

Back in October 2002 I had been given sixty Lariam tablets to cover my tour in Sierra Leone. As I was then working in the MoD in Central London, my issue of the drug was being controlled by a doctor in St Thomas's Hospital. A practice nurse had telephoned me to explain that because I was to take Lariam a doctor had to advise me on the side effects. My medical notes record:

E: Requires protection malaria.

S: Detached to Sierra Leone for one year—date of departure 6 Jan 03.

Rx: Lariam Tablets 250 mg 1 weekly 60 tablets.

P: No contraindications to taking Lariam. Advised on use of medications and side effects.

I had never heard of Lariam (a synthetic quinoline anti-malarial) and the doctor told me that the antimalarials I had taken for earlier service in Pakistan and Africa were ineffective against the strain of malaria now prevalent in Sierra Leone. He said I should expect to encounter a range of side effects, especially disturbed sleep and vivid dreams, but these should only be transitory. However, about one in 25,000 users experienced serious psychotic reactions and, therefore, I should start taking the drug a couple of weeks before departure to ensure tolerability. Those odds seemed fine to me.

The advice that in the event of such a reaction I should stop taking the drug was noted, but it did strike me later that such a judgment might be beyond the capacity of someone suffering serious neuropsychiatric damage. I didn't lose my sanity; however, as predicted, I immediately experienced vivid and colourful dreams. But as another sufferer has said, any novelty from such psychotropic dreaming quickly wears off.

We had a great deal of work to do with 3 Brigade and Lariam was not an immediate concern. I trusted that the lesson of our medic's malaria had been learned. But no sooner had I made the point to the team that it was essential that we adhere to all anti-malarial defences, including the weekly Lariam regime, than I received a much more disturbing report. While on his leave flight back to England on a civilian airliner, the medic's condition had rapidly deteriorated.

Thankfully, a colleague travelling with him recognised that immediate hospitalisation was essential. That was a life-saving decision. The medic was not suffering from malaria; rather, he had contracted Lassa fever. For some time he remained seriously ill in the Royal Free Hospital's Department of Infectious and Tropical Diseases in London. [2] While, apparently against the odds, he made some recovery he could certainly not return to Sierra Leone. Indeed, it would be unlikely if he would ever be fit enough to remain in the army.

––––

Flag poles bearing the Union Flag and the flag of Sierra Leone stood as sentinels atop the small set of steps descending to the IMATT HQ in Leicester Square. A long, pristine whitewashed bungalow with a pale green corrugated iron roof, one end provided the offices of the brigadier commanding the IMATT and his staff. At the other end, beyond the armoury, was the medical centre. Thus it was that on my next visit to Freetown, having dealt with a range of operational matters, I called on the doctor.

My primary concern was for the team medic. The initial prognosis was far from encouraging. Furthermore, it seemed that the medical and operational chains of command in the UK were more concerned with the embarrassment of the import of a notifiable disease into Britain and the adverse publicity now attaching to the Ministry of Defence. Why hadn't Lassa fever been diagnosed in Freetown? And why, therefore, had the infected individual been allowed to travel on a civil airliner? Apparently, the desired course of action would have been to deploy a military aircraft to Sierra Leone with medical and isolation facilities on board.

Such issues, thankfully, were neither within my competence nor responsibility. But I did offer the observation that Lassa fever did seem tricky to diagnose locally and, more importantly, had there been such a delay in travel necessitated by rather bureaucratic medical and flight protocols, the patient would more likely have died. As I was to learn over the coming years, the problem too often isn't really the *problem.* Securing reputations and careers (and profits) will often out-trump the soldier's well-being.

In the pristine clinical environment of the medical centre I had a crash course in Lassa fever, was given a once-over, and the team were each given a thermometer in order that we could check our temperatures on a daily basis.

Second on my agenda was snakes. There is a general rule that if you are bitten by a snake that cannot be identified, and if it is safe to do so, you should kill it so that better informed medical action can follow. We would routinely chance upon snakes of various colours and sizes. A particularly close encounter in Kenema was at about eighteen inches when I disturbed one under the tap of our water bowser when filling my water bottle. In the heat of the day it seemed quite docile and may have been sleeping. I eased away and then watched its three foot and rather fat body slide away.

In the few moments it took to find my camera, it had disappeared over the dusty ground whose colour it seemed to match. Its dark markings, according to one of my Sierra Leonean officers, suggested it was a puff adder. I thought, therefore, it would be helpful to have a guide to the venomous snakes of West Africa. The medical centre couldn't help but suggested I might go into Freetown and try a bookshop or a library. In those days, we couldn't simply Google such questions. The bookshop/library option was as absurd as it was unhelpful.

And I also needed to have a proper discussion about Lariam. And that's when I was given the line that opens this chapter. Perhaps unusually, I did take the trouble to read the information leaflet contained in each packet of pills.[3] We all knew that Lariam could cause some very peculiar side-effects, but as the months passed it was quite clear that the prevalence and severity of the side-effects were far more common than suggested by the manufacturers, the Swiss pharmaceutical company, Roche. I was also concerned that, if we completed a full tour of duty, we were being required to take the drug in excess of the 12 month limit stipulated by the manufacturers.

I was rather patronisingly reminded that the strain of malaria in Sierra Leone was particularly dangerous and potentially deadly. Lariam, I was told, was the only effective anti-malarial drug for our theatre of operations. I had, at that time, no reason to doubt the doctor or that to think that the Surgeon General's 'risk assessment' was fatally flawed. Only when I returned home at the end of my tour did I learn from civilian medical practitioners that other, and safer, anti-malarials were freely available.

Thus it was that I was unwittingly drawn into a web of medical negligence founded upon the conceited arrogance of successive surgeon generals. Along with the rest of the field chain of command, I became complicit in the imposition of a toxic drug regime upon subordinates who looked to their leaders to keep them safe and well. We failed them. Tennyson said of the Charge of Light Brigade "Not though the soldier knew someone had blundered" and most of us know how the poem proceeds. In due course I did "reason why" but in the stiff resistance of the cannons of service chiefs, the surgeon general and ministers.

And I never did get an answer about the snakes.

# Chapter 2
## Of Mice and Men

*As a result of its toxic effects, the drug is quickly becoming the "Agent Orange" of this generation, linked to a growing list of lasting neurological and psychiatric problems including suicide...Public Health England has a responsibility to protect the travelling public from the threat posed by dangerous medicines, and should carefully reconsider its recommendations in light of mefloquine's neurotoxicity and its association with risk of permanent neurological injury and death... Mefloquine toxicity is also a potentially life-threatening condition that is fully preventable by use of safer daily antimalarials.*

*-Dr Remington Nevin, epidemiologist and expert consultant in the adverse effects of antimalarial drugs,*
*The Independent, 27 Sep 2013*

After returning from West Africa, I suspected there was something quite wrong with me but the complacent advice continued to be that things would clear up over time. After all, don't all drugs have side-effects? That mantra turned out to be a very handy trope conveniently deployed later by ministers trying to bury an inconvenient truth; but at that time I remained unaware of the implications of their duplicity. Side-effects should, eventually, pass, and even if they don't, were those less tangible or measurable reactions, like Lariam dreams, really such a big deal? This seemed to be a question that no one was willing to answer, or even address, when I was first trying to manage my increasingly volatile nightly imaging.

In an interview recorded in 2015 for the BBC Radio 4 documentary *The Lariam Legacy*[1], the presenter, Victoria Derbyshire, with all due sensitivity, posed the question that Lariam dreams were, after all, just dreams. She was, of course, both correct and playing a journalistic devil's advocate. However, unlike normal dreams or nightmares, their impact was unlike anything I had ever experienced. Dreams should not instil senses of unease and negativity that can pervade throughout the following day while wrecking every night. Unfortunately, Lariam dreams were but a part of the toxic mix I was struggling to manage while serving in Sierra Leone. (We'll be looking more closely at Lariam dreams in the next chapter.)

On 15 April 2003, I was driving home from Gatwick Airport for a spell of leave from Sierra Leone. The crowded overnight Monarch Airlines flight from Freetown had eventually taken off at 9.30 pm. With a short stop at Banjul in The Gambia, and regular in-flight passport checks and little sleep, we landed at 6.45 am. I set off for Yorkshire in a hire car and, a few hours into the journey, pulled over for a break at the M1 motorway services at Trowell in Nottinghamshire. Then, after a short sleep in the car—no dreams—I awoke with absolutely no idea who or where I was, or what I was doing in that totally unfamiliar car. It's hard to say how long that total loss of recall lasted, perhaps less than a minute—I simply don't know.

Sixty seconds may not seem that long but try timing it and imagining a complete erasure of cognitive function. It was a profoundly disturbing, almost frightening, experience. But I was lucky; it passed. For others, such Lariam-wiping of the memory card would be the portal to a living nightmare. (A particularly striking account can be found in David Stuart MacLean's autobiographical account of Lariam toxicity[2]) At the time, I didn't make the connection with the drug and was blissfully unaware that I was in the vortex of a sordid tale of pharmaceutical subterfuge, involving commercial gain and deceit.

But later in the year, as other side effects induced outbursts of anger I had never previously experienced and began to scare my family and friends, it was clear that Lariam was the problem. So where had this drug come from and why should such a widely used medication now be described as a pharmaceutical "Agent Orange"?

———

Malaria is caused by a parasite called *Plasmodium,* a unicellular organism that can infect a variety of vertebrate hosts, including humans. It is neither a virus nor a bacterium. The parasite uses an intermediate host organism to complete part of its life cycle, the most commonly known being the malaria-carrying *Anopheles* mosquito. There are several forms of the malaria parasite, the most common being *Plasmodium falciparum*, *Plasmodium vivax*, *Plasmodium ovale*, *Plasmodium malariae*, and *Plasmodium knowlesi*[3,4] According to the World Health Organisation, in 2018 there were 228 million cases of malaria globally and around

400,000 deaths. *Plasmodium falciparum* is by far the most prominent form in Africa and prevalent also in South-East Asia and the Western Pacific region. *Plasmodium vivax* is also present in South-East Asia and is the predominant malaria parasite in the Americas.[5]

Transmission of the malaria parasite via the bite of a female mosquito is the initiating factor for malaria infection in humans. Once in the bloodstream, the parasite moves to the liver and undergoes the first portion of its life cycle—called the exo-erythrocytic cycle. During this stage the malaria parasite infects the liver's cells, replicates, and eventually bursts the liver cell to release a multitude of immature trophozoites, or ring-stage parasites (so called by their characteristic 'ring-like' appearance when viewed down the microscope) into the blood stream. It is during this next stage, the erythrocytic cycle, that the host develops the characteristic symptoms of malaria as the parasite continues to invade blood cells, replicate and rupture them, causing a breakdown of the host's immune system and release of gametocytes (the mature reproductive phase of the parasite's life cycle) into the blood stream.[6]

The blood-borne stage of the parasite life cycle induces the distinctive feverish symptoms of malaria, resulting in severe chills and sweating, headaches, muscle pain, weakness, vomiting and diarrhoea. In very severe cases this can lead to death in less than 24 hours, or if infection crosses the blood-brain barrier, then cerebral malaria can ensue—the primary killer of children under 5 years who contract malaria in endemic regions. In addition to the fever, the rupture of red blood cells can cause severe anaemia, while cerebral malaria can lead to seizures, brain damage and coma.[7,8] There is no doubt that this is a serious and life threatening disease, particularly in countries where access to healthcare is limited.

Digressing slightly, I believe I may have experienced malaria myself, although one of the less dangerous forms. I say 'may' because the event was almost entirely self-diagnosed. It was during my United Nations service in Georgia in 2001. Georgia is a very low-risk area for malaria and antimalarials are not considered necessary in that region. During a particularly intense period of insurgent, partisan and criminal activity, as well as cross-border incursions, in which many locals lost their lives, for about three days I had hourly turns of fever, followed by a deep chill and then a severe headache, although I cannot recall the exact sequencing. The working conditions were, thankfully, nothing like those experienced by the British Army in the monsoons of the Burmese jungle in the Second World War and I was able to work through it.

Whatever I had certainly seemed inconsequential when compared to the death and destruction we were trying to prevent. I was 'self-diagnosed' because our German military doctor was one of the bodies we needed to recover and repatriate after one of our helicopters was downed by a hand-held antiaircraft missile. We lost nine friends and colleagues that day, including Dieter, the first German soldier to die in a combat zone since 1945. Carrying or handling corpses is unpleasant, but sadly not uncommon, work for the armed forces; furthermore, at close quarters, the stench of Georgian bodies in fairly advanced states of decay seemed to linger much longer than any of the symptoms of my malaria, or whatever else it may have been.

There is no doubt that finding preventative treatments, or prophylactics, as well as drugs that could kill the malaria parasite during active disease, has long been a medical imperative. Malaria's history can even be traced to ancient Hindu and Chinese scripts. In the military context, the disease may have caused, or at least contributed to, the death of Alexander the Great; his final campaigns in Mesopotamia certainly took him to areas where malaria was endemic.[9] But it was the 17th-century Spanish conquistadors and Jesuit missionaries in South America who appear to have first noted a natural curative effect that could be derived from the bark of a local tree, the quina-quina.

Legends vary, but the Countess of Chinchon is generally credited with bringing quinine to Europe in 1638. While in Peru, she had contracted a fever and, adopting a South American Indian practice, consumed quina-quina bark and recovered. She returned to Spain with samples of the bark (from which quinine is derived) and the tree was later named Chinchoa in her honour by the 18th-century Swedish botanist Carl Linnaeus. During the 19th century, purified quinine was to become the primary therapy for malaria, providing recovery for up to 98 percent of those treated.[10]

During the First World War, military planners became increasingly concerned about the impact of malaria on operations. It was heavily compromising operational success in a number of different global theatres. In the German East Africa campaign, malaria infections had a massive effect, with hospitals totally overwhelmed. With multiple single admissions, cases mainly of malaria and dysentery accounted for a staggering 240 percent of the force, while wounds represented only about three percent.[11] For the British, the problem was especially acute in Macedonia (Northern Greece and Southern Bulgaria) and the Middle East. According to the Ministry of Defence, from the front in Macedonia alone, malaria caused the evacuation of 146,000 personnel.[12] Malaria was becoming a major military problem that all governments were keen to solve.

The truly global nature of the Second World War again demonstrated the catastrophic damage malaria could have on warfighting potential, notably in Africa, but especially in the South East Asia and Pacific theatres. Up to one third of the American force attempting to defend the Philippines from the Japanese invasion of 1942 succumbed to malaria. It is believed that the rate of infection in the Pacific went on to reach 4,000 per 1,000 US soldiers in one year.[13,14] General Douglas MacArthur, the Supreme Commander Southwest Pacific, was so concerned that he noted:

*This will be a long war if for every division I have facing the enemy, I must count on a second division in the hospital with malaria and a third division convalescing from this debilitating disease!*

The situation was equally dire for the British in Burma where the annual rate for malaria across the 14th Army reached eighty-four percent, and was even higher in some of the frontline units.[15] If the war was to be won, it was now vital that effective counter-measures be developed and embraced as an essential component of military capability.

Before the Second World War, quinine continued to be widely used to combat malaria. It was both effective and thought to be well-tolerated, having only what were considered to be a few mild side-effects. The Dutch East Indies had, meanwhile, become the main source of supply of quinine. Java chinchona bark was more fruitful than South American, making quinine essentially an Amsterdam-based and controlled product. Supplies to Britain were thus lost when the Nazis invaded Holland in 1940. The subsequent fall of Java and the other Dutch colonies to the Japanese in 1942 finally ended any other Allied access to quinine.[16]

The use of mosquito nets and other bite prevention measures, and even the extensive use of insecticides such as DDT, could only do so much, and the loss of quinine was arguably as strategically damaging for the Allies as was the denial of oilfields to the Germans. And as the Germans were forced to develop synthetic fuels, so a similar American programme would produce chemically-based anti-malarial drugs. With its industrial might and a formidable chemical industry, the United States was quickly able to find a solution. It was a drug called quinacrine that had, ironically, originally been developed by the Germans. Billions of doses were produced and supplied to troops under the trade name of 'Atabrine'.

Also known as mepacrine, Atabrine did not come without a cost. The calculus of war and the imperative of defeating the Japanese would have demanded many risks in physical combat. And such risk-taking would have extended to weapons development and the logistic supply chains. Similarly, in the medical services, Atabrine use was to demand a payoff between force protection and collateral damage to some of the soldiers it was meant to shield. While it certainly proved to be a highly effective prophylaxis in the fight against malaria, Atabrine quickly began to signal some very disturbing side-effects. As well as arguably tolerable instances of nausea and diarrhoea, there were increasing reports of neurological and psychiatric damage ranging from nightmares to psychosis. [17,18,19]

Interestingly, quinacrine was marketed in the US without ever having undergone US Food and Drugs Administration (FDA) approval, until 2016 when it was finally abandoned due to its extensive adverse event profile. In its review meeting in March 2016, the FDA Pharmacy Compounding Advisory Committee noted that "Quinacrine has been supplanted by more efficacious and less toxic drugs and is no longer used to treat this condition."

It has now been feasibly suggested that the soldier famously slapped for cowardice by General Patton in Sicily in 1943, and immortalised in Franklin Schaffner's 1970 biopic starring George C Scott, may have been suffering from the effects of Atabrine toxicity. Patton actually slapped two soldiers that day and it is clear that they were in hospital recovering from malaria.[20]

Malaria was seriously degrading Allied operations in Sicily and, while the island was secured within two months, US hospital admissions for malaria (21,482) exceeded battle casualties (17,375). Atabrine, which was ordered to be taken in suppressive doses by all troops, was issued with the soldiers' rations. Dosing regimens were varied, but by 1944 had settled on daily consumption in all Italian malarial areas.[21,22]

Equally plausible are claims of the nearly lethal effect Atabrine had on one of Britain's outstanding wartime leaders, General Orde Wingate. Wingate (who was decorated with the Distinguished Service Order and two bars) took Atabrine during his service in East Africa. Shortly afterwards he attempted suicide by stabbing himself in the neck. He would almost certainly have died had he not been quickly discovered by another officer and hospitalised.[23,24,25] Later, when leading the Long Range Penetration Groups (better known as the Chindits) deep into the Burmese jungle, Wingate was renowned for both his personal courage and his unconventional and erratic behaviour.[26]

Shortly before his death in a plane crash in March 1944, both the Chief of the Imperial General Staff, General Sir Alan Brooke, and his commander in Burma, General William Slim, recorded their concerns about Wingate's mental state. Brooke said, "It looks as if the strain of operations had sent Wingate off his head."[27,28] One might now suspect that he was, in fact, suffering from Atabrine toxicity.

Atabrine doubtless made a major, and perhaps even decisive, contribution to the defeat of the Japanese. But its use involved poorly informed regimes of enforced compliance along with a lack of willingness to properly assess the associated risks and the damage it was causing.[29] British officers thought not be rigorously enforcing consumption of Atabrine were summarily removed from command. This was the historical embryo of an unfortunate and enduring medico-military culture that was to become, in many ways, as invidious and pernicious as the disease it was meant to control.

Shortly after the Second World War, a different drug, chloroquine, was adopted as the next generation anti-malaria medication.[30] Chloroquine's genesis was, however, pre-war. German scientists hunting for more efficacious antimalarials synthesised the 4-aminoquinoline antimalarial compound chloroquine in 1934. It appeared to be equally effective as Atabrine and was adopted worldwide, both as a prophylactic and as a treatment for malaria infection. Importantly, it was considered to be a safer alternative to Atabrine, lacking the severe neurotoxic side-effect profile of Atabrine but not without a risk of psychosis and seizures. And, as time passed, it became apparent that chloroquine also possessed a significant cardiac side-effect profile now appearing relatively frequently in patients given high doses for malaria treatment.

Unfortunately, as we have now seen with the widespread use of antibiotics, unregulated or profligate use of a drug can lead to problems with drug resistance in the organism it is being used to treat. By 1961 the most deadly form of the malaria parasite, *Plasmodium falciparum*, had become resistant to chloroquine and this was soon to become highly problematic for the American Army in the Vietnam War. With tens of thousands of servicemen afflicted, rates of malaria infection were becoming unsustainable and a serious risk to operational success. As in the Second World War, conflict was once more the engine for medical research.[31]

———

The United States Walter Reed Army Institute for Research (WRAIR)[32] is located in Silver Spring, Maryland, just within the Washington DC Beltway. With a history dating back to the late-19th century, it is now a modern, multi-storey biomedical research organisation, administered by the American Department of Defense. Named after Major Walter Reed, an army physician who advanced the field of infectious diseases research at the beginning of the 20th century with his work on another mosquito-borne disease, yellow fever, WRAIR has expanded to encompass a global reach, with affiliates in West and East Africa and across South East Asia. Silver Spring is also home to the FDA, responsible, in America, for assuring the safety, effectiveness and quality of drugs, vaccines and other biological products.

Revolutionary in its inception and tracing its origins back to 1848, the FDA was created in 1906 to regulate the registration of pharmaceutical products in the USA. The FDA's regulatory role in managing drug registrations came to the fore after the international disaster of thalidomide in the 1960's. The United States avoided a generation of children being born without limbs or with dramatically shortened appendages by recognising the toxic effects of this drug before any other country, and putting in place a regulatory body to prevent such a disaster ever happening on its shores.[33] Despite this exalted history, the FDA is now criticised as something of a 'tick-box' organisation for the global pharmaceutical industry, with FDA approval essentially giving a global seal of approval for any drug that has sufficient industry backing to pass its somewhat depleted process of scrutiny.[34]

Within the WRAIR is the Center for Infectious Disease Research (CIDR), concentrating on diseases of military importance such as malaria and dengue fever. According to the WRAIR website, the CIDR works at the interface of scientific specialisms and product development. A key role is to meet the challenges that infectious diseases pose to American national security. Their scientists monitor the rates and development of viruses and bacteria across the globe and

42

use that intelligence to inform deployed commanders of the threats posed to their personnel. Data collected on infectious disease outbreaks are then also used to inform product research and development programmes.

Hardly surprising is the enduring interest WRAIR has in malaria which it sees as one of the most serious of the various infectious diseases encountered by American armed forces serving overseas. It has been estimated that currently the annual cost to US defence from malaria-enforced medical evacuation and treatment could be over US$ 4 million, while lost working hours could be as high as 21,000 per year. This is despite an advanced range of countermeasures including insect repellents, impregnated uniforms and the use of chemo-prophylactic drugs. The persistent rate of malaria infections is believed to be due to three factors; regional drug resistance, poor adherence to personal protection measures and a lack of adherence to drug regimes. Thus, the WRAIR believes that:

*A safe, durable and efficacious malaria preventive will eliminate the burden of compliance and the associated side effects of daily or weekly chemoprophylaxis, (and) overcome regional drug resistance to currently available antimalarials... Protection against malaria infection improves unit readiness and mission success.*

And so, drawing on their corporate experience and earlier research into malaria vaccines, their mission now is "to develop new vaccines and biologics in collaboration with global and US government partners to reliably prevent malaria infection in military personnel." A noble cause.

An important second arm of the WRAIR is the Center for Military Psychiatry and Neuroscience (CMPN). The CMPN focuses its activities on the protection of the brain health of the fighting force before, during and after operational deployment. The work of CMPN scientists takes them into training systems aimed at improving psychological resilience and performance. They also explore sleep hygiene and its relationship to performance. Blast and direct trauma to the brain is another major area of investigation where, for example, the CMPN claims to have contributed to the identification of blood biomarkers for the diagnosis of concussion.

Ostensibly, and probably in many cases actually, these objectives and research themes are driven by laudable aims. There are, however, a number of potentially dangerous tensions that will arise both ethically and commercially when defence institutions appear to take the lead in medical research, especially when the driving imperative is a nation's warfighting capability. Is the real enemy the disease or is it an opposing state, or what now is often referred to as a non-state actor (read terrorist or a 'so-called state')?

The lesson from the war against Japan in the Pacific is surely that we must not be seduced into unacceptable or even unknown levels of human collateral as the therapeutic payoff for military effectiveness. So what controls are in place to ensure that trials, experimentation, and the development of pharmaceutical products in particular, meet ethical, moral and internationally respected standards?

More formalised in their structure since 2018, WRAIR has long conducted what are known as Phase I and Phase II clinical trials. These are internationally recognised tools applied by research institutions across the globe to provide the necessary clinical data for drug registration. Phase I trials focus on a drug's safety and, in a modern clinical study, would generally be limited to a small group of up to 15 people. Phase II trials will further examine a drug's safety but also extend to the efficacy of the drug; in other words, does it actually work? These Phase I and II trials would, of course, be preceded by a great deal of preclinical and other experimentation, and this could include testing a chemical compound in laboratory animals. Unsurprisingly, mice have been used in the early trials of many drugs, and experiments exposing mice to mefloquine were important in its development.[35] Such activities are, of course, not unique to WRAIR and may be found in respected research laboratories across the world, including some in the United Kingdom. However, the mid-20th century WRAIR drug development programmes, and their scale, were remarkable for their time, and if matched anywhere, we would probably need to look behind the Iron Curtain.

After efficacy and safety have been established through Phase I and II trials, a drug should progress to Phase III testing. This is the final phase of testing prior to submission of all trial documentation to a regulatory body, such as the FDA, for drug registration for human use. Phase III trials usually consist of a double-blinded, placebo-controlled trial and, depending on the drug and the disease, will constitute a population of hundreds, or perhaps thousands of patients. 'Double-blinded' means that neither the patient receiving the drug nor the administering clinician knows which compound the patient has been given; 'placebo-controlled' means that one group will receive the active compound and the other will

45

receive something that looks like the drug but contains no active ingredient.

In the case of infectious diseases such as malaria, the outcome should be that the active drug will prevent or cure the patient whilst the placebo will not. Frequently, these gold standard Phase III trials measure success in terms of fewer deaths, reduced severity of disease or accelerated recovery times in the treatment group, with no such gains in the placebo group. A Phase III trial will also monitor the rates and severity of adverse events, the technical term for a bad reaction to the drug in question. Adverse events may be anticipated but should not exceed acceptable limits. A drug can fail the threshold for registration at this point by simply being too dangerous for people to take, even if they are sick, and this is an entirely possible outcome.

Perhaps entirely legitimately, WRAIR currently actively recruits healthy human volunteers to take part in its studies. It is to be hoped that such trials are both necessary and would conform to proper, internationally recognised ethical standards and protocols. But the history of American research into anti-malarial drugs suggests a much darker and sinister story.

We know that from the early 1960s WRAIR was receiving huge US federal resources in order to fund its antimalarial drug programme. Driven largely by the imperatives of the Vietnam War, it seems that the Institute examined over a quarter of a million candidate compounds. Allocated the experimental number WR 142 490, one particular compound (later to be known as mefloquine or Lariam) became what has since been described as one of the main progeny of the WRAIR malaria investigation programme.[36] Perhaps both surprising and disturbing, the first reported trials of mefloquine were conducted on prison inmates. These were performed at the Illinois Stateville Correctional Center and at the Maryland House of Correction, Jessup, and reported in 1975 and 1976, respectively.

Academic, and especially medico/scientific, research should be governed by strict ethical protocols. I am acutely aware of these requirements from my own recent doctoral research involving engagement with some elderly and vulnerable people. It is essential to construct robust frameworks within the research programme that will protect patients and volunteers enrolled in clinical trials. Since 1964 these have been enshrined in the Helsinki Declaration codifying the ethical principles for medical research involving human subjects.[37] The peer-reviewed papers describing the Illinois and Jessup penitentiary experiments are not particularly forthcoming regarding the informed consent of the convict volunteers although they do confirm some ethical oversight by the Human Investigation Committee at Rush University, Chicago, and an independent University of Maryland committee.[38,39]

Stateville Correctional Center had been complicit in this ethically questionable research since the 1940s when it supported American wartime studies into antimalarial drugs. The formalised nature of the arrangement between the prison system and a body of scientists from the University of Chicago seems to be confirmed by the existence of what a 1975 report describes as the "Laboratory for Tropical Diseases at the Stateville Correctional Center, Joliet, Illinois."[40] Who needed mice when the state penitentiaries were apparently full of willing men apparently keen to volunteer, and thus able to atone for their crimes by doing their bit for the war effort? It appears that Stateville eventually provided around 4,000 participants, with various studies involving batches of tens or even hundreds of men.

Astutely noted by Bernard E Harcourt[a] in 2011, for the researchers, the inmates "were as close to lab animals—to caged lab animals—as one could possibly hope" and where the so-called volunteers were being infected with the most virulent forms of malaria. Given the nature of what was going on, it can hardly have been surprising that the Stateville experiments were cited at the Nuremberg Trials by defence lawyers for Nazi doctors implicated in German experiments on prisoners of war and captives in concentration camps.[41] Stateville geese and Dachau ganders.

Prison-based experimental practices raise serious moral questions, beyond the obvious difficulties of either informed consent or coercion. Stateville remains a maximum security prison and in the 1940s it housed some of America's most notorious killers, one of whom, Nathan Leopold, would both take part in and help to administer the experiments. Leopold, and other murderers and rapists, would then even use their involvement in the trials as a form of moral capital in later pleas for sentence reduction or parole.[42]

Eventually, according to the New York Times (28 April 1974), the various American university ethics committees could no longer convince Allyn R Sielaff, the director of the Illinois Department of Corrections. Condemning such experiments on prisoners as both immoral and unethical,

---

[a] Julius Kreeger Professor of Law, and Professor and Chair of the Department of Political Science, The University of Chicago.

Sielaff ordered the end of Statesville's involvement in the programme. The Jessop penitentiary, described as notoriously dangerous, was vacated in 2007. Its subsequent demolition involved the use of labour from other prisons whose inmates had, allegedly, been certified in asbestos removal.[43]

Although probably first synthesised by 1969, WR 142 490 (or mefloquine) would not be available as an antimalarial drug before the Vietnam War had ended. The drug clearly remained of strategic importance to the US Department of Defense, but there still remained a major barrier confronting production and marketing. There were Congressional rules which prevented the US military from operating in the commercial sector. Thus it seems that a deal was made between the US government, WRAIR and the multinational pharmaceutical company, F. Hoffmann La-Roche (now Roche) which allowed the drug giant to manufacture and sell the drug. The details of the arrangement have never been made public but it seems likely that the company was given free access to WRAIR's trial data.[44]

This presumably represented a massive saving for F. Hoffmann La-Roche in terms of research and development costs. Mefloquine acquired the brand name of Lariam and was approved for use by the US FDA in 1989.[45] It may be no coincidence that in 1984 the US Army Medical Material Development Activity (USAMMDA) was established. Its role is to develop new drugs and vaccines. The process, according to the USAMMDA website, "takes promising technology from DOD, industry, and academia to US Forces, from the testing required for US Food and Drug Administration (FDA) approval or licensing, to fielding and sustainment of the finished product." They also invite unsolicited private proposals for medical products with the intention that the US Government may enter into a contract for research and development.[46]

On 5 October 1989 a product licence for Lariam was also granted in the United Kingdom.[47]

It may seem extraordinary, but in both the USA and the UK, the drug had now been licenced, and was being sold to the public, having evaded essential elements of blinded or randomised Phase III studies which should have involved a group of healthy civilian volunteers. In fact, the first of such randomised controlled trials, using generally travellers, was not reported until 2001; that is some 12 years after the drug had been licenced.[48,49] And that was only after there had been growing reports about Lariam's ominous and damaging psychiatric side-effect profile among populations of both military and civilian users. Even shortly after its marketing, Lariam was causing serious unease, concerns that would eventually be borne out as the drug's neurotoxicity took hold on so many unfortunate and un-warned consumers.

Equally disturbing is the apparent absence of what are known as longitudinal studies of all the human guinea pigs subjected to the prison trials. A longitudinal study would have involved follow-on observations of all of those participants and could quite reasonably be expected to have alerted the researchers to the true nature and scale of Lariam's side effects. Unfortunately, however, yet another problem arises from the use of these inmates for the study of potentially neurotoxic drugs in advance of their exposure to the general public. Criminals such as Nathan Leopold should not be considered as healthy volunteers. We need a closer look at both Stateville and its convicts.

Stateville was opened in 1925 as a maximum security prison for males. It can accommodate over 3,000 inmates and has housed some of America's most notorious and violent offenders. It was also a site for executions, first through the use of the electric chair and later by lethal injection. In 1998 the Illinois death row moved to the Tamms Correctional Center.[50]

Of particular historical and social interest is that Stateville was designed to incorporate a specific controlling strategy for some of its inmates known as the panopticon. The panopticon was a prison structure developed by the social reformer Jeremy Bentham in which prisoners would be housed in cells in an outer wall, observed by a guard in a central observation tower. Key to the concept was that the prisoners would never know when they were being observed. The perceived omnipresence of the gaoler's gaze would impose a regime of self-imposed compliance.

As described by the French philosopher Michel Foucault, it was 'a functional mechanism that must improve the exercise of power by making it lighter, more rapid, more effective, a design of subtle coercion'. Panopticism in other guises has been seen as a tool in the structures of power and manipulation across other state institutions.[51] Specifically, Stateville's panopticon was its 'F-House', with a central armed tower surrounded by multi-storey cells. The F-House was closed in 2016 but retained because of its historical significance. In England it might have become a listed building. In 2020 it was, according to press reports, reactivated in order to isolate Stateville prisoners suspected to be infected with Covid-19 .[52]

Nathan Leopold was convicted in 1924 at the age of nineteen, along with his close friend, Richard Loeb, who may also have been his lover. Highly intelligent, studying law and from a privileged background, Leopold and his accomplice kidnapped and murdered a 14-year old boy, apparently stimulated by self-gratification and an attempt to commit a perfect crime. They were each sentenced to life for murder and ninety-nine years for kidnapping. Loeb himself was murdered in Stateville in 1936, in a razor attack allegedly prompted by sadistic sexual advances he had made towards another inmate.[53,54]

Narcissistic, a fantasist and probably highly manipulative, Leopold was employed in the prison hospital X-ray lab before being recruited to the Chicago University malaria trials. In an astonishing series of ethical and research compromises, Leopold and others acted as study technicians and secretaries, as well as gatekeepers exercising power over other prisoners' participation in the project. Prisoners such as Leopold were permitted to experiment on other prisoners and sometimes even on themselves.[55] To put it mildly, as Nathaniel Comfort says, "such participation demonstrates a remarkable blurring of the line between researcher and research subject, between investigator and captive."[b]

The academic research staff appear to have been seduced into a working environment of co-dependency. Flattered, and

---

[b] For a more detailed examination of these activities see the papers Nathaniel Comfort (2009) The prisoner as model organism: malaria research at Stateville Penitentiary; and Bernard E Harcourt (2011) Making Willing Bodies: The University of Chicago Malaria Experiments on Prisoners at Stateville Penitentiary.

to some measure even controlled, by Leopold and his peers, the relationship seems to bear comparison with the hostage/captive 'Stockholm Syndrome' which was first recognised in the 1970s just as the Stateville experiments were being drawn to a close.

Leopold also had a determination, even an obsession, to be infected with malaria. He wanted to experience "the real thing". Perhaps he was driven by sadomasochistic observations he made of other sick inmates experiencing temperatures of 106 degrees; they were expected to tolerate these levels of fever for up to five days before being given experimental medication. And he went to extraordinary lengths to ensure that he would become a subject as well as a technician.

The chemical compounds being trialled by the University of Chicago were called 8-aminoquinolines and this piece from Comfort quoting Leopold is especially revealing:

*The 8-aminoquinolines were known to be dangerous; the brand-new ones would, of course, be more or less unpredictable...Everyone was just a little frightened of the 8-aminoquinolines.* One of the new drugs, SN-8233, he went on, *turned out to be a wildcat.*

Leopold apparently suffered two heart attacks while participating in the Stateville experiments and heart failure was subsequently to be acknowledged as a known side effect of some synthetic antimalarials. Longitudinal studies would have provided much-needed data about the physiological side effects of these novel and dangerous medications. The extent to which longitudinal studies could have identified the neurotoxic hazards is much less clear given the already disturbed and violent nature of so many of the trials' subjects.

Nathan Leopold was paroled in 1958 and died of heart failure in 1971.

That is how Lariam was developed.

———

It would be many years after Lariam was licenced, and following many appalling acts of violence and suicide, that Phase III trials would begin to expose the true nature of this pharmaceutical "Agent Orange". Of course, no individual or institution would ever countenance such shameful practices or unethical research in the 21st century? And surely once the truth began to emerge no one would want to continue to impose this 'horror movie in a pill' on human beings? Tragically, complacency, greed, hubris, and stupidity are enduring human characteristics. It seems that one side effect not generally noted in the medical literature is that of institutional deafness. In fact, to the mice and men in the research programmes we should not forget to add the three monkeys.

# Chapter 3
## Joining the Dots

*For in that sleep of death what dreams may come.*

*Hamlet, Act III, Scene i*

A volley of shots rings out. There is a thumping impact in the middle of my chest as it is penetrated by a rifle's high velocity bullet. I fall, still conscious, to the ground and lie there alongside two or three of my comrades. I think they are dead. I am gasping for air but it won't come, and now the crunch of gravel describes the approaching steps of the officer in charge of the firing squad. With pistol in hand, he is coming to deliver the *coup de grace*.

By now most people would have woken up. But this is a Lariam dream and you get your money's worth. We had been through the opening scenes, making ourselves as presentable as captivity would allow before execution. We were prisoners of war. We had been interrogated but the dream didn't want to focus on that. We had offended our enemy and that was enough to seal our fate. After being marched to a piece of waste ground, we had exchanged a few muttered farewells and tried to stare down our captors in a final act of defiance. No hoods or blindfolds and too fatigued to attempt escape. And so the dream went on.

Lying there, I heard the pistol above me being cocked in preparation for the fatal shot. It came, penetrating my skull and I knew it was all over. But if I was now dead, *how* could I know? Dreams don't have rules, particularly those concocted by WR 142 490. In the surreal world of the Lariam play, I was both actor and audience. The dream concluded with some kind of externalised survey of our inanimate forms and I slowly awakened. But like the episode on the hotel balcony in Kyrgyzstan in 2003, there was no residual sense of shock or rapid pulse. WR 142 490 has given my nocturnal world a new normal; so I no longer ask why and when the dreams will stop. I don't remember the date of this particular dream, but it was fairly recent and certainly more than ten years after I had consumed my last Lariam pill.

I have Lariam dreams every night, although thankfully not always like this one. There are some, believe me, that are even more disturbing but I hope you will understand that I am going to keep those to myself. Others I am prepared to share have me trapped in burning buildings or being buried alive and, seemingly like other Lariam victims, I have the occasional encounter with a snake or a spider. A common feature of these dreams seems to be that they can access some of the most frightening, perverse or intractable fears deep in the psyche. Yet I do often get a night free of these sleeps of death.

But Lariam doesn't leave me alone at night, ever. I will often wait until the BBC closes the day on Radio 4 with my old friends *Sailing By* and the shipping forecast before attempting sleep. Dogger, Fisher, German Bight... the deceptively sonorous Lundy, Fastnet, Sole... but what storms await after the wilds of Hebrides, Faeroes and South East Iceland?

The best I can hope for is about an hour before I will wake after some bizarre nocturnal visitation. The dreams aren't always especially unpleasant—some are actually quite benign—but they nearly always conclude with some unresolved difficulty; I'm unprepared for an exam or a lecture I am about to give, or perhaps a vital piece of military equipment won't work or cannot be found. Just dreams.

I'm quite used to them now, and what others might describe as 'night terrors' don't cause me to wake in panic or fear, or to break out in a cold sweat. Even as the dream plays out its sometimes violent finale, I often find myself in some nether region between sleep and wakefulness during which I seem to know I am dreaming; I *know* this is a Lariam dream. And because I now know the cause, I no longer endure anxiety or shame for what has been going through my mind. I can even get back to sleep, sometimes to re-enter the same dream and then I will be awake once again. As so the cycle has continued, night after night, year after year.

It's not nice, but the problem is not me. These are not flashbacks and, despite the offerings of some snake-oil psychiatrists, I know this is not post-traumatic stress disorder (PTSD). How can I be so sure? Let's find some dots and make a few connections.

———

In 2008 I was stationed in Catterick Garrison in North Yorkshire, designing training for our infantry battle schools. It was my last job in uniform and I was preparing to leave the army that summer. The five years since first taking Lariam had been rather busy. I'm probably far from unique, but my service in those final few years had taken me to every continent except Antarctica, and back to a number of conflict zones and what we euphemistically called failing states. It was a time when all our forces were overstretched.

Remarkably, I even had to go back to Sierra Leone in 2005. Incredible as it may seem, the medical system wanted to give me yet more Lariam as part of the Sierra Leone pre-deployment routine. The drugs were to be issued by the same military medical centre at Shrivenham—with the very same doctor—who over the past two years had been handling my appointments with consultants at the Department of Infection and Tropical Medicine at the Birmingham Heartlands Hospital. Regarding my enduring Lariam side effects, one of those consultants had reported to the army medical services "There was nothing whatever to suggest depression and I am quite certain that this continues to be the legacy of his Lariam prophylaxis."[1] Had the military doctors not read those reports?

Thankfully, I had sufficient rank to tell the Shrivenham medical staff that under no circumstances would I consume anymore Lariam. I informed them that there was an alternative, safer drug, doxycycline. I got my doxycycline but I was to learn later that the medical centre then simply slipped back into its old routine of issuing Lariam without any regard for the prescribing regulations required for such drugs. Or had they been directed to? I was becoming increasingly aware of Lariam toxicity but could nobody else see it? Was it just some inconsequential background babble, lost in the bigger noise of the campaigns in Afghanistan and Iraq where our under-resourced and strained army was suffering 'real' casualties? Professionally, I had my own pressing issues to deal with and had made the rather naïve assumption that the Surgeon General should have been all over these Lariam issues, and competent enough to address them. That was, after all, supposed to be his job.

These were among my thoughts as I drove through the rain of a gloomy February night in 2008 from my home in North Yorkshire to the James Cook University Hospital on the outskirts of Middlesbrough. The James Cook is a modern facility with a major trauma centre. It also specialises in clinical neurological research and I was on my way for an overnight stay at the Sleep Disorders Clinic. In 2008 the science of sleep was a relatively emerging field in neurology and, since then, this highly specialised area has greatly improved our understanding of sleep hygiene and its contribution to good mental health. To put it bluntly, I knew my sleep was screwed up. Doctors at Catterick had recently prescribed medications such as Zopiclone, Clomipramine Hydrochloride and Clonazepam to help with my sleep but I couldn't tolerate them; they made my nights worse rather than better. I was to have a polysomnogram, and, a few weeks later, a magnetic resonance imaging (MRI) scan to look for any inflamed sleep centres in my brain.

The A172 Marton road has three lanes as you approach the James Cook from the south. Turning right into the main entrance I found plenty of room in the carpark. I did wince a bit at the parking charges but I guess they do need the money. Passing through the large doors, and beyond a couple of patients having a final fag before lights out, the hospital ground floor seemed airy, bright and welcoming. My directions had told me that I needed to locate the Blue Route which would take me to Ward 9 on the second floor. In a side ward I found the team who would conduct the examination.

A polysomnogram records brain activity and eye and leg movements during sleep. It can identify what is known as REM, or rapid eye movement sleep which is generally associated with dreaming. The plan was that I should sleep from about midnight until 6am. After a bit of paperwork, the procedure was explained to me and I got ready for bed. The side ward had a single bed where I would be observed from the next room. I sat down while I was wired up for the session. A number of electrodes needed to be attached to specific points on my scalp and these were duly fixed in place with a conductive paste. That was the only uncomfortable part of the whole process. Some firm pressure on the skull was required which seemed to cause a draining of all colour from my face and a feeling of faintness—but I will admit that I have never liked visiting hospitals.

Anyway, I was fine and we all agreed to go ahead. I got into the bed, the others left the room and the lights were turned off. I think I had an alarm button to use if required. Otherwise, the only other thing I was aware of before falling asleep was a small point of red light, a bit like the LED on a television. I fell asleep as planned and was officially wakened at 6.30. By seven o'clock I was on my way home and then back to work at Catterick Garrison.

I went back to the James Cook a few weeks later for the MRI scan. That was a much shorter procedure conducted by a radiologist. It involved lying on a bed that was moved into a large white tube containing powerful magnets. I lay still for about half an hour as the scanner did its work. Thankfully, I'm not claustrophobic but the electronic noise from the currents in the scanner was rather discomfiting. It was something of a Star Trek experience as I was acutely aware of my brain being clinically interrogated. There was also a slight feeling of vulnerability being immersed in this cocoon of white noise, but in a British hospital setting we rightly trust our medics and their ethics. We take that for granted, but some people in other parts of the world cannot.

Later in the spring, I returned to the hospital for a review with a consultant neurologist. The MRI brain scan results were assessed as "reassuringly within normal limits." On the other hand, the polysomnogram had revealed what was described as an unusual sleep pattern. My sleep efficiency was fairly high at around 90%. However, sleep was extremely fragmented with frequent awakenings, often from very deep non-REM sleep. My REM sleep also displayed some fragmentation. There was no snoring or excess movement, indicating that I did not have sleep apnoea or restless leg syndrome—some good news. I was shown a graph which appeared to show a series of peaks during the night which seemed to correlate with my dreams and regular awakenings. When we investigated the relationship between my general health, deployments, and any other changes in my life or circumstances, no cause other than Lariam could be identified. My military medical grading continued as Fit for Full Duties.

I had these tests for a number of reasons. First, if at all possible, I wanted to be rid of the Lariam side-effects. Five years of disturbed sleep was becoming, forgive me, a little tiresome; even if I did have the consolation that the sleep I did get had a decent efficiency score. Some more investigations might help. Second, the army had no immediate mechanism for any pension or payments for injuries acquired during service. For various and often arcane reasons, these could only be addressed after retirement or discharge. Thus, I had been advised that I needed to get all these Lariam events properly entered into my service medical records. That was one sound piece of counsel from an army doctor, delivered in a corridor outside his consulting room. And, third, there was also an army administrative requirement that a full medical examination be conducted as part of the discharge process.

There was another key motivation. While I was still fairly optimistic that my own side-effects might eventually pass, I felt it was essential that both our medical and operational chains of command be alerted to the problems of Lariam. Surely if someone was presenting (as the doctors like to say) with these long-term side effects, the matter would attract proper attention and perhaps a change of policy. The army prides itself on so-called Lessons Learned processes. Well, here was a lesson to be learned. While even at that stage I was still unaware of the horrifically global nature of Lariam poisoning, I had seen enough to know that we had a real problem. The anecdotal rates of side effects were high and what I had witnessed during my second tour of Sierra Leone, and the effect the drug had on people on other deployments,[c] had simply reinforced my worries. I felt it a point of duty.

---

[c] In 2004 a junior officer from the RAF was unable to attend a United Nations pre-deployment briefing I was giving. His colleagues informed me that he was depressed and suffering unexplained outbursts of crying. I tracked him down during the coffee break and discovered that he had just started taking Lariam.

(Remember that Sandhurst motto "Serve to Lead"?) Little did I know then the extent to which things were being covered up at the very highest echelons.

I left the army on 31 July 2008. To this day, no one from the army or the Ministry of Defence has asked me to share my experiences. Quite the contrary. But I did make one last attempt to work within the system.

———

In those days, if you had been injured during service there were a couple of options available for veterans, both of which were managed through an organisation called the Service Personnel and Veterans Agency.[d] For reasons that remain quite opaque to me, the Agency insisted that I had to apply for any redress first through the Armed Forces and Reserved Forces Compensation Scheme, a programme for which we both knew I was ineligible. Once that route was exhausted I was then able to proceed through the War Pensions Scheme. I wasn't after money. If I had been, I would have been rather disappointed: the amount I eventually received was £5,387 which, assuming I can defy the Grim Reaper for a few more years, would put the value of an undisturbed night at about the price of a cup of cocoa.

I could, and with hindsight probably should, have sued the Ministry of Defence for its neglect. I chose not to because I

---

[d] The Service Personnel and Veterans Agency was an executive agency of the UK Ministry of Defence. The SPVA provided personnel, pensions, welfare and support services to members of the UK Armed Forces and veterans and their dependents.

still retained a misplaced trust in senior officers to address the problem once it was brought to their attention. I had also yet to discover just how incompetent various Surgeons General had been, and continued to be, or the depths of deceit to which some government ministers would descend in defence of this drug. And you don't lightly take legal action against a body you have served for over thirty years and where you had always believed that loyalty was a two-way street. This dirty linen did not have to be washed in public and the subsequent War Pensions process was to prove of some value on a number of fronts.

Perhaps my first success was that I finally extracted from the system a formal diagnosis of my condition. Some of my symptoms were noted and declared as being 'Nightmare Disorder'. This is a clinically recognised illness defined by the World Health Organisation *International Classification for Diseases*.[2] It describes Nightmare Disorder thus:

> *Dream experiences loaded with anxiety or fear. There is very detailed recall of the dream content. The dream experience is very vivid and usually includes themes involving threats to survival, security, or self-esteem. Quite often there is a recurrence of the same or similar frightening nightmare themes. During a typical episode there is a degree of autonomic discharge but no appreciable vocalisation or body motility. Upon awakening, the individual rapidly becomes alert and oriented.*

I was informed of this medical finding by letter in April 2009, almost a year after my final army medical examination.[3]

I wasn't entirely surprised, but it was disappointing that my condition had not been pursued to diagnosis while I was still in uniform. I wonder why not? And it was particularly disconcerting that the diagnosis was passed to me not by a doctor but, it would appear, by a civil servant on behalf of the Chief Executive Officer of the SPVA. So I then conducted my own investigations into Nightmare Disorder. Eventually, after some institutional resistance, it was decided by a pensions appeal tribunal that my injury caused a disablement in the range of 6-14%.

Vitally, I had also got the Ministry of Defence to acknowledge that Lariam caused this damage. The admission was probably unintentional and it appears to have been subsequently suppressed by the MoD and the Surgeon General's Department. The disclosure can be found deep in the documentation preparatory to my appeal to the pensions' tribunal.[4] On Page 110, under the heading 'Comment by the Secretary of State', then Mr Bob Ainsworth, it reads:

*The Secretary of State notes the further correspondence with enclosures from Mr Marriott dated 15 August 2009. However, the Secretary of State has already accepted the use of Lariam by Mr Marriott during service and the purpose of this appeal is to determine the correct level of assessment for the resultant disablement of "nightmare disorder".*
*The Secretary of State has no further comment to make.*

No further comment and, apparently, no further interest.

My appeal was heard in Leeds on 24 September 2009. These tribunals are appointed by the Lord Chancellor and are composed of three members; a tribunal judge, a medical member and a retired service officer. Also present was a minor official from the SPVA representing the MoD. He appeared to have little knowledge of Lariam yet felt qualified to offer a comment that it was quite safe and unlikely to cause long-term damage. The tribunal members gave me a fair hearing.

I was particularly keen to stress that one of my desired outcomes was to allow the MoD to address the dangers associated with the use of Lariam. It was gratifying to learn that the tribunal supported my claim but, unfortunately, the finding seemed to stimulate no reactions from the SPVA or within the MoD in London. I'd once heard Bob Ainsworth described as 'Bob Ain't Worth It'; it would certainly appear that Bob wasn't interested.

Had Bob, or any of his staff, actually shown a bit of interest, there were quite a few things I would like to have told them. The drug was a hazard to a significant number of our soldiers; it was being issued in a manner that clearly defied both medical and military protocols and ethics; [e] and

---

[e] Article 4 of the UNESCO Universal Declaration on Bioethics and Human Rights (2005) states: 'In applying… medical practice and associated technologies, direct and indirect benefits to patients… should be maximised and any possible harm to such individuals should be minimised.' Article 6 goes on to declare 'Any preventive, diagnostic and therapeutic medical intervention is only to be carried out with the prior, free and informed consent of the person concerned, based on adequate information. The consent should, where appropriate, be express and may be withdrawn by the person concerned at any time and for any reason without disadvantage or prejudice.'

compliance was enforced by a number of highly questionable regimes, including the imposition of collective or unofficial punishments. Such penalties are crude and simply blunt disciplinary instruments, and rather difficult to reconcile with either civil or military law. I know something of the latter, having acted as defending and prosecuting officer at numerous courts martial and, later in my career, being President of a District Court Martial. And anyway, I think I generally know what is right and what is wrong.

Especially problematic for the British Army, Lariam use coincided with acts of violence, apparent suicide ideation and other erratic and exceptionally dangerous behaviours, many of which I had personally witnessed. These matters are now all in the public domain and not secrets, official or otherwise. Moral and health issues aside, the use of this medication was quite incompatible with our military fighting doctrine; in fact it seriously undermined it, affecting not just the performance of soldiers taking the drug but eroding confidence and team cohesion across whole fighting units. For many years, and while we were fighting major campaigns in Afghanistan and Iraq, this corrosion of the nation's combat capability was either ignored or covered-up—probably both. Thankfully, and despite rather than because of the MoD, the damage caused by Lariam to military performance has now been acknowledged in academia.

Beyond the physical and mental harm done to so many soldiers, independent peer-reviewed research has now definitively established that Lariam use compromised fighting power.[5] Specifically, the drug "diminishes effective decision making, the ability to follow orders, innovation, critical thinking and the cognitive readiness of both individuals and collective units."[f] I rather hope these findings, published in the Royal United Services Institute Journal in April 2020, have become required reading for those responsible for developing our military plans and operations.

Perhaps the Director General of the Defence Medical Services (we no longer regularly have a Surgeon General) might give it a read although he may fail to grasp its significance. In 2019 the Government decided the Surgeon General's role required neither any military experience nor any clinical qualification, and could be better performed by a civilian with a background in economics and business administration.

"Something is rotten in the state of Denmark" is another oft-used quote from *Hamlet* (Act 1, scene iv). Appropriately, it is an observation made by a soldier, Marcellus, reflecting on the rife corruption plain to all but generally ignored. What other Denmarks might Shakespeare cite today? Sadly, there are multiple candidates, here and abroad.

———

As I was to discover over the years, the period of Mr Ainsworth's silence was very significant. He was Secretary of State for Defence from June 2009 until May 2010 and before that spent two years as Minister of State for the Armed Forces. This was, of course, at the height of the US 'War on Terror' shaped by the Bush/Blair alliance; the days when the interpretation of international law was 'modified' by our

---

[f] See P Bathie (2020) Military Safety: A Systems Perspective on Lariam.

Attorney General, Lord Goldsmith, to better align with the views of the Pentagon, Donald Rumsfeld and George W Bush. And it was during this period that some extremely alarming reports were beginning to surface about the use of torture at the United States detention facilities in Abu Ghraib in Iraq and at Guantanamo Bay, Cuba. These were the days of Weapons of Mass Destruction, dodgy dossiers and a process known as 'rendition'.

In the $20^{th}$ century, the word rendition would usually have inspired thoughts of the artistically creative; an interpretation or performance of a fine piece of prose or music. (But there was always Caesar, lurking somewhere in the background, hoping for something to be rendered unto him.) Today, and perhaps pleasing to Caesar, a darker definition is very much in the ascendant. The war on terror gave us the term 'extraordinary rendition', defined thus in the Oxford English Dictionary:[6]

*(especially in the US) the practice of sending a foreign criminal or terrorist suspect covertly to be interrogated in a country with less rigorous regulations for the humane treatment of prisoners.*

And now even the adjective 'extraordinary' has become largely redundant. In the current military idiom, rendition refers to the forceful and usually clandestine apprehension of suspects by state entities or agencies operating beyond the scrutiny of domestic or international law. So it was that from 2002 around 780 men (including some minors) were to be spirited away from various parts of the globe and taken to the US naval base at Guantanamo Bay.

Guantanamo Bay (or Gitmo in US military parlance) is a little piece of America on the southeast coast of Cuba, leased under an arrangement dating from 1903. Cuba is, technically, the sovereign power. However, the United States enforces its right to govern the territory, a right it clearly did not intend to cede to the Castro regime during the Cold War and one that Cuba does not recognise but is powerless to change. For the USA, this arrangement presents an interesting and serendipitous legal anomaly; any actions conducted on the territory appear to be insulated from US laws. The base was thus an ideal location for a secure compound in which to detain inmates collected under the rendition programme. The inconvenience that the 1903 agreement apparently required that the base should only be used as, or modified to the meets of, a coaling and naval station, does not seem to have prevented the construction of the War on Terror's special prison/detention facility.[7]

A mark of a civilised society is how it treats the people for whom it is responsible. This must extend beyond the general population and should include humane regimes for those it has incarcerated, either through domestic law or because of the exigencies of war. The moral authority of the Western Allies at the end of the Second World War was enhanced and not eroded by how they dealt with German prisoners of war, including the surviving upper echelons of the Nazi regime implicated in the most horrific of war crimes.

It is for good reason that the Geneva Conventions and the Laws of Armed Conflict exist and must be respected. Suspected terrorists, until proved guilty, are just that— suspected. It may be that high security controls will be imposed along with loss of liberty, but degradation of prisoners has no more legitimacy in modern armies than it had in the Second World War as routinely applied by the SS or the Imperial Japanese Army. That moral imperative was lost to the Bush presidency and Donald Rumsfeld in their management of the prison at Guantanamo Bay.

Wars are not an impersonal subject to me. Along the way, I have lost a number of friends and colleagues to enemy or terrorist action. A soldier's response is always likely to include anger. But we are educated in decency in our schools and families, and then trained in uniform to behave with professionalism and dignity. I had known for years that the Americans had run a loose ship at the Guantanamo Bay Naval Station but it was only while researching this book that I discovered just how institutionalised their base behaviours had become.

State-endorsed dehumanising of captives is at best a retardant to operational and strategic success. The torture of prisoners at Gitmo, which in some cases led to their deaths, was not simply unproductive, it was too often counterproductive. It's not for this book to critique all the behaviours of the staff at Guantanamo Bay: for a proper insight I would strongly recommend the testimony of Staff Sergeant Joseph Hickman[g] who, as one of the camp guards, witnessed the abuse and then had the courage to expose it while his government mobilised all their resources to supress his story.[8]

By far the most disturbing revelation by Hickman concerned the deaths of three detainees on the night of 9 June

---

[g] Joseph Hickman (2015) Murder at Camp Delta. A Staff Sergeant's Pursuit of the Truth About Guantanamo Bay.

2006. It should be clear to the meanest intelligence that these men were killed as a result of torture, and probably while undergoing interrogation in a secret block away from their cells, even if their deaths were not intended. The official line, however, was that the prisoners, who would have been housed in separate cages, with wire and plexi-glass walls, and under almost constant observation, had managed to hang themselves. Yet somehow their bodies remained undiscovered for almost two hours.

The detention centre commander, Rear Admiral Harry B Harris, presented these 'suicides' in a briefing to the world's press as acts of a coordinated protest by smart, creative and committed men who had thus engaged in an act of asymmetrical warfare against the authority holding them.[9] In an ultimate act of state subterfuge later discovered by Hickman, the bodies of the deceased were returned to their families with their necks removed, presumably to avoid any independent autopsy questioning the officially recorded cause of death.

I had often observed, when working with them, how American officers liked to quote Churchill. There is a particular phrase that Churchill is believed to have used about truth having to be protected by a bodyguard of lies. The Pentagon and Rumsfeld seemed to like that one. Sadly, when it comes to dirty truths, our own MoD is not so bad at that game either; but more of that later.

Admiral Harris's assertions of 2006 are no more convincing than an independent film of the prison that the Americans allowed in 2019 and which can be accessed on

YouTube.[h] In that film it is asserted that the abuses of many years ago no longer happen. That's all in the past. The prison commanders rhapsodise that there are now no interrogations, only "voluntary interviews"; Churchill to Orwellian Newspeak in one easy bound! During the filming, none of the journalists was allowed contact with any prisoner and the all accommodation they were shown was unoccupied.

The film is worth watching but not for the reasons the American authorities intended. Personally, I found it reminiscent of a notorious Nazi propaganda film of 1944 which attempted to convince the International Red Cross and the wider world just how contented, active and well everyone was in the Jewish ghetto/labour camp of Theresienstadt. But returning to Hickman's story and events in the 2000s, there was something even more chilling going on.

To get his story out, Staff Sergeant Hickman had to leave the army. There were no internal routes for him to use and he took the incredibly courageous step of approaching a professor of law, Mark Denbeaux, then director of the Center for Policy and Research at Seton Hall University Law School Newark, New Jersey. By 2009 Denbeaux had already conducted a number of investigations into the Guantanamo detainees, drawing heavily on US official papers. Partly inspired by the expectation that a new Obama presidency would fulfil its promise to close the camp, [i] Hickman

---

[h] Guantanamo Bay: World's most controversial prison. Free Doc Bites. Free Documentary. 30 Oct 2019.
youtube.com/watch?v=SHctHcGCdlM

[i] It seems that even President Obama could not shut it down throughout his eight-year tenure and the prison continues to operate.

embarked on a collaboration with Denbaux and his research students.

Towards the end of an exceptionally forensic examination of all the available official documents, they made one particularly startling discovery: not only was it quite clear that detainees were continually being subjected to physical and mental abuse and torture, they were also being administered mefloquine, that is Lariam/WR 142 490, in notably high doses.

In a compelling report published in 2011, Professor Denbeaux and his team established that all detainees were being given mefloquine upon their arrival at Guantanamo.[10] Either as a treatment or for the prevention of malaria, the use of mefloquine would have been quite remarkable for a number of reasons. Many detainees were taken from regions where the malaria risk was low. Furthermore, mefloquine may not have been the appropriate medication for the strain they may have been harbouring. Detainees were given the drug before any tests confirmed whether they might even be infected, and there was no credible public health threat arising from any possible importation of malaria to the island. Moreover, the US Centers for Disease Control and Protection had clearly identified that there was no malaria in Cuba and hence no reason to protect prisoners from contracting the disease once they arrived. It was presumably for that reason that no one else on the base was taking any antimalarial medication.[11,12]

According to in-processing medical records, prisoners were being given an initial oral dose of 750 mg of mefloquine/Lariam/WR 142 490, followed twelve hours later by a further 500 mg. This represents *five times* the dosage for prophylactic use. The drug was given to men whose medical background, had it been consulted, would have confirmed that the drug was simply too hazardous for them to consume. And to confound the felony, when inmates complained of serious problems such as anxiety, nightmares or suicidal thoughts, doctors did not consider mefloquine as a cause despite these being known and dangerous side effects. Rather, it seems that the men were being diagnosed with some form of adjustment disorder or with anxiety and passive-aggressive personality traits. These conclusions have been based on the records of two individuals that somehow came into the public domain and were thus accessible to Denbeaux.

Given that wider public health concerns and the welfare of the inmates were not plausible reasons for the enforced consumption of mefloquine, there remain only two likely reasons for such abuse of medical ethics. One is that the psychotropic nature of the drug, especially when administered in such high doses, is such that it would render inmates more amenable to interrogation. That would represent a form of chemical waterboarding. A second, and closely related purpose, could have been to provide data for drug experiments conducted on humans.

According to the American records accessed by Professor Denbeaux, one of the three men who died on 9 June 2006 had not only consumed mefloquine but had indeed reported nightmares and suicidal thoughts. In his report, after reiterating that mefloquine was first developed by the US military, Denbeaux includes this comment in his findings:

*Mefloquine is a quinolone [sic], a drug family the CIA experimented with under a project called MKULTRA that studied psychotropic drugs for behavioural modification for use as a weapon and interrogation tool.*

Was it possible that the use of mefloquine at Guantanamo was another manifestation of these CIA experiments? In the 2019 video, the two senior officers at the Guantanamo prison, Colonel Gabavics and Rear Admiral Clarke, assured us that these dirty research programmes were all in the past. Something about all of this was strangely familiar and I needed to dig a little deeper.

———

The scandal that was MKULTRA was exposed in the 1970s during the Carter presidency.[13] It was a clandestine multi-programme research project run by the CIA from 1953 until at least 1963. Its main purpose was to evaluate the potential of psychedelic drugs such as LSD for the purposes of mind control, interrogation and even torture. It operated within a highly decentralised structure in order to maintain secrecy and evade accountability. Using locations such as so-called safe houses, CIA operatives conducted human experiments, often on unsuspecting citizens or highly vulnerable subjects who had no idea they were participants in any trial, even when they succumbed to the hallucinogens they were surreptitiously given.

The project involved numerous organisations, perhaps recruited unwittingly, including universities, pharmaceutical houses, hospitals, state and federal institutions, and private research organisations. Over the life of the project, "additional avenues to the control of human behaviour" were explored. They included radiation, electroshock, various fields of psychology, psychiatry, sociology and anthropology, graphology, harassment substances, and paramilitary devices and materials.

Although the CIA had ordered the destruction of all of MKULTRA's records in 1973, sufficient papers existed in other government repositories to enable a joint investigation in 1977 by the US Senate Select Committee on Intelligence and the Subcommittee on Health and Scientific Research.[14] In his preamble to the Joint Committee's Report, the Chairman, Senator Daniel K. Inouye, made these remarks:

*It should be made clear from the outset that in general, we are focusing on events that happened over 12 or as long as 25 years ago. It should be emphasized that the programs that are of greatest concern have stopped and that we are reviewing these past events in order to better understand what statutes and other guidelines might be necessary to prevent the recurrence of such abuses in the future. We also need to know and understand what is now being done by the CIA in the field of behavioural research to be certain that no current abuses are occurring.*

Given that no one was held to account for MKULTRA, nor, so far, for what was subsequently put in place at Guantanamo by the Bush/Rumsfeld administration, this statement appears both naïve and complacent.

Much of the evidence presented to the Committee was provided by the then Director of the CIA, Admiral Stansfield

Turner. Turner gave this personal assurance: "Let me emphasize that the MKULTRA events are 12 to 25 years in the past. I assure you that the CIA is in no way engaged in either witting or unwitting testing of drugs today." Curiously, regarding human experimentation, there seems to be no acknowledgement of the Nuremberg Code by either CIA Director Admiral Turner or the Joint Committee. The Nuremberg Code, mainly American authored, was established during the Nuremberg Trials of Nazi researchers and physicians with the expressed intent of codifying the ethical principles of research involving human subjects.[15] The first of its ten principles, which would have been a very useful starting point for the hearing, is worth presenting in full.

*The voluntary consent of the human subject is absolutely essential. This means that the person involved should have legal capacity to give consent; should be situated as to be able to exercise free power of choice, without the intervention of any element of force, fraud, deceit, duress, over-reaching, or other ulterior form of constraint or coercion, and should have sufficient knowledge and comprehension of the elements of the subject matter involved as to enable him to make an understanding and enlightened decision.*

*This latter element requires that before the acceptance of an affirmative decision by the experimental subject, there should be made known to him the nature, duration, and purpose of the experiment; the method and means by which it is to be conducted; all inconveniences and hazards reasonably to be expected; and the effects upon his health or person which may possibly come from his participation in the experiment.*

*The duty and responsibility for ascertaining the quality of the consent rests upon each individual who initiates, directs, or engages in the experiment. It is a personal duty and responsibility which may not be delegated to another with impunity.*

The evidence presented to the Joint Committee was alarming not simply because of the CIA's wide-ranging criminal activity, but also because of the extent of similar research across other national entities, and notably various CIA collaborations with the Department of Defense. The report makes reference to:

*"Subprojects involving funding support for unspecified activities conducted with the Army Special Operations Division at Fort Detrich."* It also states that *"Under CIA's Project MKNAOMI,"* the Army assisted the CIA in *developing, testing, and maintaining biological agents and delivery systems for use against humans as well as against animals and crops.*

In their report, further Joint Committee scrutiny of the volunteer and surreptitious human testing showed that the US Army Chemical Corps was conducting its own research into LSD; this was for two particular reasons. The first was to evaluate the potential of LSD as a chemical incapacitant. The second was to collect data on the utility of LSD in field interrogations. Significantly, it would appear that these experiments were also being extended to non-American populations in Europe and the Far East. But the research hub itself was much closer to home, located in a United States Army facility in Edgewood, Maryland. A closer look at Edgewood will be vital in understanding the prevailing research and development culture in the United States. It will also throw a light on the murky relationship between secret government programmes and the pharmaceutical industry.

Edgewood Arsenal is located within the wider military complex known as Aberdeen Proving Ground. It provided an isolated location at the head of Chesapeake Bay but one that remained geographically convenient for the Pentagon, WRAIR and other government agencies in Washington. It was initially established to provide the US Army with a means of studying the effects and utility of the gas and chemical agents they had encountered during the First World War. But it was after the Second World War that it began to engage in secret programmes that should have been an affront to any self-respecting doctor or scientist. After the war, in common with the Russians, the Americans had acquired a number of German chemical formulas and, according to the *New Yorker* magazine (12 December 2012), some of the Nazi scientists who developed them, and began to work with them at Edgewood. As well as LSD, Edgewood was investigating mustard gas, the nerve agent sarin and PCP (phencyclidine). PCP, now with the street-name Angel Dust, was originally developed as anaesthetic but was abandoned because it caused hallucinations and delusions. Those were exactly the characteristics that made it attractive to Edgewood. Thousands of military subjects passed through the various Edgewood programmes of the 1950s and 60s. The studies were terminated in 1975.

A number of recent sources have turned their attention to the Edgewood projects and the propensity of the US Army Chemical Corps to receive samples of drugs rejected by pharmaceutical companies because of their unacceptably dangerous side effect profiles.[j] [16] One company implicated in this practice was F. Hoffmann-La Roche. Their involvement was lauded by the particularly influential and bizarre Colonel J S Ketchum, an Army psychiatrist spearheading much of the research at Edgewood.

Colonel Ketchum joined the army in 1956 and during his career worked mainly at Edgewood and Walter Reed. He had a particular fascination with hallucinogenic drugs and reportedly was a regular user of Dexedrine, (dextroamphetamine), a chemical stimulant that is now largely prescribed for its positive impact on patients with narcolepsy and ADHD, and sometimes used to stimulate weight loss in the morbidly obese. It is also said that he used other recreational drugs. He defended his research and methods by describing them as "a noble cause". He left the army in 1976 shortly after the Edgewood programmes were terminated. Married five times, he died in 2019.[17]

A particular difficulty facing Edgewood occurred when LSD testing was ended after it was assessed, unsurprisingly, as being too unpredictable to be used as an incapacitating agent. As Ketchum himself wrote, the research programme was then reinvigorated when the Chemical Corps accessed another compound, 3-quinuclidinyl benzilate. It is more

---

[j] See David Livingstone (2015) Transhumanism: The History of a Dangerous Idea, and Lukasz Kamieński (2017) Shooting Up. A History of Drugs in Warfare.

commonly known as BZ and produces an anticholinergic delirium, a non-specific syndrome of cognitive dysfunction and hallucinations. BZ became a major focus of Ketchum's work with human subjects as he explored its deleterious effects on the ability of the soldier to perform even basic military tasks. The compound could be administered orally but, importantly for chemical warfare, also in a gaseous form. Of BZ, Ketchum noted in his own memoir: [18]

> *In 1952, Hoffman-La Roche Inc. chemists created a possible ulcer drug called RO2-3308—not bad for ulcers, but better at causing hallucinations. Within a decade, Chemical Corps workers were loading this remarkable substance into experimental munitions. They gave it a shorter name: "BZ" (no doubt shorthand for "benzilate", a subset of the glycolate chemical family). Credit Hoffman—La Roche Inc. with "serendipity".*
>
> *After testing BZ extensively in animals, the Medical Research Laboratories gave very small doses to volunteers and obtained only minimal effects. As doses approached half a milligram (i.e., 5 or 6 micrograms per kilogram of body weight), however, hallucinations started to appear. It was potent and it worked!*
>
> *Not only did it work, but its effects lasted a long time.*

One might observe that along with the formulas and scientists the Americans had imported from The Third Reich, they also acquired some disturbing research values. With friends like these who needs Mengeles?

What is likely to remain unresolved is the nature of the business relationship between the US Department of Defense and Hoffmann-La Roche. It seems curious that reject pharmaceuticals, intended to heal, should be peddled to military research complexes seeking to exploit the damage they can inflict on humankind. There is clearly something of an ethical dilemma but presumably not sufficient to cause ulcers for Colonel Ketchum or the Chairman of Hoffmann-La Roche. But the curious becomes a little more sinister when we consider the possible *quid pro quo*. With no evidence to the contrary, we must assume that in the 1980s Hoffmann-La Roche was gifted all of the intellectual property pertaining to WR 142 490.

From a business perspective, and discounting any obvious moral compromises, Hoffmann-La Roche appears to have made a sound investment. Here a couple of other observations can be made. The first is that there is little evidence of any other pharmaceutical company being offered, or being interested in, the opportunity to exploit WR 142 490. The second is that as the side effects of Lariam started to raise serious public concern in America, the drug was given a full endorsement by the US authorities. The subject was discussed in a Voice of America broadcast on 17 May 2001.[19] The piece included an interview with a Colonel Wilbur Milhous, introduced as one of the military scientists who developed mefloquine/WR 142 490 at WRAIR. Milhous claimed that the US Army's experience of the drug had been good but stated that the public criticism of Lariam was causing the government to fear that Roche might pull the drug off the market. To protect the drug, Milhous declared, "health officials promised Roche they would continue to back the use of Lariam, despite the reports of adverse effects."

If there was no formal business relationship between WRAIR/Department of Defense and Hoffmann-La Roche, there is at least something of an odd symmetry at play. Pharma develops a medicine that cannot be used because of its psychotropic nature. The licence is passed to the US Army in order that it can exploit these by-products. Later, an anti-malarial drug with psychotropic side effects bounces back the other way. The company makes a lot of money.

———

The final chapter of Staff Sergeant Hickman's book is titled "America's Secret Battle Lab." It is quite clear that a key purpose of the Guantanamo Prison, and perhaps later *the* primary one, was to provide a laboratory of human subjects for a continuation of the former clandestine programmes of the CIA and the US Army. Mefloquine was a major component of the mental and physical conditioning of prisoners prior to torture and interrogation.

Mind-numbing, in all senses.

# Chapter 4
## Bydand

*A Scots word meaning 'Steadfast', not to run away from danger, to keep going whatever the difficulties.*

-*The Gordon Highlanders Museum Website*

In the autumn of 2008 I became an archaeologist, enrolling as an undergraduate at the University of York. There can be few more inspiring places to study archaeology. Nestled in the heart of the medieval city, the archaeology department occupies the King's Manor. Among a rich Roman heritage, the King's Manor itself can be traced back to the 13th-century residence of the Abbot of St Mary's, the richest Benedictine Abbey in the North of England. After the Reformation it became the Headquarters of the Council of the North. It then suffered significant damage in the Civil War and is now a fascinating assemblage of medieval and post-medieval architecture. With its wooden floors and mullion windows, the quiet of the library is only disturbed by the peal of York Minster's bells just the other side of the ancient city walls.

The first serious archaeological textbook I read, just before my studies began, was called 'Digging the Dirt. The Archaeological Imagination', written by Jennifer Wallace, a lecturer in English Literature at Cambridge. I had my own copy and would regularly revisit it over the coming years through my masters and doctoral studies. In discussing the recent past, war crimes and genocide, Wallace is eloquent on the role of the forensic archaeologist in defying attempts by governments to deny or erase the past.

The archaeologist "plays a vital political role in revealing what is… inescapable when the general trend is to evade responsibility."[1] 'Digging the Dirt' was inspirational to the budding archaeologist and, subliminally, to my wider pursuit of the truth. I was to dig a lot of dirt with my physical and metaphorical trowels. In archaeology, everything is about context. For my investigation of the Lariam scandal, the context was about to set by two particularly harrowing stories.

On a Saturday morning in Northallerton, in North Yorkshire, I met Bea Coldwell for a coffee. I had last met her in 2007 at our daughters' school speech day, with her husband who was about to deploy to IMATT, Sierra Leone, for a year. We served in the same regiment and our paths had occasionally crossed over the years. They looked very happy and I chatted with him about Sierra Leone while our wives went to look for our girls. A year later, Bea's life was in shreds. Lariam had wrecked their lives. This is what she told me.

———

We were a normal, happy family. Not without problems, but happy enough. He had at last made lieutenant colonel, but it had been a struggle. Our younger daughter's recent brush with cancer had taken a toll, but the four of us loved each other and we were content, and he and I were confident enough in each other to have decided that an unaccompanied one-year posting to Sierra Leone presented no danger to our marriage. And the extra pay would always be welcome. So in mid-August 2007 he took his first Lariam pill, in preparation for his departure at the end of the month. I can't recall that there were any noticeable changes in his behaviour; I think all army families will say that as we prepare to send our men off to war, or wherever, we retreat into our own thoughts, he considering what lies ahead, and setting up a joint Facebook page where he could share photographs, and for my part checking that I knew how to complete a boarding school allowance claim, or that the car insurance was up-to-date.

The girls and I were old hands at the goodbyes. They'd been at boarding school since 2002, and we'd seen him deploy to Iraq twice in the past four years, but there were tears from all of us at the airport. Of course there were. Tears and hugs and reassurances and "I love yous" and "be safes" before we watched him disappear up the escalator to Departures. And naturally a really good howl in the car before setting off back to Catterick.

The next week passed in a flurry of packing for the girls' return to school just across the Pennines and getting used to being just the three of us again. He rang every day to say how much he loved and missed us all and posted dozens of photographs of his living accommodation, which he shared with the IMATT doctor, ███████████, and the teeming mass of Freetown. He was really excited at being in Africa, although from early on he was quite dismissive of the locals and their army, and agog at the persistence of what the army refers to as "nightfighters", i.e. prostitutes, who swarmed around foreigners in Freetown's drinking holes. His boss was a friend of ours from Germany fifteen years or so ago,

Brigadier ███████████, who had a Special Forces background so I was confident that he would be looked after; the only thing that rattled me was an evening call in mid-September when he said: "Listen to this: we've just taken our Lariam", and held out the phone so that I could hear the strange baying sounds his colleagues were making.

The first real alarm bell sounded in the second week of October when he spoke in a cold, detached tone that chilled me, but we were back to normal the following day, as far as I can remember. Around the same time, I saw on the Facebook page an affectionate hearts-and-roses-type emoji from a woman and, like a dolt, just thought how sweet the locals were. And so life went on, both there and back home in Catterick, as we counted away the days. I went to work, saw friends, visited our daughters most weekends. The nights drew in, and the girls came home for a week at half term.

My younger daughter's health continued to improve and her lovely new hair to grow, and suddenly it was December and Daddy was coming home for R&R on our 18th wedding anniversary. Only Daddy didn't sound as excited as we were. Having flown to Gatwick overnight and caught the train up to Darlington, he was exhausted and seemed angry and resentful at being back in North Yorkshire in December. Very unusually, he was aggressive with the girls and withdrawn at the party I had organised.

Christmas was unmemorable, except for a row we had on Boxing Day, after which he didn't speak to me again except to say that he was returning early to Sierra Leone and that I could take our daughter to her cancer check-up at the John Radcliffe in Oxford on my own. And he just left.

2008 was a horror. This was someone I simply didn't know. I had to explain to the girls, then aged 13 and 15, that Daddy wasn't coming home again, and that I had no idea why. We exchanged emails; he denied vehemently my accusation that he was having an affair ("I would never do such a horrible thing to you and the girls") but wasn't able to explain why he had done what he had done, nor what were his plans. Separately, he was telling the girls that I had caused the collapse of the marriage.

It was then that I recalled what the army doctor in Shrivenham had reportedly said as he prescribed him the Lariam in August: "It might make you go mad", and immediately something clicked. Eureka moment. I emailed him and reminded him of that conversation—telephoned him too and begged him to change prescriptions, but was told that the IMATT MO had dismissed my theory and that Lariam was to be continued. The rows went on for several weeks, culminating in a particularly vicious one that led to my making a suicide attempt which was thwarted by the unexpected arrival of a friend at my door. Thank God for friends.

I even contacted ███████████, now returned from Sierra Leone. ████████ dismissed my worries: no, my husband was not having an affair ("no secrets between boys" is what he told me) and no, no problems with the Lariam, although he had taken himself off it because of sleep problems.

In April I consulted a lawyer, but decided to hold off petitioning for divorce. I loved my husband, we were both Catholic and I wanted to keep my family together. I wrote to the Catholic Bishop to the Armed Forces, the Rt Rev Tom Burns, explaining the situation and asking for his help in securing a judicial separation, rather than a divorce. I also asked him to raise the whole issue of Lariam at his next meeting with the Chief of the General Staff. I received a rather limp reply: "I am shortly to retire and were I to write to General Dannatt on your behalf they would put my letter on hold until I had left the Forces, or simply regard me as a 'lame duck' Bishop." He suggested that I make contact with the Surgeon-General, Louis Lillywhite, and to this end, to press his point, he enclosed a stamped envelope addressed to General Lillywhite. [k]

Some mutual friends also contacted the Chief of the General Staff, Richard Dannatt, asking for some help. His response was surprising, particularly considering that in the later 1990s his own son had fallen victim to the same drug. His approach was that this was personal business between me and my husband and he would take no action.

Accusations and denials went back and forth between us until August, when he came home for R&R again and I moved in with a neighbour, leaving him with the girls in their familiar home. He came to see me one afternoon, and we sat in the garden while he went out of his way to provoke me until I lost my temper and screamed at him, whereupon he produced a tape recorder from his pocket and said "Once more for the tape, *bitch*?" before leaving.

---

[k] The bishop retired in July 2019, when he said: "I feel unworthy to have been chosen by the Lord to be a priest and then a bishop, to navigate waters that have become increasingly challenging, yet day by day were filled with so many graces. I thank the Lord, as well as clergy and people, for so many blessings, and ask forgiveness for my failings".

He took the girls to see a Batman film that night and as I walked past our house with the neighbour's dog, I saw that he'd left every window open, and let myself in to close them. In his dressing room, laid out where the children could see it, was a book about how to leave everything behind and do what you really want to do. I wish I could remember the detail. But more importantly, in the top of his day-sack, where he always kept his secrets, I found a piece of evidence which confirmed my hunch about an affair.

I confronted him with this item the following day and he admitted, unapologetically, that he had indeed been having an affair with the woman who had posted the emoji ten months ago. My reaction was to laugh: here, surely, was the evidence that he had lost his mind. A local 'bar hostess'? In a country where AIDS is rife? I made him sit down with the girls and tell them what he'd done. Then I threw him out, called my lawyer and launched the divorce petition on the grounds of his adultery. Then I boil-washed his bedding. Twice.

I was tested for AIDS, Hepatitis and various other nasties at the med centre in Catterick not long afterwards and had one of the worst weeks of my life waiting for the results. In the meantime, ████████ were doing their own detective work and asked a mixed-race friend to send a "friend request" to my husband's Freetown girlfriend, which was accepted. The next time I met them, they showed me photographs of my husband and the (according to ████████, former prostitute) girlfriend he had so long denied.

The thing I can tell you for certain is that the man who was my husband would never have behaved like this. He was a decent—if slightly weak—officer and family man who loved his three girls. He had a strong moralistic streak: when the (married) housemaster of the girls' Catholic prep school had been caught *in flagrante* in 2003, he'd written (but not posted, at my insistence) to the headmaster, demanding the dismissal of the housemaster, saying that the man had "behaved appallingly in betraying his family" and that to leave him in post would set a bad example to "children at a crucial stage of their moral development." Here was a recently-promoted Lieutenant-Colonel who, presumably, had issued stern warnings to the men under his command about having sex with the locals whilst doing that himself. How the hell had this been allowed to happen, with a special forces Brigadier in command, and my husband sharing a house with the MO? How indeed. I rang again to update him and he called back a little later, having been through his photographs and, presumably, seen what he should have noticed at the time. So much for SAS observational skills. But, despite this, he remained unsympathetic and unhelpful, and distinctly unfriendly. Similarly, nothing from our own Regiment. Nothing. Not a word.

When the affair came to the attention of his new boss in the autumn of 2008, he became very ill and was medically evacuated back to the UK. I spoke to the consultant neurologist charged with his care twice (before my husband's lawyers intervened); it seemed that neither Lariam, nor my husband's affair with a Sierra Leonean woman had been mentioned to the consultant by the IMATT MO.

A quick Google of British Army+Lariam produced my first breakthrough: a paper entitled "The rise and fall of Lariam and Halfan", authored by Lt-Colonel Ashley Croft, RAMC, which cited 19 deaths causally associated with Lariam use and went on to describe its rushed development by the Walter Reid Army Institute of Research in Washington DC.[2] Lariam was released onto the market that year without any human tolerability trials being carried out. Can you believe it? So here was a senior British Army doctor writing about a dangerously neurotoxic drug, four short months before that same drug was prescribed to my husband by another doctor contracted to the army.

I contacted Ashley Croft and we spoke for over an hour. He said my husband's behaviour were "classic symptoms of Lariam derangement" but also warned me that his opposition to the army's use of Lariam had threatened his own career and that he would be unable to offer much help. He did, however, give me one little gem: out there, somewhere, is an army widow called Jane Quinn, who had corresponded with the Surgeon-General's department in 2006 following the Lariam-cited suicide of her husband.

There was something else niggling away inside my head. Hadn't another Fusilier officer fallen ill after taking antimalarials a few years ago? Weren't our daughters at the same school? Maybe we could form a team?

———

Bea's story was sickening and depressing but, sadly, did not surprise me. Ideals such as the Military Covenant and Duty of Care become an embarrassing inconvenience when they venture into the murky world of damaged minds, non-battle casualties and former service families who have no advocate to help them pick up shattered lives. She had asked for help and everyone, including the Chief of the General Staff, the Surgeon General and even the Army Chaplains

Department, simply wanted to hit the delete button. My coffee was cold and so was I. I wanted some time to go through my diaries and records and we agreed to meet again the following weekend.

At the next of what would be many meetings over the years, we talked about Jane Quinn, a most remarkable and courageous woman whose life, I was to discover, had been totally devastated by Lariam. Jane's was an utterly horrific story and not just because of the immediate effect Lariam had on her life and the lives of her two young daughters. She was a widow and the shabby treatment she received from the Ministry of Defence is nothing short of a national disgrace. Jane was now in Australia, rebuilding a life for her girls after Lariam had killed her husband.

Over the years we have all become firm friends with a determination to uncover the truth. Jane must have been feeling especially raw back then but, with a bravery that would shine on any battlefield, she responded to our emails and agreed to join the fight. Jane has since become the most extraordinary advocate for Lariam-damaged veterans in Australia and across the world. She is now a senior academic in an Australian university. Her story has been summarised in a number of media but I recently asked if she would share some of the details of the day when she discovered her husband had committed suicide.

Here, in Jane's words, is what happened when WR 142 490 hit her family.

———

## Scotland, 2006

It was a Saturday, 11 March 2006, a Saturday much like any other, except it wasn't.

We were a young family, our life had been ordinary enough for a couple that met and became childhood sweethearts, eventually marrying in 1995 when Cameron was a young Lieutenant in the Highlanders. He was initially a Gordon Highlander, a regiment formed in 1881 but steeped in an illustrious history that went back to 1794. Their motto 'Bydand' *was* the regiment. Amalgamations of regiments in the infantry were occurring across the board in the 1990's and the Gordons and the Queen's Own Highlanders were joined in 1994 creating the new regiment 'The Highlanders'.

Cameron had been proudly commissioned from Sandhurst in 1991 after having to prove his worth as an officer candidate through the rigorous proving ground that was Rowallan Company, and was a Scottish soldier through and through. We had known each other since we had met through a mutual high school friend at fourteen and bar some other dalliances, some significant, we had been an inseparable couple ever since.

The difference on that fateful day in March was that Cameron had woken out of sorts and agitated after another night of Lariam dreams. When I say that it was different, actually it wasn't. These nights of broken sleep, tossing and turning, and crying out, had become part and parcel of our married life. They had been a feature of our existence since Cameron had taken Lariam for a live firing exercise in Kenya in 2001. The dreams bothered him and he was always moody and irascible after them. Initially they had been frequent, nightly or every other night, but after a few years they seemed to dissipate slightly, only seeming to manifest if he was particularly stressed, or tired, or both.

I had often asked what these dreams contained but he would never tell me. The lurid, vivid nightmares associated with taking Lariam for antimalarial prophylaxis had become somewhat infamous over the previous decade and many, many soldiers reported similar bizarre dreams, some that were real enough to sound almost like psychosis. What I didn't realise was how very common these were, and that they could be a portent, or 'prodromal', for more serious neuropsychiatric issues. He would not tell me what the dreams contained, just saying 'you don't want to know' with a meaningful inflection and intimating that often they contained myself, and our girls. I guess the thought of what scenarios might include all of us in such horrible nightmares put me off pushing for further details, but also suggested that the tenor of the dreams was too horrible to repeat.

Prior to taking Lariam, Cameron had not been a 'dreamer' in the sleep sense, but I certainly was. It was one of the notable differences between us. Frequently, I would have extraordinary or memorable dreams. I have dreamed vividly since childhood including having repetitive dreams of the same scenario for years and years, and he had marvelled that I could frequently remember my dreams in detail and recite their often bizarre or hilarious content the following morning. He did not experience dreams in that manner until taking Lariam. After Lariam, vivid, memorable dreams became a feature of his very existence, and not a pleasant one.

So this was a typical post-Lariam dreams morning. Cameron was subdued and irritable after a poor night's sleep, but it was the usual Saturday morning in a small house in

Scotland with two young kids who were full of life and happy to have their dad at home after many years of him being away with the army or work. At this time Cameron was working from home having recently set up a new business venture with two ex-military colleagues, one who worked for HSBC in risk management, and another who was located in Russia working for a private security firm.

The business, called Scio Consulting Ltd, was a military risk analysis venture that aimed to provide global security reports to the banking and finance sector, as well as other entities, working in locations that could represent risk through local military instabilities or other insurgent activities. It had taken some time to get off the ground, but after a few months of networking and pressing hands, the first contract had come in and the team were working on the necessary background intelligence to get the report to the customer. Although things were starting to come to fruition, money was tight and Cameron was definitely feeling the pressure that any emerging business owners might experience.

I, on the other hand, had huge faith in him and his colleagues, and was simply delighted that the contract was on the table and the team were working. I felt that this was a good sign. It validated the decision to leave his previous role, and that even if the business did not turn over big bucks, certainly we would be financially stable. I was working full-time as a research scientist at the University of Edinburgh, having finished my PhD in development neurosciences a few years earlier, and both our trajectories seemed finally to be heading in a common direction, and one where Cameron could potentially spend more time at home than in his previous roles which essentially had him living away from the family home for most of our married life.

Cameron had left the Army in late 2004. At that point in time, he had become increasingly disheartened by the erosion of the trust of the British public in their military after taking part in the Iraq invasion, commonly referred to as 'Gulf War II'. He had volunteered to go and had landed a plum position, British military liaison officer stationed with a US contingent on the southern border. Whilst he loved the work, his homecoming had left him disappointed and disillusioned. In hindsight, this may also have been somewhat the impact of an increasingly altered thinking process due to the long-term impacts of Lariam and the constant interminable dreams, but it was hard to place his level of disappointment at the time. It was almost as though he was embarrassed at having been part of the coalition forces that toppled Saddam Hussein's regime in those critical few months in 2003.

The 'war' began in March and was all over (so we thought) by July, during which time thousands of British, American, Australian and other coalition forces swarmed into Iraq taking over all military strongholds and causing the downfall of Hussein's despotic regime. Despite this great military achievement, Cameron returned home enervated. British soldiers were being castigated for the failure to find the infamous 'weapons of mass destruction', and for brutality towards prisoners. The commonplace use of roadside bombs that had harmed both military targets and civilians had left him feeling that the victory was pyrrhic. There was no flag-waving in the streets on his return, no victory parade, just an overwhelming feeling that the British Army had been used for political gain rather than justifiable military need.

The emerging story of British military involvement in Gulf War II and the relationship between British Prime Minister Tony Blair and the then US President George H.W. Bush, may now validate some of his feelings, but this was not publicly known at the time. He just came back flat, deflated, having seen some fairly appalling behaviour and felt a lack of public integrity for the invasion. This tempered his ability to really engage with the career he had loved up to that time. After a brief stint in Whitehall as a Ministry of Defence desk jockey, he decided to try his hand in civvy street. I had hoped that this was to be a new era for him and his career, but also for us as a family. Sadly, through a series of twists of fate this was not to be the case, and I am sure that Lariam had a hand in it all.

———

After retiring from the Army as a Major in 2004, Cameron took up a role as a strategic business manager for the primary healthcare management firm founded a few years earlier by his mother. With his personnel management experience, erudite manner and friendly good looks, Cameron transitioned into this new role easily. However, after eighteen months or so, it was clear that the boom era for practice management was over, with changes in the internal funding models to the NHS and primary healthcare system making it harder for practices to engage consultancy services. Practices were being encouraged to amalgamate into multi-GP conglomerates. With business retracting, Cameron took the leap to be his own boss and enact the business idea that he had been forming for some time with an old Highlander friend, and their company Scio was born.

As I say, this was a blissful time for me and the girls. After 10 long years of having a husband who invariably was living somewhere other than the family home, we were finally together. Cameron had left the family business just prior to Christmas in 2005, convenient as I also managed to take a fall from my horse, who decided to try ice skating on a frozen puddle, and fractured the head of my radius. With a painful break and my right arm in a sling I was off work for 6 weeks and unable to do much other than painfully point and lift a teacup, but Cameron was home to help and the girls and I were finally a full time family, like everyone else. It felt wonderful, broken arm and all.

After six weeks at home my arm was mending, and we settled into the daily routine of family life. Kids to school, me to work, and Cameron at home developing the business. Initially, there were some trips to London, mainly to the City, to meet people working in the banking sector with interests in the Middle East, Russia, and the old Yugoslavia, but after some initial networking, the first contract was on the horizon and Cameron was at home compiling information and waiting on the contract to be signed.

There was no doubt he was stressed, he was smoking incessantly and drinking more than I would have liked, in fact much more than was healthy, but he was home and at least I felt I could support him as he made the transition to being self-employed and getting a business up and running. After all, information was my business too, albeit it scientific journal articles and data on numbers of cells in different areas of the brain, so handling and managing information was what we were both now doing and I felt that I could support him in his ventures. So the days passed, one by one, and we seemed to be making progress in the right direction.

However, things were clearly not alright. How could they be? After all, randomly and without warning he was dead. And it is only working backwards that I can now see some of the warning signs that were telling me that he had not been himself for some time. I guess that that's the trouble with Lariam, the change in personality, the altered behaviours, somehow become normal, but they are not normal, and with Cameron living away from the family home for so many years, the changes had been intangible but had altered his thinking in many ways, including fundamentally altering his ability to self-regulate his own feelings and behaviour with fatal consequences. After his death, a medical colleague of mine described the event of his passing as a 'psychotic episode', and I think that is correct.

———

In hindsight there had been something wrong for some time. I just hadn't understood the signs at the time but they were there. I have come to understand now, having talked to many hundreds of veterans who have taken Lariam and suffered long term neuropsychiatric consequences, that these changes in mind-set and behaviour are very, very common. The increasing anger and inability to hold his temper in check had been an escalating feature. It almost seemed that he could 'hold it together' for business, but when he returned home and let his guard down the least thing could result in a disproportionate response.

Some toys left in the middle of the living room floor, muddy boots worn across a clean floor, a broken pair of glasses, the person who took a parking space outside the shop he was trying to visit one Christmas Eve that resulted in a police charge for aggravated assault—a completely uncharacteristic road rage incident. It took some careful legal wrangling and vouches of perfect character to avoid a criminal charge, something that would have been highly detrimental for his career at that point.

He became increasingly angry and paranoid. People were watching his work, they were looking at him and talking behind his back. He wasn't valued at work, and other people were coming to steal his job. He became increasingly hard to convince of his own self-worth, which for a man who had always been supremely confident was a significant change in personality. He was not earning enough, his house was not big enough, his car not new enough. He compared himself to friends who had old established country families, and city jobs, and, no, we did not have those things, but we had two beautiful children and lived in the most beautiful part of the world, and that was enough for me.

His appetites increased in various ways. His drinking seemed to be ever-increasing, and he went from smoking one pack a day to two. He seemed so confident and in control on one hand, but totally unable to control other parts of his life at all. On occasions I was actually scared for my safety and that of my girls, and made a number of calls to the Samaritans to ask for help. However, after these nights of rage and anger, he would be contrite and hold me saying that nothing like that would ever happen again. Until it did happen again, and we would go through the same routine, not often, but often enough for it to be frightening and concerning.

I was perplexed and worried but had no idea what to do to help my husband. This was the mid-2000s and no one talked about 'PTSD' in those days, nor was the crisis in military veterans' mental health even discussed, and I had no contact with any other military families so I had no benchmark to tell if this was normal behaviour for someone in the Forces or not. Equally, as appearances were very important to him, this was not something we ever discussed with anyone outside. I had no idea that abuse could extend beyond the physical, and although he punched walls, broke doors, and expressed his anger in other ways, I never felt he would deliberately hurt me or the girls—accidentally maybe, he was certainly rough with them at times and I protected them from him when I knew that he was out of sorts, but actual danger, never.

All I did know was that this was not the man I knew, not the man who was a wonderful and caring husband and father, not the man I had seen grow up from a teenager to a man, and leader of men in his beloved Gordon Highlanders. I put it down to the stress of feeling disenfranchised from the job he loved, and was sure that if he could just be *home* that this would change, and that all would be well. And initially, I was right. But then that fateful Saturday came and our lives changed forever.

———

So Cameron awoke from a night of Lariam dreams. We only had a few plans for the day, the girls had their usual Saturday afternoon riding lesson at our local riding stables, and Cameron had planned to meet up with his father to watch the Six Nations rugby at the pub that afternoon. His father also lived in our small village of West Linton in the Scottish Borders, having retired at 65 and headed north. He was also making the most of Cameron being home to help him train his new black Labrador pup to the gun, a talented bundle called Dbhuva, so the pair would meet every morning to work together to get the pup trained in recall and retrieving with toys and then bird dummies to get her used to 'picking up', the job she would be doing when she was older at one of the local shoots.

The girls were up and about early, as usual. ███, 8, bright and bubbly, blonde and quirky with a wicked sense of humour, was getting us organised with Saturday morning television, and ███, 5, with dark ringlet curls and a powerhouse of action, was helping clear the morning dishes and organising her boots and hat for her riding lesson. March in the Scottish Borders is generally cold, frequently wet, but also a transitional time of year. After the long winter months where the sun would only begin to show its face after 9 am before beating a hasty retreat by 3.30 pm, the days were starting to lengthen and early daffodils were beginning to poke their heads through in the gardens and verges in and around the village.

West Linton, with a population of approximately 1,500 at that time, was a beautiful, picturesque Scottish village, with a strong local community. We had moved to the village in 1996, just before we found out that we were going to be parents, and bar a short stint in Lisburn in Norther Ireland, where ███ was born, I had lived there continuously at Cameron's insistence as he wanted his children to grow up in Scotland. During this

104

time he had moved around, from posting to posting. There were several tours of Northern Ireland including one in Armagh in an intelligence role, a training platoon commander posting at Catterick, Junior Staff College in Warminster, then a posting to HQ Scotland at Edinburgh Castle before Iraq and Gulf War II.

On his return from Iraq, he finished his posting in Edinburgh and transitioned to a position in Whitehall as well as undertaking a selection course somewhere secret. So although he was always on the move from job to job, location to location, the one piece of stability was always returning to West Linton for his weekends and holidays. This was the place he 'came home' to, the place he felt most safe and secure.

Despite my being the one living in the village, he was definitely the one that people knew. A real socialite, he was a frequent visitor at one of the local pubs and seemed to know everyone, a trait that his younger daughter seems to have inherited from him. I was very much the working mum, juggling two kids as a 'single' parent and working full time in academic research at Edinburgh. It was hard work, but we were both committed to giving the girls the best start in life we could, and for him that meant Scotland, Scotland, Scotland. So, on that Saturday in March it was the usual Saturday morning routine. Kids, breakfast and then plans for the day. Or so I thought.

——

That morning Cameron was definitely out of sorts. He was irritable, took frequent breaks 'outside' to smoke as no one smoked inside the house, and couldn't seem to settle to eat or sit to read the Saturday morning papers. He said that his eyes were troubling him and that he couldn't see properly, which was definitely unusual, but I didn't question further. He had a regular prescription of contact lenses and also wore glasses in the evening or when off-duty to read or watch television; however, he had recently had his prescription checked and apparently all was well so it seemed odd that his eyes should be troubling him on this particular day.

He sourced his contact lenses from the optometrist based in our local Edinburgh Costco, as being both good value for money and convenient as co-located with Sainsbury's (a regular Saturday morning shopping trip location). He was agitated that he wouldn't be able to see the rugby game properly that afternoon and so we decided to take a trip into Costco to see if we could get his prescription checked.

I had said to him that Saturday morning was usually busy at the optometrist but he insisted that he would be able to do a 'walk-in' appointment, so I got the girls ready in winter boots, coats, gloves and hats and we piled into the car and took the 20-mile scenic trip, along the edge of the majestic Pentland Hills south of Edinburgh, to Costco on the edge of the town.

Costco for the girls always meant the chance to look at the toys and books. So while Cameron headed to the eyewear section, I took the girls in for a browse. They each chose a book, and we returned to the entrance area to find Cameron agitated and annoyed that the receptionist at the optometrist had told him that he could not get an appointment, and the earliest they could do was Thursday of that week. He was angry, storming out to the car, with us following meekly behind. He put his foot to the metal and drove home at top speed.

Luckily, the girls noticed nothing but I was concerned with his somewhat reckless driving and agitated demeanour, so when we got home I suggested that the girls and I would go to the park and he could head around to his Dad's place to pick up the pup and take her out. Usually, some time out training the dogs helped him settle when he was like this, and he agreed to the plan.

The girls and I headed out to the swings, and after a cold hour or so returned to a quiet house. Surprisingly, Cameron had not gone to collect the pup but had left a note to say he was meeting his Dad in the pub early, at midday, and would be back later, after the rugby. I was relieved that he now seemed to be having a better day than the one that had begun, and got started with organising the girls lunch before heading out to the riding stables for their afternoon lesson.

Riding was cold but enjoyable. Both girls did well, ▆▆▆▆ on lead-reins and ▆▆▆ steering her pony herself, including over some small jumps. As a horsey mum, I was proud that they were getting to grips with riding, and taking part in activities, but we were all glad to get home. Even 45 minutes in a biting wind is enough for anyone. When we got back to the house, all was quiet.

The girls settled down to DVDs and books, whilst I prepared dinner: pork loin chops, mashed potatoes and cauliflower cheese—good wholesome winter food. The hours ticked by and I kept an eye on the time, knowing that the match started at 3.30 pm and therefore should finish just after 5 pm. It was a Six Nations match, Ireland versus Scotland, so there would be a fair few punters in the pub to cheer the national side on. I was hoping that Cameron would leave quickly after the game, having gone up early, so that we could eat dinner together.

Five-thirty pm came and went, and then 5.45 pm. I sent a text to Cameron's phone—'Are you home for dinner soon?', but no reply. By 6 pm, the girls were hungry so we sat and ate, and I made a plate for Cameron and put it in the oven to stay warm. I'd started the washing-up and the girls were lounging tired in the living room when finally Cameron returned home. He didn't say anything when he came in, just took off his coat and headed for the kitchen table where I made a place and put his dinner on the table. I turned my back and continued to finish in the kitchen talking over my shoulder as I did so.

'Who won?' I said.

'Ireland.'

'Ah, ok. Was your dad there? And Tim?' Tim was a good friend of Cameron's and someone he always looked forward to seeing. No answer.

I carried on with some small talk, but didn't get much of a response. When I turned round to say 'Hey, come on, tell me how things were at the pub', Cameron was just sitting there, totally still. The room seemed black around him. I went over and put a hand on his shoulder and squeezed and said 'Hey, eat your dinner, it will get cold. I'm going to run the girls a bath'. He didn't move, just didn't say a word. I figured that the disappointment with the optometrist, and then a loss at the rugby had constituted a bad day.

I'd get the girls bathed and into bed—Cameron hated bath time as it was noisy and messy— and then we'd just chill out with a movie and get an early night. I went through to the living room and sat next to the girls on the sofa, one under each arm, and watched the end of their Disney movie with them. After a little while, I heard Cameron get up from the table and go out of the front door. This was a usual routine for him after dinner as he would go outside to have a post-prandial cigarette, usually sitting in the porch if it was cold, or leaning against the old wooden struts if the moon was bright and sky was light, pulling on a cigarette which he usually put out in one of the flower pots and then put the stub in the outside bin.

The porch was a feature of the house. It wasn't original but had been added on to the old stone bothy cottage sometime in the mid-20th century. 'Hansel and Gretel' would describe the porch, with its pitched roof and large oak beams supporting the arch to the doorway that were painted in very traditional white and black, wattle and daub style. Inside on either side was a low wooden bench; an ideal resting place for rods and guns, wellington boots, and for me, riding gear that smelt too horsey to bring inside. Sitting in the porch, on the right hand bench seat at that time was a rope halter and a set of rope reins, brought home to be washed ready for their next ride out. I loved the porch, it was a beautiful feature of the property, probably the reason that we had both fallen in love with this quirky mish-mash cottage.

After 10 minutes or so, Cameron came back into the house and headed up the stairs. The layout of the house was eclectic, having been constructed from an amalgamation of two adjacent properties, a single-story old bothy cottage dating from about 1890 making up the kitchen, dining room and living room, and the upstairs being of a second more 1900's Edwardian style house, where the bedrooms, bathroom and attic were located. Cameron headed up the stairs and into the spare room which was immediately above the living room in which we were sitting.

The spare room was the attic of the old cottage, with a steep pitched ceiling, wooden floors and a skylight window that opened out over the porch and garden. It was also the room that housed a relatively unused cross-trainer and all of Cameron's clothes and hiking gear. A keen walker, he still kept all of this in good condition and sorted it regularly, even if it was less used now than he would have liked. It was also the space where he would take himself for a nap if a few too many beers had been consumed at the pub in order not to disturb me or the girls after a night out.

I heard him go in, move around for a little, and then the footfalls ceased. I assumed he had gone for a lie down, which was not unusual, and thought nothing more of it other than that I would give him a little bit of time and then see if he was ok.

Once the movie ended, about 10 minutes later, I hustled the girls up the stairs to the bathroom and turned on the taps. While they stripped for the bath I gathered their nightclothes, and a book for bathtime. I readied their room for bed, turning down sheets, closing the curtains and making sure the heater was turned up a little to keep them warm. Once the bath was run, they both popped in and I sat on the toilet seat next to the bath and read them a story. ████████'s favourite was *The Very Hungry Caterpillar* by Eric Carle, an old favourite of many generations, so we read through all the food the caterpillar had eaten and then I left the girls to play with their bath toys and went to check on Cameron.

The spare room was immediately across the hall from the bathroom and I opened the door and peered in. The view into the room was partially obscured as you had to go down a step and around a corner to get into the main area, but I could see the double bed from where I was standing and there was clearly no one in it. I went to our main bedroom, again no one was there. That was very odd. Where was he? I checked the girls' room but as I had only been in there minutes before I knew that he wasn't in their either.

Now I was getting increasingly agitated. I went downstairs, and looked out the front door. Perhaps he had slipped downstairs and I hadn't noticed whilst I was in the bathroom. Again, I couldn't see him. Then I saw his plate untouched on the table and became suddenly frightened. Where was he? Was he hiding? This was too odd. I jumped up the stairs taking two at a time and went back into the spare room. Coming into the room my eyes were on the bed, thinking maybe I had missed him under the covers, or that he was on the other side where my view was slightly obscured, and in turning around the corner, I almost walked straight into his hanging body.

His head was bent towards the floor, his tongue protruding, and he seemed to be sagging at the knees. I froze, but then reacted, if this was a joke it was a very poor one.

'Cameron, what are you doing?' I said faltering, and rushed to hold him. I grabbed him by the waist, expecting his eyes to open and a mischievous grin to cross his face, but it didn't happen. He stayed limp in my arms, a dead weight, and I realised this was no joke. I looked to see how he was caught and not falling to the floor. There was a rope around his neck and it was hooked over the window latch on a small skylight, an old pitched window, in the corner of the room.

I pulled at the rope to see if I could dislodge it, but it wouldn't shift. It seemed to be caught on the improbably small piece of metal. I tried to lift him, panicking now, saying 'Oh shit, Oh shit' over and over under my breath, knowing that the girls were only feet away and I couldn't have them walk in on this macabre scene. With the after effects of my broken elbow still being keenly felt, I didn't have the strength to lift his limp body to release the cord that held him to the window latch, it was no good, I couldn't seem to move him at all. But I had to get him down. My heart was now racing, but all I could think of was that I needed to call an ambulance, and I needed to cut that rope.

I raced down to the kitchen and grabbed a small knife and my mobile phone. I ran back up the stairs and cut the rope above and behind his head. His body dropped to the floor with a heavy thud, and I knew two things. Firstly, there was no way the girls hadn't heard that something odd was happening, and secondly that he had tried to take his own life. As quickly as I could, I cut the rope around his neck.

Once it was in my hands I had a horrible realisation, these were the rope reins I had left in the porch. It didn't compute how they could now be so elegantly tied into a noose, looking like something out of a movie. I threw it across the room, as far away from me as I could. I didn't want my girls seeing the elegantly tied noose, perfectly constructed with all the skill and expertise of a mountaineering aficionado. With shaking hands, and talking to him all the time 'Cameron, wake up, please wake up, don't do this to me, wake up', I dialled 999.

'Hello, fire, police or ambulance,' a voice said.

'Ambulance, and quickly, O please help me, my husband has hung himself,' I felt that my heart was burning as I heard the door open behind me and a little voice said, 'Mummy, is everything ok? We heard a noise'. It was ██████, out of the bath and wrapped in a towel, staring at me.

'Daddy's hurt,' I said. 'I'm calling the ambulance, can you get your little sister out of the bath and get her dressed please? Can you help Mummy do that? I have to stay here with Daddy.' I tried to keep my voice as calm as I could, I knew if I panicked that ██████ would be frightened, and what was happening to their dad now was enough for us to deal with. I needed to look strong so that they would feel safe even if something totally extraordinary was happening. Mothering instinct kicked in to protect them from the worst.

██████ nodded sagely and turned back across the hall. I heard her helping her sister out of the bath and down to their bedroom. In the meantime, the ambulance staff had come onto the phone and were starting to give me instructions as to how to do CPR. One, two, three, four, five, six, seven, eight, nine, ten chest compressions, then hold the nose and blow deeply into the mouth. And just keep going. I did as I was told.

The girls came back down the hallway and opened the door again. I had to keep going with CPR, I couldn't stop, but equally I knew that an ambulance was some time away. The two local ambulance stations were Galashiels, and Edinburgh Royal Infirmary; even blue-lighting they would be at least 30 minutes. I couldn't have these two young children standing watching me try to revive their father for all that time, I needed some help.

'██████, can you go and get the phone from the kitchen counter and bring it to me, we'll try to call Grandad?' I asked her as I kept going with CPR, one, two, three, four, five, six, seven, eight, nine, ten chest compressions, then hold the nose and blow deeply into the mouth.

████ zipped down the stairs with ████ in tow and came back moments later with the phone. I was still talking to the ambulance worker on my mobile, pleading for an ambulance to hurry, all the while them giving me reassurances that the ambulances were on their way and that I was doing everything right. I fumbled Cameron's father's number into the phone. It rang, and rang, but no answer. He must still be at the pub I thought. I couldn't send the girls to the pub, but I could ask them to alert our neighbours. Across the way, literally maybe 20 feet from our front door was our neighbour's house. These were a lovely couple, he was a local businessman and she owned the hair salon next door to their house. They knew the girls from many years of cutting their hair and I knew I could send the girls to ask them for help finding Cameron's father.

'████', I said as calmly as I could. 'Take ████ and go and knock on Alan and Tracey's door and see if they can go to the pub to look for Grandad. Tell them that Cameron is ill and can they find him to come and help.'

One, two, three, four, five, six, seven, eight, nine, ten chest compressions, then hold the nose and blow deeply into the mouth. The girls turned and went hand in hand down the stairs, and I heard the front door open. For a moment, it was just me, him and the ambulance lady on the end of the phone.

'Why is he not coming round? It's not working!' I wailed at the phone. 'Oh please can the ambulance come quickly?' My heart was beating out of my chest, tears streaming down my face, and all the time I kept up the rhythm: One, two, three,

114

four, five, six, seven, eight, nine, ten chest compressions, hold the nose, blow deeply into the mouth.

I looked at his face. He looked exactly the same as ever— his lips now had colour, his fingertips had gone from blue to pinkish. I was doing something right but he wasn't waking up. This wasn't what usually happened in Casualty, when people did CPR and the person came back to life. Why wasn't this happening for me? I didn't understand. One, two, three, four, five, six, seven, eight, nine, ten chest compressions, hold the nose, blow deeply into the mouth. I looked at his clothes, they were the same as the ones he had been wearing out— a grey wool polo neck jumper, and Levi's jeans, with his RM Williams boots. Cameron always dressed well, even when he was dressing down, but for the first time I noticed the urine stain that had spread down one leg of his trousers. I didn't realise at the time but this was the sign that I should have realised that no amount of CPR would bring him back.

He had lost autonomic control of his bowels, usually the last event after complete loss of consciousness, when death must have been imminent. I had simply been too late to save him. I found out later that I had approximately 6 minutes between him losing consciousness and my being able to revive him, and even if I had, he might have been permanently brain damaged. I'm not exactly sure how long it was, but it was certainly longer than 6 minutes between him heading upstairs and me finding his lifeless body. That he had hung himself in the room above my head was not an indication that he had intended to be stopped or found in time. There was no reason, and no note. It simply made no sense.

Moments later, the girls returned. They had found Alan and he had gone straight out to see if he could find their

Grandad. Then all of a sudden I heard deep footsteps on the stairs and a paramedic appeared in the small doorway of the attic room behind where the girls were sitting tightly together on the step, watching me give CPR to their father. I will never forget that feeling—my desperation reaching out to that man in blue who appeared so large in the doorway 'Oh my god, please help me, help him.'

The paramedic stepped into the room and lifted me by my elbow from the floor. 'Don't worry, we'll take over from here, you take the children downstairs.' I looked behind him and another paramedic was coming up the stairs with a large case of medical equipment. With both relief and despair, I reached for my mobile and thanked the ambulance lady who had stayed on the phone with me the whole time, and took the girls downstairs. I found out later that the whole ambulance service room had stopped when I had been on the line. One of the workers on roster that night was from our village, knew me and my daughters, and the whole room was visibly affected. I can only imagine what it must have felt like to listen to my desperate voice, my counting every chest pulse of CPR and the call centre team knowing that the likelihood of revival was zero.

I took the girls downstairs and we sat on the sofa and I curled them one under each arm, just as we had done about an hour before, and I cried silent tears of terrible grief. At that moment two police officers arrived, looking stern and official. One headed up the stairs and the other sat on the sofa opposite me and spoke reassuring words— that I shouldn't worry, the ambulance men would be doing their best for my husband, and that he was also there to help. I couldn't speak, I just cried. At that moment, ▮▮▮ did an extraordinary thing. She got up

116

from the sofa and went to the toy box in the corner of the living room.

'We need a story,' she said. 'stories make it better.' And with a composure well beyond her eight years she started to read one of her books out loud. My tears kept falling, and the policeman looked as though he might lose his composure too. Then at that moment one of the most awful things happened. The phone rang. No one moved to answer it, it wasn't the time for small talk so after a few rings the answering machine kicked in. It was Cameron's voice, loud and clear, answering the call with the recorded message.

'Hello, you've reached the Quinn household. None of us can take your call right now but if you leave a message we'll get back to you as soon as we can.'

We all froze. There was a terrible moment like he had walked back into the room from the dead. The policeman leapt to his feet and headed for the phone. He took it from its cradle and turned the answering machine off. 'I'm so sorry. Don't worry, I'll stop that for you,' he said kindly and I could not have felt more grateful for his tender concern. ▮▮▮▮ continued to read, her gentle voice rising and falling with the lines from the children's book.

After some interminable time, there was a footfall on the stairs. The second ambulance man came a few steps down and looked at me, and then at the policeman and just shook his head. 'I'm so sorry,' he said. I opened my mouth but no words came out. Just tears. And I held my girls and sobbed.

The door opened behind us and Cameron's father came rushing into the room with our neighbour behind him. He came straight to me and held me and the girls.

'What's happened, what's happened?' he said.

'He's dead, Bill. I don't know why.' I saw his face crumble in front of me, and then look at the policeman. The policeman nodded and the father headed up the stairs to be with his son.

Time blurs after that. The police suggested that I take the girls to their Grandad's house so that the ambulance men and morticians could do their work. We collected coats and jumpers and they drove us together in a police car the 500 yards to Cameron's father's small terraced house in the village. Cameron's father stayed at the house and helped the morticians tend to remove his body. I know they washed his face and hands and made sure he looked presentable. The ambulance men had tried to revive him with adrenalin and defibrillation, but we were all too late.

The following morning as I cleared the detritus of their work, I found the wrappings from various tubes and needles, and swabs where they must have cleaned his chest to make a good contact for the defibrillator. There was also a strange smell in the room, a sweet smell that has only ever come back to me once when I felt his presence very strongly on a walk in the hills a few weeks after he died, and one I have never come across since. It lingered in the room for several weeks after he died, as I slept there every night hoping to feel his presence or receive a visit giving me some explanation of why he had done such a thing, but there was no visit and no explanation.

The girls were taken to a kindly neighbour whose kids they knew from school and I spent several hours giving a statement to the police. No, I had no idea why he had taken his life. He had left no note, had given no warning. I told them of his dreams the night before, that he had been out of sorts that day, but that he had never been suicidal or ever even intimated thoughts in that way—bar once when he was taking Lariam, but that had been years before. They took their notes, and eventually left. I can't imagine a worse job and their kindness and humanity has stayed with me to this day.

Friends hearing the news started to arrive at the house to console the grieving family. We phoned my family and Cameron's mother to call them to the village, we were numb with shock and pain. Eventually, I put the girls to sleep together in their room at their Grandad's house and lay on the bed in their main bedroom. It must have been midnight or 1 am, or later.

I tried to sleep, but sleep seemed not to come, but I must have fallen into a fitful rest eventually as after some time I awoke and went to the window and opened the curtain. Somehow the terrible night before had ended and the sun had risen. I still have no idea how that could have happened; when my whole world had ended. It must have been 5 or 6am and the sun was just rising and the world was white. A deep blanket of snow covered the ground, and the village had descended into a deep silence.

———

'Google' Jane Quinn and you will find something along the lines of:

Charles Sturt University. Associate Dean (Research) Faculty of Science/Associate Professor in Veterinary Physiology. Co-founder of a multidisciplinary research team investigating the effects and mode of actions of chemicals, both naturally-occurring products and synthetic compounds, causing toxicity to domestic species, plants and the environment.

A/ Prof Quinn works extensively with military veterans exposed to quinoline antimalarials, to gain a better understanding of the neuropsychiatric health conditions that can be caused by this exposure. She is the Scientific Adviser for the Australian Quinoline Veterans and Families Association (QVFA) and has provided evidence on the effects of these drugs to both the Australian and UK governments. She regularly liaises with government authorities, the pharmaceutical industry, Ex-Services organisations and the media in this capacity.

My definition of Jane Quinn:

*A borders lass, steadfast, will not run away from danger, keeps going whatever the difficulties.*

# Chapter 5

## Swerve to Lead

*I should add that I have some personal experience of this drug but, on balance, am content to go with the formal advice.*

*-General Sir Richard Dannatt, Chief of the General Staff,*
*21 January 2007*

In a penetrating and disturbing 2017 documentary film 'Mefloquine: The anti-malarial drug investigation', the producer and narrator, Cailean Watt, has to make repeated requests to the MoD for an interview.[1] Cailean had discovered multiple inconsistencies and apparent serious malpractice across a range of governmental and commercial bodies. The MoD won't speak to him and Cal offers the astute line, "The Ministry of Defence were appearing defensive."

Cal was also on something of a personal journey as he, too, had taken Lariam when backpacking abroad with friends. After taking his fifth tablet, the drug hit him badly. Cal describes an overwhelming feeling of terror and an episode where he says "I had no idea who or where I was." One of his companions recalls that Cal was becoming increasingly paranoid and had lost his grip of reality. She recounts how he had become withdrawn from the group and at one stage he even assumed an alias. She goes on to say, "we actually had a conversation about whether or not you might try and kill yourself." Thankfully, Cal has now recovered although he admits that occasionally he still does have bad days, even weeks— I know what that feels like. Cal took his Lariam in 2005, the year before Cameron Quinn hanged himself.

In the film, Cal is eventually granted an audience by the MoD. They don't put up a minister or a particularly senior officer but he is able to interview a Group Captain Andrew Green, a medical officer with the appointment of Armed Forces Director of Infection Prevention and Control. Group Captain Green argues that it was essential for the army to embrace Lariam in the 1990s because there was so little else available: had the Group Captain not heard of Doxycycline either? [1] Certainly the Surgeon General, Air Marshal Paul Evans, seemed unfamiliar with it. He had struggled, and manifestly failed, even to pronounce 'Doxycycline' when interviewed on the BBC Today programme by John Humphries on 25 September 2015. (The MoD's 'Defence in the media' blog for that day avoided the drug's name when covering the Evans interview. Sadly, the Defence media team's credibility took another hit as they could not even spell 'Air Marshal' correctly.) [m] [2]

Group Captain Green was evasive. His faltering responses to Cal plead that the data about adverse reactions to the drug

---

[1] Group Captain Green is also curiously silent on the fact that his own service, the Royal Air Force, banned Lariam use among pilots and aircrew because of its dangerous side effect profile.

[m] This criticism is not a cheap shot at poor journalism. Rather, the Blog entry is consistent with a very casual approach taken by the MoD towards truth and accuracy when discussing Lariam, as we will see.

could not be easily measured (so we ignore them?), and he denied, even at that late stage, that the extent or severity of side effects were sufficient to cause military doctors to stop advising the use of mefloquine. But when discussing Lariam, the Ministry of Defence had been long practised in evasion.

Evasive and defensive. And somewhat patronising. That was the MoD's response to Cameron Quinn's suicide when it was brought to their attention in the summer of 2006 by Jane and the Procurator Fiscal for Lothian and Borders, responsible for investigating the death.

———

While slowly coming to terms with Cameron's death, and even in the months before, Jane had learned that many people appeared to be suffering from Lariam toxicity. And the problem extended well beyond the British Army. Depression and imaginings of violence were among the effects endured by many of those offering her support and condolence. They ranged from a volunteer in the US Peace Corps to a teacher of English in the West African state of Benin; people whose lives had been shattered by the Lariam/WR 142 490 compound and who were now stalked by the fear of suicide.

With a clear need to investigate Lariam's role in Cameron's death, the Procurator Fiscal, Mr xxxxxx xxxxxx, wrote to the Army Medical Directorate on 22 June 2006 to ask some questions about the prescribing of antimalarial drugs for soldiers exercising in Africa.

The Procurator Fiscal received an uncharacteristically expeditious response from the MoD, dated 3 July, something rarely repeated over the coming years. The reply was from a

Dr S N Galbraith.[3] Notably, Mr xxxxxx's queries had been immediately passed to Dr Galbraith who was the Head of the Medico-Legal Department of the Army Medical Directorate. It was perplexing to Jane and Mr xxxxxx, but with hindsight perhaps unsurprising, that Dr Galbraith should have been instructed to respond on behalf of the MoD. The legal shutters were coming down.

The Galbraith letter is an extraordinarily tart and defensive composition devoid even of the common courtesy of an offer of condolence for Jane's bereavement. It certainly appears more legal than medico. And my own experience suggests that it would have been an exceptional feat of staff work to have been able to conduct a satisfactory investigation into this matter within five working days. Equally noteworthy is that Dr Galbraith did not sign the letter herself. As this single page document really does deserve some close scrutiny, it is presented in full as an appendix at the rear of this book.

In her opening two paragraphs, Dr Galbraith stated that, in general terms, the Army's use of antimalarial drugs was informed by, and compliant with, the national guidelines of the Health Protection Agency (later Public Health England and now the Health Security Agency) and the Advisory Committee on Malaria Prevention (ACMP). She also referred to a Ministry of Defence Consultant in Communicable Disease control who worked on such policies. That individual transpires to have been a then Wing Commander Andrew Green. Perhaps he might have been asked for a comment? But had Dr Galbraith engaged in some fairly basic research herself, she should have been aware of a key document which showed quite clearly that the Ministry of Defence, in the use

124

of antimalarial drugs, deviated markedly from the ACMP guidance. That document was the Surgeon General's Policy Letter on malaria prevention, due to be revised at the time of Jane's queries.[4] That policy letter does contain some confusing contradictions but, concerning chemoprophylaxis, it is quite clear about regulations for Joint Service exercises and operations:

> *The Permanent Joint Headquarters (PJHQ) [n] is to issue an instruction on malaria chemoprophylaxis for all joint or potentially joint deployments to geographic regions where malaria presents a risk to health. PJHQ is to carry out an area-specific risk assessment, and to determine the most appropriate antimalarial regimen.*

While the Policy Letter itself did not dictate explicit drug regimens for specific areas, it certainly laid that requirement upon the Joint or Single Service commands. And, as confirmed by their own medical staff, Lariam was the Army's default choice for antimalarial prophylaxis for British military personnel in African regions until at least 2015.[5] Thus, the Army was clearly not compliant with the guidelines set by the ACMP. It was using a predetermined regimen for chemoprophylaxis and, by definition, could not have been using the vitally important prescribing protocols required of such drugs.

---

[n] Located at Northwood, Middlesex, and just north of London, PJHQ is the tri-service organisation overseeing all armed forces deployments.

Chloroquine resistant antimalarials are included in the range of "prescription only" medications which should only be given following a one-on-one consultation between a qualified doctor and the patient. Presumably Dr Galbraith was aware of these important safety protocols. The most superficial of investigations would have confirmed that the MoD did not, "in general terms", follow "medical practice as laid down by... Public Health England." What she was saying was simply incorrect. She should have known better and her letter raises further suspicions about the integrity and safety of the MoD's Lariam policy.

Jane and the Procurator Fiscal had been particularly concerned about the significant body of anecdotal evidence of "Lariam days"; those days when troops were collectively given the drug, following which many would experience bad reactions. Dr Galbraith claimed to be unaware of "Lariam days". She further states "It is likely that I would be aware of them as I was closely involved advising in a group action against the Ministry of Defence brought by servicemen deploying to Sierra Leone who had been prescribed Lariam in 2000."

Here, Dr Galbraith is simply imposing a burden on the concept of credibility that it should not be expected to bear. It is almost inconceivable that the Army Medical Directorate should have been unaware of "Lariam days", regardless of Dr Galbraith's professed ignorance. There are two essentials to address here; the effects of the drug in the hours after the soldiers had consumed it and the fact that the drug was being imposed through what were, in essence, unethical and illegal Lariam parades.

Regarding the side effects of the drug, British health and defence ministers had already been regularly challenged about the efficacy of Lariam. The MP, Jean (now Baroness) Corston had spent many years exposing the hazards of Lariam and the long-term damage it had inflicted on so many travellers. Let us give Dr Galbraith the benefit of doubt and assume that she was, somehow, unaware of the public and parliamentary concerns about Lariam poisoning. These quotes, however, from Baroness Corston in 1997 from a debate she initiated in the House of Commons are illuminating [6] and tend to signpost the institutional evasion that was being continued years later by the MoD. But somehow the Medical Directorate remained in the dark. Perhaps Hansard [o] wasn't on their reading list.

*I asked a series of parliamentary questions last June, and was told by the Department of Health that revised guidelines were still being developed by the malaria advisory committee [MAC] and that no publication date had been set. I assumed that the MAC was a statutory body, but it turns out to be a self-selecting volunteer group of about 40 experts, which has met eight times since 1980. I asked again in early February when the committee would report, and was told by the Minister for Health that the consultation process was "taking longer than anticipated".*

*It is important to ask what advice GPs give and what they say about Lariam. Dr David Chisholm of the British Medical Association GPs committee, when asked whether*

---

[o] The official record of debates in Parliament.

*he would take Lariam, said on BBC television: I would be reluctant to, because of the information that is reported to me and to all doctors about its safety profile and its side effects. Some of these side effects are serious and extremely unpleasant. It must be admitted that there are disputes about the prevalence of side effects. Hoffman-La Roche has always claimed that the rate of serious side effects, defined by the company and by the WHO as leading to death, prolonged hospitalisation or significant disability, as one in 10,000. Dr Gordon Cook, an expert on malaria at the Hospital for Tropical Diseases, has described that as "sheer nonsense".*

*All the information that I have sought to date from the Department of Health regarding the number and nature of trials that have been done on Lariam before and since licensing has been refused.*

*This matter has the makings of a Government health scandal.*

(In 2017, Baroness Corston remained "staggered that people who are serving now are (still) being given Lariam".[7])

While stretching credulity, it may be possible that the Surgeon General and his staff remained in ignorance of the amnesia, psychotic episodes, paranoid delusions and terror attacks cited by Baroness Corston and independent medical experts. But it would seem most unlikely that the Head of the Medico-Legal Department of the Army Medical Directorate would have been unaware of an important legal case of 1997, that involving a Sgt Colin Murray of the Royal Engineers who had been convicted by Court Martial of the civil offence of wounding another soldier during an off-duty fight in Nairobi, Kenya.

Sgt Murray was on a military exercise and had been taking Lariam. He had a long record of blameless service and his violent behaviour was, according to his commanding officer, quite out of character. While taking Lariam, Sgt Murray experienced nightmares of spiders and bouts of anxiety but, without explaining why, the members of the Court Martial refused to accept that the drug may have been a causative factor.

The Court Martial determined that Sgt Murray should be imprisoned for six months, reduced to the ranks and dismissed from Her Majesty's service. That sentencing was subsequently overturned by civilian judicial review where credence was clearly given by Lord Chief Justice Bingham to expert medical evidence that Sgt Murray's violent behaviour was plausibly driven by Lariam.[8] That evidence had been presented to the military court but inexplicably ignored.

And are we to believe that the Head of the Medico-Legal Department of the Army Medical Directorate would have been unaware that soldiers in areas such as Sierra Leone and Afghanistan could not tolerate the drug's side effects? In 2002 Johnny Aisbett, my predecessor in Sierra Leone, informed his military doctor that every day that he took the drug, he experienced 24 hours of severe mental and physical exhaustion, as well as nausea. His medical records contain the following entry:

*13/03/02—Wishing to stop Lariam. Having problems with mood swings and temper. Altered sleep pattern and vivid dreams slowly getting worse. Short term memory loss.*

*Takes on Mon[day]. Advised of options and to try Doxycycline 100mg. Advised of side effects.*

This, and many other similar cases, had apparently not crossed the radars of the Army Medical Directorate and Dr Galbraith. And what of the suggestion that Dr Galbraith was personally unaware of Lariam parades, those "Lariam days" when the drug was simply forced on soldiers, whether they wanted it or not. Might that be credible?

The legal aspects of such drug enforcement regimes had recently been studied by Dr Galbraith herself in papers she had authored in the Journal of the Royal Army Medical Corps in 2000.[9,10] Dr Galbraith was exploring the tensions that could have arisen during the First Gulf War of 1991 between medical ethics and operational necessity; would the government have had a legal defence for imposing on soldiers vaccination against chemical or biological weapons that they might encounter on the battlefield?

In this context she observes, regarding military law, that the Army Act, 1955, "has not been used to coerce servicemen to undergo particular treatments they do not wish to partake in without their consent. If it were, the Ministry of Defence could risk action in battery."[11] Furthermore, in the 1950s, after it was alleged that servicemen abroad were stopped from going on leave having refused routine vaccinations, the Secretary of State for War had made it clear that existing instructions emphasised that vaccination and inoculation were voluntary.[12]

So it seems fair to conclude that Dr Galbraith had a professional and well-informed interest in this topic. And the same volume of the journal in which her articles were published included a paper in which an army doctor, serving in a battalion deployed to Sierra Leone, declares that it was the policy to impose Lariam compliance through supervised consumption parades.[13] Unofficial (that is illegal) punishments were employed as a form of coercion. The author of that paper, Major Nigel Fraser, RAMC, the medical officer (RMO) of the Second Battalion, The Royal Anglian Regiment, is almost boastful:

*We initially started a daily 'LARIAM parade' but it proved impossible to get all personnel in one place at one time despite the CSM's best efforts.* [p] *We settled on a system which placed responsibility on commanders to report daily to the Regimental Aid Post (RAP) and notify the duty medic, after witnessing their men taking their tablets. This was ticked off on a master board and the RMO then 'named and shamed' non-compliant personnel, in the evening 'O' group.* [q] *The plentiful supply of really unpleasant jobs and the firm convictions of the chain of command ensured that the system worked. There was a 'no questions asked' policy on issuing further mefloquine and insect repellent from the RAP to ensure that compliance was not affected by junior soldiers losing these items.*

---

[p] CSM. Company Sergeant Major. A warrant officer responsible for administration and discipline in a company (about 100 men).

[q] Orders Group. An executive and planning meeting, chaired by the Commanding Officer.

Are we to believe that Dr Galbraith only read her own published papers and that neither she nor any of the Medical Directorate was aware of what was happening in the field? Major/Dr Fraser and his commanding officer do appear to have exposed the Army, *prima facie,* to charges of what Dr Galbraith describes as battery. (Note that mefloquine was *issued* in the same manner as insect repellent.)

Absent from Major Fraser's article is any consideration of the possibility that one of his patients might have been intolerant to Lariam. It would certainly have been a statistical anomaly for all personnel in the unit to have been devoid of side effects indicating that an alternative was desirable or perhaps even essential. Trashing the basic tenet of patient confidentiality, and the denial of alternative medications, surely breach the most fundamental of medical ethics. This was not the Burmese jungle of 1944 and what is described in the RAMC Journal appears to go well beyond medical negligence.

Finally, scrutiny of Dr Galbraith's reference to "a group action against the Ministry of Defence brought by servicemen deploying to Sierra Leone who had been prescribed Lariam in 2000" suggests that, once again, the Head of the Medico-Legal Department was offering only at best a superficial engagement with the truth. Jane was intrigued by this statement and asked Dr Galbraith to elaborate. After all, this was, apparently, a matter in which Dr Galbraith "was closely involved". Galbraith declined to expound any further and referred Jane to the Army Directorate of Safety and Claims.

Subsequent responses Jane received from the MoD indicate that the group action which Dr Galbraith mentioned was not, in fact, related to the side effects of Lariam.

According to the MoD's Directorate of Safety and Claims, the Ministry of Defence "did receive a number of claims for compensation from service personnel" but these were from individuals "who alleged that due to the Department's negligence they contracted malaria during a deployment to Sierra Leone."[14] These cases appear to have had nothing to do with side effects but concerned the MoD's failure to provide antimalarial drugs. Furthermore, this failure had been formally acknowledged.

According to a report provided by the MoD to Parliament's Defence Select Committee in 2000, an Army Board of Inquiry had established that 200 personnel were, indeed, sent to Sierra Leone without anti-malaria tablets. (We will learn much more of this deployment in a later chapter.)The report states that the situation was remedied through local procurement of a French drug until that was "replaced by supplies of the preferred British drug, mefloquine."[15] Presumably someone "closely involved" in those cases would have been well aware of these details.

A reasonable conclusion to draw from the MoD's response to Jane was that this was a problem they did not want to address; throwing up misleading inferences from recent cases might help to deter any thoughts of legal action. Certainly, the implied assumption that Jane's enquiries were pecuniary was falsely based, and to her, grossly insulting. But clearly, the MoD had something to hide. Anyway, Jane was not giving up.

In the summer of 2006, Jane pressed for some elaboration from Dr Galbraith. Three months passed and she heard nothing. The Army Medical Directorate had seemingly lost something of its remarkable staff zeal. In November Jane sent a prompt to Dr Galbraith, but Jane also decided that it was necessary to alert the Army Command to what was going on. Thus, she wrote personally to the Chief of the General Staff (CGS), General Sir Richard (now Lord) Dannatt.[16] Her engagement with Lord Dannatt had two important outcomes, one immediate and the other taking a decade to emerge.

The first was a spur delivered to the flank of the Army Medical Directorate which prompted a more detailed exposition of the Army's antimalarial policy. The second was to uncover one of the most egregious deceits of the Lariam scandal and the abdication of leadership at the very highest level. Someone had forgotten the motto 'Serve to Lead'. Jane's letter to Lord Dannatt makes such an important plea that it, too, is included in full as an appendix. However, it is worth highlighting here this essential paragraph:

*The overriding reason for this letter to you, General, is to ask you to investigate my concerns and, if Lariam does predispose soldiers to developing severe mental reactions, then take action to ensure that another Army wife and family does not suffer these same catastrophic consequences.*

Jane received an acknowledgement from the CGS in which he expressed his desire to be able to address her concerns directly and to be able to give Jane the answers that she was seeking. Doubtless prompted by the CGS's interest, Jane was sent a lengthy despatch from Wing Commander Green, the MoD's Consultant Adviser in Communicable Diseases.[17] Copies of that letter were sent to the Chief of the

General Staff, the Deputy Chief of the Defence Staff (Health), and Dr Galbraith at the Army Medical Directorate.

An almost four-month delay in addressing Jane's questions was explained by Wing Commander Green as the consequence of her letter being lost in the post somewhere between Dr Galbraith's office in Surrey and his own in London. (Over the years we were to find that the postal system around, and within, Whitehall seemed to be exceptionally unreliable.)

But before getting into the presentation of policy being offered on behalf of General Dannatt, I would like to pick up a metaphorical trowel and scrape away some of the topsoil of Wing Commander Green's seven-page tome. Archaeologists are good in dirt and we are particularly keen on context and dating. In this particular trench there are a few matters that make me uncomfortable. Perhaps a minor issue to the layman is that the letter gives the UK licencing date for mefloquine as 1990. It was, as we know, given its UK licence in 1989. But where Wing Commander Green should certainly be more careful is with his claim that the drug was initially popular as it offered once-weekly dosage schedules in contrast to the alternative once-daily regimes available at that time.

It was, in fact, initially unpopular because of its rather complex dose regime, a factor that prevented its use during the 1990/91 Gulf War.[18] At that time, the drug was only consumed weekly for short visits to risk locations. For longer stays in endemic areas the dose was reduced to bi-weekly after the fourth dose. A variation to the UK licence for a change to an enduring weekly regimen was only approved in October 1991.[19] And in discussing mefloquine and suicide, Wing Commander Green says, "The manufacturer of mefloquine is unable to state if there have been suicides associated with mefloquine use."

Did he not know, however, that there had been such a British military suicide in 1995? And was this something else that had escaped the attention of Dr Galbraith? This later quote from Dr Ashley Croft, former army doctor and a consultant public health physician and medical epidemiologist with a special interest in infectious diseases and tropical medicine, is particularly disconcerting.[20]

*On or around 20 December 1995, a UK soldier who was taking mefloquine during an Army-run clinical trial killed himself. This came at an acutely embarrassing time for the MoD, since the previous month the BBC television programme* Watchdog *had highlighted the neuropsychiatric dangers of Lariam. As the Defence Committee was recently informed, the MoD seemingly panicked and concealed from the responsible authorities (Coroner, the Committee on Safety of Medicines) this fatal outcome in a controlled clinical study.*

This statement, repeatedly made, has gone unchallenged by the Ministry of Defence. But let's see what Wing Commander Green did say about Lariam/ mefloquine policy.

*Mefloquine is an extremely effective drug at preventing malaria in the parts of the world where British troops deploy. Alternative drugs are either ineffective due to drug resistance (chloroquine and proguanil), have problems with other adverse events and compliance (doxycycline), or have limitations on length of use (atovaquone/proguanil). In the operational military setting mefloquine is easy to take, being a once weekly dosage. The drug is classed as a "prescription only medicine" (PoM), and is issued with the patient information leaflet (PIL) which gives detailed information about the drug and possible side effects. Adverse events are required to be reported by military Medical Officers to the MHRA in common with standard United Kingdom medical practice.*

*For operational missions guidance is given on the choice of malaria chemoprophylaxis for Force Protection. This is necessary both for logistic supply reasons and medical, since different treatment protocols will be needed for patients who develop fever when taking different prophylaxis. Individual servicemen will always have alternative drugs offered to them if they are unable or unwilling to take a specific medication.*

It is quite clear that the MoD policy deviated significantly from the ACMP guidelines and in some cases, perhaps, for pressing operational reasons. But why continue with the false assertions? Intriguingly, there is, effectively, an admission that Lariam was the drug of choice. This "prescription only medicine" was being issued and without recourse to the expected prescribing protocols. And the suggestion that individuals would always be offered an alternative is simply irreconcilable with what was happening in the field—but let us suppose that Wing Commander Green does not read the Journal of the Royal Army Medical Corps either. He had done his bit and the CGS had a policy that had been explained to Jane.

General Dannatt wrote to Jane in January 2007. Again the letter is produced in full as an appendix. It is quite skilfully and sympathetically crafted and ostensibly offers a considered rationale for the use of Lariam. 'Ostensibly', for it is probably one of the most misleading and brazen of many public statements defending Lariam. It is also something of a stain on the office of Chief of the General Staff. In an earlier letter (22 November 2006), General Dannatt gave Jane the assurance that "the care of the soldiers and officers under my command is my prime concern." Let's see how he measured up to that responsibility.

With a few notable exceptions, senior officers are often quite resistant to reports from subordinates that are critical of resource constraints, poor equipment or, in this case a bad drug. In many cases, they feel they may have to wait until retirement before they feel able to express their own concerns. That is part of a political and career-driven culture that is too often a drag on the moral courage of generals. Regrettably, unfortunate soldiers pay the price. But a particularly interesting facet of the Lariam tragedy is just how many retired officers, including former service chiefs, later felt it their duty to 'go public' about Lariam when we managed to break the story in the national press in the autumn of 2013.

The Dannatt letter of January 2007 reconfirms the policy of Lariam selection. General Dannatt also offers some assurances about the management of the drug and its side effects. But they are simply contradicted by the stated formal military policy, what was actually happening in the field in 2006 and what was so clearly portrayed by Major Fraser's earlier report from Sierra Leone. Did the CGS actually believe what he was writing to this recently bereaved widow? Who was briefing him, other than Wing Commander Green? Crucially, what did the Surgeon General, Lieutenant General Louis Lillywhite, have to say? As we will shortly see, apparently not very much. But let's concentrate first on General Dannatt's personal assurance in his letter to Jane. He says:

*I should add that I have some personal experience of this drug but, on balance, am content to go with the formal advice.*

He doesn't elaborate on what his personal experience of the drug was but it would be reasonable to draw the conclusion that, probably having taken Lariam, General Dannatt was aware that it produced some nasty side effects. He was, however, content to go with the formal advice. ('Formal advice' were the words he chose.) The inference was that the policy was sound and soldiers, including himself, should continue to take Lariam. That was certainly Jane's understanding. And why not? After all, this was a man who regularly espoused a strong Christian belief within his soldiering ethic and he would, a few years later, publish an autobiography titled "Leading from the Front."[21]

Sadly, as far as we can ascertain, nothing was done during the Dannatt tenure to properly investigate the matter. But after he retired, and presumably wanting to get on the right side of the argument, he was quick to jump on the bandwagon in 2013, making a call in the press for Lariam use to be banned by the MoD because of its association with suicide and psychosis.[22]

By then, Bea, Jane and I were beginning to muster significant support in the media and our major breakthrough came when the Independent journalist, Jonathan Owen, produced a series of excoriating reports, revealing the extent of the scandal in the Armed Forces. One of Jonathan's headlines read "The Lariam scandal: Former head of army calls for ban on malaria drug." And his copy opened with the line "General Lord Richard Dannatt demands action after concerns that Lariam can cause suicide." I suppose being a Christian, General Dannatt must be permitted a Damascene conversion.

But perhaps I am being unfair to General Dannatt. Might he perhaps have tried to do something when CGS? In October 2013 I wrote to thank him for his contribution to Jonathan's article and to ask if Bea and I might meet him and explore how our campaign might be advanced. We would, of course, be representing Jane, now in Australia. I received a disappointing and rather terse response, indicating that I might as well have asked Bob Ainsworth to get involved. He simply said:

> *Thank you for your letter dated 11 October in which you commented on the continued use of the anti-malarial drug Lariam, by the MOD. As the Independent newspaper correctly reported, I am firmly against the use of this drug, and am endeavouring to persuade the MOD to share this view.*

Wives and widows and damaged veterans were too insignificant for this Christian luminary. Was this the same compassionate General Dannatt who was quoted in the

Eastern Daily Press the year before, after becoming president of the Norfolk YMCA?[23]

*The motto of the Royal Military Academy, Sandhurst, which I attended some years ago, is 'Serve to Lead'. Serving an organisation like the YMCA in order to lead others to a better opportunity in life is, I think, really important.*

*We always say look for a role model in leadership and the person who was the most obvious servant, who set out to lead, was Jesus Christ, who did the most menial task in washing his disciples' feet, thereby earning the right to lead them.*

General Dannatt wanted nothing to do with us (or our feet) and I wondered why. So I decided to present the MoD with some Freedom of Information (FoI) questions to see if we could find out how engaged General Dannatt and General Lillywhite had been, if at all, with Jane's call for action to prevent more harm to soldiers and their families. (When serving, I was once advised by a civil servant, who was both a pragmatist and a bit of a cynic, about FoIs. He pointed out that the MoD's requirement was only to respond in the most minimal fashion. It may be obvious, he said, what the questioner wants to know, but if they haven't specifically asked, don't offer anything. So I do try to craft my questions carefully.) Here are the questions I raised, along with the MoD's answers:[24]

Please provide copies of all correspondence that took place between the office of the Chief of the General Staff, the Defence Medical Services Directorate and the

Defence Medico-legal directorate relating to death of Major Quinn.

*A search of records held has yielded no information within the scope of this part of your request.*

Please provide copies of correspondence that occurred during the years 2006, 2007, 2008 and 2009 between Gen Sir Richard Dannatt and the then Surgeon General, the Defence Medical Services Directorate, including the ACMP member Wing Commander Andrew Green, and others regarding the use of Lariam/Mefloquine in UK troops.

*A search of records held has yielded no information within the scope of this part of your request.*

Please provide copies of correspondence or any minutes of any interaction that took place between 2006 and 2009 between the Ministry of Defence and Public Health England concerning the use of Lariam/Mefloquine.

*A search of records held by the MOD and Public Health England's Advisory Committee on Malaria Prevention has yielded no information within the scope of this part of your request.*

Please provide copies of any correspondence or communication that took place between Gen Sir Richard Dannatt, his staff, staff of the Defence Medical Services

Directorate and the Surgeon General regarding the death of Major Cameron Quinn.

*A search of records held has yielded no information within the scope of this part of your request.*

Nothing—absolutely nothing. These responses appear to deny the existence of even the correspondence that must have passed between General Dannatt's office and the Defence Medical Services. Wing Commander Green did assure Jane in his letter of 28 November 2006 "I have copied this letter to the Chief of the General Staff." This looks more like washing of hands than washing of feet.

The year 2016 was a bad one for the reputation of Lord Dannatt. Victoria Derbyshire and her team at the BBC had been covering the Lariam story closely and a piece presented in August would demolish his integrity in the eyes of those afflicted by Lariam.[25] Dannatt was interviewed by Joanna Gosling and she established that his 'personal experience' of the drug was, in fact, second hand. Years previously he had seen how it had affected his son, Bertie, when he had taken Lariam for a recreational visit to East Africa.

That gave the General a determination never to take Lariam himself. He explained that he always told his staff and doctors that he would take anything else, but not Lariam. He had seen what it had done to his son and, understandably, did not want to expose himself to the same risk. Joanna challenges him, however, pointing out that as head of the Army he presided over a body that insisted his subordinates did take Lariam. He hesitates and admits "Yes... ah...ah... that is true." He is pressed further to explain his conduct and responds "The organisation hadn't reached a settled view on whether Lariam was more beneficial..."

The sentence is left hanging, a powerful metaphor of shame, not lost on Jane or the rest of us. What is so unforgiveable is that the Chief of the General Staff had his own misgivings about Lariam/WR 142 490 reinforced by the tragedy of Cameron Quinn's suicide. He was effectively using his highly privileged position, authority and now inside information, to keep himself safe from the Agent Orange of this generation. But according to his letter to Jane he was "content to go with the formal advice." Well, he was content for everyone else to be put at risk. This was the Western Front generalship of Blackadder's Melchett alive and well in Whitehall, London SW1A 2HB.

# Chapter 6

## On Se Leve!

*In being unwilling to stand up and argue the case publicly,*
*they are also cowardly.*[1]

*-Dr Liam Fox, Secretary of State for Defence, 29 May 2011*

I'd been awake for some time and now the early morning
sunlight was filtering through the fabric of our small tent. A
few indistinct shadows suggested a gentle breeze and that at
least the insect world had stirred. My young French
companion was still sleeping deeply and, as far as I was
aware, he had not been disturbed by my regular awakenings.
As I've said, Lariam never leaves me alone at night, not even
when camped at over 2,000 metres in the French Alps. It was
a tight squeeze but I managed to get to the zip, open the tent
flap and stick my head outside.

It was the middle of July 2009, but the nights and early
mornings were still cold at that altitude. Our tents were
sparkling with the dew that also covered the alpine meadow
and a few drops fell refreshingly onto my forehead and down
one cheek. After blinking and shading my eyes to adjust to the
first dazzle of daylight in the mountains, there was a little time
to take in the view while all was still and quiet. Below the
rapidly-rising sun and far to the east, the skyline was

dominated by the serrated peaks of the Queyras range, capped with snow and close to the Italian border.

Somewhere in-between, and lost to sight, were the wooded valleys and slopes we had scaled to get to the Serre de L'Homme, high in the Ecrins National Park, a fabulously remote land of mountains between the Rhone-Alps and Provence-Alps-Cote d'Azur regions. What we hadn't been able to carry on our backs during our half-day and exhilarating climb to the site had followed on a team of donkeys who had now departed for lower pastures and hopefully less strenuous summer activities.

Beyond the lush grass the ground dropped quite steeply to a nearby alpine lake. Further, and to either side, the massive ice-sculpted grey and bare mountains enclosed everything like an open-air Gothic cathedral. Under a dome of blue sky, nature was busy in this short season: edelweiss, alpine sea holly and purple gentian waiting to be discovered among the stones and in the verdant carpet; inquisitive marmots scuttling over the rocks but always maintaining a discreet distance; a far-off chamois seemingly defying gravity while traversing some precipitous outcrop; and, up in the dizzying heights, a circling eagle. We were on the upper extremity of the Fournell Valley, camped among the rocks of glacial moraines and at the limit of ancient human settlement.

"On se leve… on se leve…" That was the gentle summons to wake and start the day from the team leader, Dr Kevin Walsh, as he passed through the tiny encampment rousing the group of mostly French archaeologists from their slumbers. Anything more strident would have simply been wrong in such a peaceful alpine idyll. I pulled on my hiking boots, grabbed a towel and my washing gear and headed to the stream, a silver course of water fed by the melt from the ice and snow still holding their final bastions, secure in the darker slopes and corries where even the midsummer sun could hardly extend its rays. A cold morning plunge can have a marvellously dispelling effect on WR 142 490 dreams.

I had just completed my first year as an archaeologist at York and during our field school on a Romano-British site on the outskirts of the city I had learned that Kevin, one of our tutors, was looking for a volunteer to join his investigations in the French Alps. Kevin is a landscape archaeologist with a particular interest in high-altitude human activities and was then in the middle of an extensive examination of sites in the northern Mediterranean and the Alps. This season, Kevin and his partner Florence Mocci, an archaeologist from the Centre Camille Jullian, Aix-en-Provence, were investigating alpine pastoralism, with a focus on Bronze Age (c. 2400 BC to 900 BC) stone animal enclosures at these extreme heights.

This was a fascinating but slow and painstaking endeavour. Excavations during our eleven night stay at the Serre de L'Homme were limited to two fairly small trenches. In terms of classic finds, I think they only yielded one tiny fragment of worked flint to the excited cry of "Regardez! C'est un selix!" But we were involved in what archaeologists and historians call the *Longue Durée.* This certainly wasn't a project that would have fitted the three-day constraints of a Channel Four *Time Team* television programme which was then popularising archaeology on Sunday afternoons.

Our work was to record the scatter of rocks which, to the casual observer, might not have suggested any human agency in their roughly circular arrangement. Along with pollen core samples that Kevin and Florence had extracted from the lake's sediments with an earlier team, we would also be collecting soil samples and carbonised wood, all of which would help to paint the picture of human manipulation of these landscapes, from the first incursions of Mesolithic (Middle Stone Age) hunter-gatherers to the transhumance farming of French medieval life. Context and dating are key archaeological skills and so, too, are patience and persistence. Usually, if you are looking in the right direction, you will, eventually, be rewarded.

Accessing the past and buried truths can be the work of many seasons; perhaps even half a lifetime. There may be many unexpected obstacles and new routes to explore. What's more, life can become uncomfortable on a number of fronts, especially if you are going to challenge some cherished and well-established orthodoxies. I turned these ideas over in my mind during the long descent as, after twelve days of fieldwork and archaeological companionship, we bade farewell to the Serre de L'Homme. With cloud now shrouding the upper valley and its millennia of secrets, we returned it to the marmots. A few hours later, in bright summer sunshine, we were enjoying cold French beers in the delightfully quaint medieval village of Vallouise.

———

A couple of weeks later, I was at home preparing for the appeals tribunal I would be attending in Leeds in the autumn. At that stage I was quite unaware of how shamefully Jane had been treated but it wouldn't be long before I too began to find out just how many people involved in the Lariam scandal would be unwilling to stand up and argue the case publicly. I agree that such people are, as Dr Liam Fox might describe them, cowards, and many are much worse than that. For the moment, however, I needed to review my approach and ask some broader questions about Lariam.

I had already discovered some more disturbing facts and I wanted to be much better informed before I appeared in front of the tribunal. The evidence of Cameron's suicide that had been placed before General Dannatt should have been what an archaeologist might describe as a 'Staffordshire Hoard moment'.[r] Perhaps, one day, Lord Dannatt and General Lillywhite will explain why it was not. Back then, however, I was only working my way through Lariam's pollen core samples and charcoal remains. The skeletons would appear later.

An especially worrying and perplexing discovery was that a number of the common side effects, including something as ostensibly insignificant as restlessness, were described by Roche as 'prodromal'; that is they were clinical warning signs of the possible onset of something much more serious. In such cases, Roche mandated that the drug had to be discontinued and an alternative medication should be substituted. How had I missed that? And how, in God's name, had it been missed by the Surgeon General and every doctor implicated in his

---

[r] The Staffordshire Hoard is the largest and one of the most important collections of Anglo-Saxon gold and silver ever to be found. The hoard had an immediate and enduring impact on our understanding of what is popularly (if erroneously) known as the Dark Age. It was, coincidentally, discovered in July 2009, by a metal detectorist, in a field near Hammerwich, Staffordshire, and close to the Roman road, Watling Street.

policy? This vitally important information had been known since 2002, and perhaps even earlier.

Online, I had found a copy of a letter Roche had sent to every doctor in the USA in September 2002, drawing this issue to their attention.[2] That warning was then almost immediately followed up in a revision to the company's summary of product information, a document essential for any prescribing doctor and also available online.[3] Under a heading 'Information for Patients', doctors were unequivocally directed:

> *that if the patients experience psychiatric symptoms such as acute anxiety, depression, restlessness or confusion, these may be considered prodromal to a more serious event. In these cases, the drug must be discontinued and an alternative medication should be substituted.*

Looking for some clarity about how this information had been used by military prescribers and physicians, in early August I wrote to Bob Ainsworth (the uninterested Secretary of State) and, using the Freedom of Act, asked if the MoD complied with those directions relating to prodromal symptoms and, if so, since when.[4] This was one of a number of questions I posed. By the time of my tribunal in late September, I had received no response, despite Mr Ainsworth clearly knowing that my case was to be heard and that there would have been a pressing need for some answers. But remember that this was a man who had already said that he had "no further comment to make."[5]

It would, in fact, take until the summer of the following year (almost twelve months) to extract a proper response, and then only after the MoD had been found to be in breach of the Freedom of Information Act in their failure to respond, and having been twice directed by the Information Commissioner to provide some answers.[6]

In the intervening months, the MoD had indulged in a series of evasions, including fanciful excuses to my MP, William (now Lord) Haig, whom I had asked to intervene on my behalf. Lord Haig had once been leader of the Conservative Party and was a former Minister. He would soon occupy the post of Foreign Secretary, one of the most senior offices of state in the United Kingdom. This was the state of affairs as explained to me by Lord Haig in January 2010 when he was occupying the Opposition benches in the House of Commons.[7]

*I wrote to the Secretary of State for Defence on your behalf about this issue on 2 October 2009 and again on 27 November. No correspondence has been received from the Ministry of Defence, however, a telephone call was received on 1 December to advise that both letters had been received and passed to the FOI unit for reply. Unfortunately, no reply has been received.*

*A further letter has been sent to Mr Ainsworth to remind him that my letter is still outstanding, which I hope proves helpful.*

Ainsworth would not respond to me and now he was ignoring my MP. As 2010 wore on it did strike me as odd that a Secretary of State should, three times, deny a senior parliamentarian: this was starting to become rather Biblical.

But this would be far from the MoD's only act of contempt for Parliament.

———

There was a General Election in June 2010 and a coalition of Conservatives and Liberal Democrats came to power. Gone, we hoped, was the New Labour Blair/Brown era sullied by the manipulations of unelected and unaccountable advisers such as the Downing Street Director of Communications and Strategy (aka spin doctor) Alastair Campbell. Public trust in government was at a nadir and there was now an opportunity to sweep away many of the deceits of the past decade. The 2000s had been the era of the Iraq War, Weapons of Mass Destruction and the mysterious suicide of the troublesome government scientist, Dr David Kelly. These events had defined much of the prevailing culture of our government (and especially the MoD) and, as they coincide with so much of the Lariam scandal, they deserve at least a little of our attention.

Dr David Kelly was a scientist and biological weapons inspector of international renown and his story is a compelling one. An adviser to, and employee of, the MoD, he had significant expertise in the weapons programme of the Iraqi regime of Saddam Hussein. One of his roles was to provide advice to the Defence Intelligence Staff and to the Secret Intelligence Service on Iraq. He had serious misgivings about the veracity of the Blair government's statements about Iraqi Weapons of Mass Destruction, a position entirely vindicated in the later Iraq Inquiry, eventually published in 2016.[8] Essentially, the prospectus for the Iraq War had been founded upon a fallacy and, frustrated by the government's spin, Dr Kelly appears to have been at the heart of a public exposé of institutionalised deception. After being himself exposed as a press source or whistle-blower, David Kelly then unexpectedly died on 17 July 2003.

The official verdict remains suicide. His body was found in woodland near his Oxfordshire home with cuts to the left wrist. Toxicology reports indicated the ingestion of a significant number of Coproxamol tablets, which may have contributed to Dr Kelly's death.[9] On the day he died he had responded to a supportive journalist in New York in an email referring to "many dark actors playing games." The circumstances of his death remain controversial, not least because key evidence, or rather the lack of it, is being withheld from the public. This includes the absence of fingerprints on items that were said to be agents in his death, such as the knife used to lacerate his wrist.[10]

Years later, Dr Kelly's body was quietly, and unusually for a Christian burial, exhumed one night and cremated.[11] The extent to which the authorities continue to evade legitimate concerns about the integrity of the government is amply displayed in a Freedom of Information response about Dr Kelly's death produced by Thames Valley Police.[12] This is what the Chief Constable, Francis Habgood, had to say:

*Response*
*This request is being refused under Section 12(2) of the FOIA. Section 12 of the FOIA allows that public authorities do not have to comply with section 1(1) of the Act if the cost of complying would exceed the appropriate limit. In accordance with the Freedom of Information Act,*

*this letter represents a Refusal Notice for this request. This information is not held in an easily retrievable format and would require a manual search of the full file. It is estimated that this would exceed the appropriate 18 hour time and £450 cost limit.*

*Section 16:- Further advice and assistance*

*Under the provisions of the FOIA legislation, Thames Valley Police are obliged to disclose recorded information and not necessarily answer questions or confirm/deny statements. Under Section 8, the majority of the elements of your request are questions and therefore, not deemed to be valid under the provisions of the Act.*

My former colleague in the Civil Service would have marvelled at this exemplar of evasion. Once again, I have decided that the full document, which includes all the original questions, is worthy of inclusion as an appendix.

How exactly Dr Kelly died is not for me to determine but his would have been one of many British deaths resulting directly from false, poorly interpreted or deliberately manipulated intelligence. The subject is much more comprehensively covered in the book *An Inconvenient Death* by Miles Goslett.[13] What is germane is that his death was caused by malpractice at the highest levels of government and that the authorities have never permitted a full and independent coroner's inquest. The political mantra of that time was that people's lives could be subordinated to the outcomes of 'sexed-up' documents and suppression of the truth.

---

By 2010, my MP William Haig had, indeed, become Foreign Secretary and I hoped that the incoming coalition government led by David Cameron and Nick Clegg might have sufficient reforming capital and zeal to give us something cleaner than its shoddy predecessor. Mr Haig agreed to discuss the handling of my Lariam questions at a constituency surgery and, accompanied by Bea Coldwell, I set off on a late sunny August afternoon to meet him at Church House in Hutton Rudby, about twenty minutes' drive from home.

Hutton Rudby is a charming North Yorkshire Village with avenues of lime trees providing pleasant shade. It was easy enough to pick out Church House on a path raised above the main road nestled in between some former weavers' cottages. Dark four-wheel drive SUVs parked outside with what looked like suited minders were a fair indication that we had found the right place. Inside Church House, formerly a Methodist Chapel and now the church hall for All Saints, we were greeted with a welcome cup of tea while we waited for our appointed ten minutes with Mr Haig. I needed to collect my thoughts.

Some peculiar things had happened in the preceding months. Bea and I had uncovered more irregularities and we were beginning to wake up to the possibility that the Surgeon General's department and people in the MoD were trying to hide something. But were the ministers of the new administration aware of what was going on? Having, even with Mr Haig's interventions, been completely blanked by Bob Ainsworth, I had decided to submit a complaint to the Information Commissioner in order to get some answers. The result was, as I have said, that in late March 2010 the MoD was found to be in breach of the Freedom of Information Act by refusing to answer my questions. And then when I compared the various statements emanating from the MoD, it was clear that someone was not telling the truth.

Very much to my surprise, the Information Commissioner had told me that the MoD claimed to have responded to my August 2009 letter to Mr Ainsworth on 8 October 2009. Really? I had received no such letter and, had that been the case, why did the MoD not simply say so in response to at least one of three written inquiries sent to them by Mr Haig between October 2009 and January 2010? And why could Mr Haig not have been advised of that answer in a phone call during which his office staff discussed the matter with the MoD in December 2009?

The Information Commissioner kindly passed me an electronic copy of the MoD's alleged answer. It was, indeed, dated 8 October 2009 and was from a David Holdridge in the Surgeon General's Department, but was unsigned.[14] What appears to give the lie to the MoD position is that they claimed to have sent that letter to me as an attachment to an email. At that stage, I had only corresponded with the MoD by Royal Mail and had not provided them with any email address. I did then ask Mr Holdridge for a copy of the signed original letter but that request was ignored. Nor did I receive a copy of the alleged email or any confirmation of which electronic address they might have used.

The '8 October' letter itself was quite inadequate and failed to answer a number of key questions that had been posed, perhaps most importantly one relating to the prodromal nature of some Lariam's side effects. I had written to Mr Holdridge on 23 March 2010 (the day after the Information

Commissioner had passed me the composition dated 8 October), presenting once more my unanswered questions. That time I used Special Delivery and the Post Office confirmed that the letter was delivered to the MoD two days later on 25 March. Almost seven weeks later I still had no response and once again asked the Information Commissioner to intervene. I did eventually receive another answer from Mr Holdridge in July 2010, although that letter carried the date of 27 April 2010.[15] And it contained one particularly startling and disconcerting admission. Regarding Lariam's side effects it said "MOD is unaware that there are prodromal symptoms or side effects with mefloquine that portend a more serious problem."

I had also been in contact with Mr Haig about the MoD's tardiness and had asked him to raise the matter with the new Secretary of State for Defence, Dr Liam Fox. A response from Dr Fox in July 2010 was curious and raised further suspicions. Dr Fox appeared to be unaware that his Department had been found to be in breach of the Freedom of Information Act. Rather, he appeared to be following the discredited narrative that there had been no delays in any of the correspondence. Either he had been incorrectly briefed or he was knowingly attempting to mislead. Something needed to be sorted.

As you only get ten minutes at a constituency surgery I had taken the trouble to provide the new Foreign Secretary with some background papers. I didn't want to overwhelm him but it was important that he should have the opportunity to read into the subject and see how important it was. He could also pass these to his counterpart at Defence. I had already asked him to look at a key paper 'A lesson learnt: the rise and fall of Lariam and Halfan' authored by Dr Ashley Croft, perhaps the UK's leading expert on Lariam use by the MoD: it was barely four pages.[16] To that I added a press article referring to the Sgt Murray case and others involving soldiers,[17] and another piece covering Cal Watt's experience.[18] And I also gave him a copy of a short email Jane had sent in 2006 while still raw from Cameron's suicide. Here is part of what she said:

> *I am now beginning to find the energy and will follow this issue up with the British Army who, as you can imagine, are being particularly evasive to both my and the coroner's questions regarding the prescribing Lariam to soldiers in the aftermath of my husband's death, particularly those on active service who may have access to live firearms. I am so scared that what has happened to me will continue to happen to other forces families, and others, who have been prescribed this drug as part of their work. I feel I need to try to do something about this situation, however insurmountable this problem may be.*

Any Defence Minister who has read this *cri de coeur* and ignored it, as so many have, is base and shameless. There can be little doubt, as we will see in a later chapter, that their lamentable failures cost lives. No one should have died from Lariam/WR 142 490 poisoning, and certainly not after 2006. There was a chance to put a stop to the blanket prescription of Lariam to our troops in 2010 and, as I said in my letter to Mr Haig before our meeting, "I hope you might be able to facilitate a meeting with an appropriate minister and staff to discuss my concerns."

Refreshed by our tea, Bea and I were ushered into a side room to meet Mr Haig where he was seated at a small table with a note-taker. In all my dealings with him, I found Mr Haig scrupulously courteous and he listened to my case. His personal characteristics define him above many of his political peers. In fact we probably had more than ten minutes, perhaps closer to twenty, and we left believing that, presented with Lariam's clear implication in so much misery, the MoD would be sure to engage with us. A week later Mr Haig wrote to me to say that he written to Dr Fox summarising what I had said and would let me know what response he received.

And Dr Fox's response to my request for a meeting? With increasingly typical delay, although this time only six weeks, Dr Fox suggested that there was no new evidence to address saying "I do not therefore believe there would be anything to be gained from arranging a meeting."[19] Perhaps the widow of a later hanged Lariam suicide would disagree. A few years on the MoD would rue Dr Fox's claim "that there is no evidence of undue complacency or failure of duty of care by the Department."

So much for being willing to stand up and argue the case publicly, or even within the sanctity of his own office.

I did receive further letters from Mr Haig and one from 2014 contained text that somehow did not appear to have been crafted by him.[20] It didn't ring true and included passages that had the trait of 'cut and paste' about them. He seemed to be conveying a departmental line. One phrase in particular stood out and it was becoming very familiar:

*If compelling evidence is produced from the body of global scientific evidence regarding the toxicity of mefloquine, then it is likely that the UK license would be reviewed and advice from the ACMP may change.*

In fact it had been deployed years earlier by Wing Commander Green in a 2007 letter to Jane Quinn. The only difference was that 'will change' in 2007 had changed to '*may* change' by 2014. Those words were something of a favourite within the Surgeon General's Department. They were also casually used by junior ministers attempting to defend the MoD's continued use of the drug. Mark Lancaster (Parliamentary Under Secretary of State and Minister for Defence Personnel and Veterans) deployed it in a letter to Rishi Sunak (then my MP) in 2015. And it was used twice by Anna Soubry (Minister of State for Defence Personnel, Welfare and Veterans) in answer to MPs' questions on behalf of their constituents: one to James Brokenshire on 19 October 2014 and the other to David Laws on 21 March 2015. In June 2015, it popped up once more, this time in a letter to me sent on behalf of the Chief of the Defence Staff, General Sir Nicholas Houghton.

Let's just pick up on General Houghton for a moment; the head of our Armed Forces in 2015. I had written to him in April of that year asking that he might turn his attention to the Lariam problem in the light of the *Lariam Legacy* programme that had recently been aired on BBC Radio 4. Again, I took the precaution of having my letter tracked by the Post Office Special Delivery service. After an overnight transit from Yorkshire to London, it then took five weeks from arrival at the MoD's Main Building in Whitehall to migrate the handful of floors to the CDS's desk. I received an acknowledgement but, lacking the moral fibre to provide any answers, General Houghton delegated the matter to a subordinate who further delegated the reply to an unnamed individual in the Surgeon General's secretariat.

Around the same time, Bea, having also recently written to General Houghton found herself seated beside him at a lunch in North Yorkshire. She engaged him in conversation and also asked if he might consider investigating what was becoming variously described in the media as *The Lariam Legacy* or *The Lariam Scandal.* He would have known that the drug was heavily implicated in acts of violence, homicide and suicide not only in Britain, but in the armies of the United States, Australia, Canada and in Ireland.

The response from General Houghton was even more staggering and craven than those offered by defence ministers. He pleaded that this was a matter that he could not address while he was serving. It would have to wait until he was retired. Why? He never explained. Nor has he since attempted to help from the comfort of retirement. In her own words Bea says "the next time I met the brave General, he attempted to hide behind his wife and child." It seems that as far as he was concerned, Lariam suicides would just have to continue.

Returning to our ministers, we must acknowledge that the Soubrys and Lancasters of the Westminster world, and their predecessors such as Kevan Jones, were, at best, middle-rankers and were bound to do their bosses' bidding. Unfortunately, they seemed unable or unwilling to deploy any more independence of thought in this matter than they displayed in the letters that had presumably been drafted for them. We were aware of their limitations, and their standards are exemplified by Kevan Jones. In 2009 and 2010, as Veterans Minister, he had serially defended the use of Lariam, even while acknowledging "an association between mefloquine and some psychiatric symptoms." [21]

Two years later, out of government and from the opposition benches of the House of Commons, he would, however, declare his own periods of mental ill health and depression.[22] Sadly, he had somehow been unable to translate any of this personal experience into the empathy or concern that Lariam-damaged veterans and next-of-kin so desperately needed.

Therefore, we continued in our attempts to get a senior minister to assume some leadership and responsibility. Each successive Secretary of State for Defence was apprised of Lariam's risks and asked to engage. And so the names of Fox, Hammond and Fallon can all be added to Ainsworth in the pantheon of uninterested Secretaries of State. They have no excuse. And even by the tenure of Fallon in 2015, the 'lost in post' excuse persisted. Here is Sir Michael Fallon explaining a five-month silence:[23]

*I am sorry you have not received a response to your letters of 9 October and 15 December about the use of the anti-malarial drug Mefloquine (commercially known as Lariam) by the UK Armed Forces. Unfortunately it appears these letters were not received by my Department. I regret any inconvenience my delay in responding has caused...*

———

An interesting nuance in that series of letters from Westminster and Whitehall is that by 2015 the term 'compelling *evidence*' had become 'compelling *indications*'. Yet even 'compelling indications' regarding the toxicity of mefloquine, which were in abundance by that stage, seemed insufficient to stimulate any action within either the Ministry of Defence or the Department of Health. To put this into context, let's just review what Fallon *et al* at Defence and the likes of Andrew Lansley, Secretary of State for Health from 2010 to 2012, and his successor, Jeremy Hunt, ought to have known from the abundance of medical literature available to them.

It had long been established that mefloquine was the least safe chloroquine-resistant anti-malarial available at the time. As Dr Ashley Croft had confirmed back in 2007, the inexcusably delayed double-blinded randomised trials "confirmed mefloquine's potential for causing psychological illness, and all three study reports described an excess of neuropsychiatric adverse effects in the mefloquine arm."[24] A key investigation had been that reported by Overbosch *et al* in 2001.[25] It reported that subjects who received atovaquone-proguanil (malarone), rather than Lariam, had fewer treatment-related neuropsychiatric adverse events (AEs), fewer AEs of moderate or severe intensity, and fewer AEs that caused prophylaxis to be discontinued.

In 2015, I established through another Freedom of Information request that this paper alone, which was far from a ringing endorsement of the product, remained the only clinical trial known to the NHS which determined that mefloquine should be made available to the public as a chemoprophylaxis.[26] But since 2001 there had been ample compelling indications that should have been, and perhaps were, known but somehow weren't attracting attention. There were plenty of warning lights appearing across the dashboard. Here are some, and let's concede that the first two might, just might, have been down there in the depths like the charcoal or pollen samples in the French Alps and, in the greater scheme of things, were overlooked by the guardians of our health.

The first is a study conducted among Swedish peacekeepers in the West African state of Liberia from 2004-06.[27] I probably met some of them during my second tour of duty in Sierra Leone: there was a great deal of cross-border and regional collaboration. The Swedish force had been prescribed either atovaquone-proguanil (malarone) or mefloquine (Lariam) with adverse events reported by 57% in the mefloquine group compared to 34% in the malarone group. Those taking Lariam experienced significantly more neuropsychological adverse reactions, with over a third experiencing nightmares and one-sixth depression.

The second is a case report published in 2012 by Dr Remington Nevin. This involved a 24-year-old male with no significant medical history, injuries, drug allergies or concerns about mental health.[28] His reaction to mefloquine was "characterised by prodromal symptoms of anxiety with subsequent development of psychosis, short-term memory impairment, confusion and personality change accompanied by complaints of disequilibrium and vertigo, with objective findings of central vestibulopathy."

That paper might have been expected to have been of interest to the MoD and the Department of Health for two reasons. This was, according to the author, the first published report of this "idiosyncratic neurotoxic syndrome" and that "Notwithstanding continued claims of safety, in 2009 the innovator product (Lariam, F. Hoffman-La Roche) was withdrawn from the US market, and the US military sharply curtailed the use of mefloquine in chemoprophylaxis, returning to a policy of first-line doxycycline use."

These peer-reviewed academic papers apparently didn't meet the standard set by our Surgeon General and defence ministers of "compelling evidence (or even indications) produced from the body of global scientific evidence regarding the toxicity of mefloquine." But other documents available to them irrefutably should.

At about the time when Dr Nevin's paper was published I was heavily involved in archaeological investigations in some fields next to the River Trent in Lincolnshire. I was conducting a lot of geophysical surveys trying to find subsurface evidence for the winter camp of the Great Viking Army AD 872-3 as it transited from York to the ancient Mercian capital of Repton in Derbyshire. In terms of surface and buried finds, this was a much richer site than Serre de L'Homme and, late one winter's day when I was there looking for artefacts, I came across what looked like a small piece of pottery.

Closer investigation showed it to be a fragment from a human skull. A few months later I found more scattered bones in the ploughed soil, including the unmistakable piece of a human lower jaw with some teeth still attached. Radio carbon dating placed them in the late-9th century, contemporary with the Viking occupation. Mine was a small contribution to the overall project which has proved to be one of the richest and informative of Viking sites investigated in England. Those bone finds were my own 'Staffordshire Hoard' moment. I would later experience a similar sense of excitement and discovery, but this time provoking a range of different emotions, when I learned what was slowing leaching into the public domain about the real horrors of Lariam/WR 142 490 in the next two documents.

In 2013, the Irish Medicines Board responded to a Freedom of Information request from a member of the public in Ireland.[29] Roche provided a copy of a fairly heavily redacted report, but, if any paper ever deserved such a metaphor, this was the smoking gun of the international Lariam scandal. The document was described by an American psychiatrist, Dr Elspeth Cameron Ritchie (formerly a doctor in the US Army), as a "smoking pill box".[30] The original report had been sent to the US FDA on 11 April 2012 and contained the following statement:

*Homicide [REDACTED] A patient of unknown demographics started on mefloquine (therapy details unspecified) for an unknown indication. After an unspecified duration, the patient who was a soldier experienced homicidal behaviour which led to homicidal killing of 17 [REDACTED]. It was reported that the patient was suffering from traumatic brain injury (TBI) and was administered mefloquine against military rule (mefloquine is directly contraindicated in patients with TBI as per [REDACTED] rule).*

As Dr Ritchie explains, exactly who provided the initial data is not clear but the documents revealed by the Irish Medicines Board exposed Roche as the body publishing what

166

was officially termed a "periodic update report" for this mass murder. The initial report was received 29 March 2012. The unique circumstances of this report can only credibly be fixed to one event, a multiple homicide in Afghanistan, by the American SSgt Robert Bales who had gone on a killing spree in Kandahar just over two weeks earlier.

In the dead of night he slipped out of his base, Camp Belambai, and ventured into a nearby village of mud and brick houses. There he killed four Afghans, including a little girl aged only three. Out of ammunition, he went back to Camp Belambai to replenish his weapon and then returned to fuel his deathly impulse. All of his victims were innocent civilians, including women and nine children.

SSgt Bales was subsequently sentenced to life imprisonment without the possibility of parole. A guilty plea helped Bales avoid the death penalty but it also allowed the authorities to avoid a full-fledged trial, with the case, according to Ritchie, remaining murky. Bales had previously served three tours of duty in Iraq during which time he acquired a traumatic brain injury.

It is likely that at some stage Bales had consumed mefloquine but US military authorities have never confirmed or denied which anti-malarial drug Bales had used during his various operational tours of duty. However, within eighteen months of the massacre, the US Army Special Operations Command prohibited the use of mefloquine among its personnel, acknowledging that "consideration must be made for the impact of this medication on our population."[31]

If even the Bales' case was insufficient to make the MoD wake up, what followed in 2014 shows that Hammond,

Fallon, Soubry and Lancaster were all still deep in their slumbers.

By late-2013, the European Medicines Agency (EMA) was becoming particularly concerned about the frequency of reports of possibly permanent neurologic adverse reactions to mefloquine. The FDA had also raised a Drug Safety Communication relating to the drug's neurological and psychiatric side effects. The EMA is the body responsible for the oversight of medical products across the European Union. Its mission is to foster scientific excellence in the evaluation and supervision of medicines, for the benefit of public and animal health.

The EMA directed Roche to conduct a cumulative review of their product. The outcome was a thirty-six-page report based on multiple case studies of patients who reacted badly to the drug.[32] Significantly, before the UK left the EU in 2020, the EMA was based at Canary Wharf in London. Furthermore, the chair of the Pharmacovigilance Risk Assessment Committee directing the EMA investigation occupied a similar role in the UK's regulatory body, the MHRA, so our Health and Defence Ministers could reasonably be expected to have been aware of this vitally important document.

The EMA report catalogued a series of serious reactions to mefloquine among patients who had previously been generally free from any relevant medical problems and with no history of psychiatric problems. A particular focus of the investigation was to establish how long side-effects might endure. Might they be transient or could they persist for a number of years? The case studies involved a host of disturbing and usually multiple adverse events including dizziness, vertigo, amnesia, aggression, depression, nightmares, delusions, psychosis, suicide ideation and attempted suicide. The conclusions from these investigations presented at page 31 of the report are stated quite clearly:[33]

*There is enough evidence from the presented drug safety reports, the submitted literature report and the FDA assessment report supporting a causal relationship between the occurrence of long lasting and even persistent neuropsychiatric side effects.*

*Additionally, based on the pharmacodynamic profile of mefloquine, the neuropsychiatric side effects of Lariam can be explained to a large extent by the neuro(patho)physiology and can be predicted by mechanistic aspects as well.*

*In consideration of this and the increase of case reports with long lasting side effects, there is a strong suspicion that mefloquine can cause different kinds of permanent brain damage, even under plasma concentration achieved in malaria prophylaxis.*

Something that adds to the suspicions about the government's behaviour is that this report was especially difficult to access in the United Kingdom. For at least two years Bea, Jane and I were unaware of its existence. We learned of it only through our contact in the Republic of Ireland who obtained a copy through that Freedom of Information request. Even after confirming its existence, the report could not be found on any UK website through any of the usual internet search engines. This certainly appeared to be something that Ministers did not want to stand up and argue in public. In 2019 I made multiple requests to the MoD to confirm when they and the Department of Health first became aware of the report. They simply refused to answer. The importance of that question will become startlingly clear in the next chapter.

Meanwhile, the behaviour of government Ministers, especially those in the House of Lords, seemed to oscillate between the worlds of Kafka and Lewis Carroll. A series of penetrating questions on the effects of Lariam presented by the crossbencher Countess Mar elicited responses bordering on the bizarre and suggestive of a brazen disregard for the evidence and the well-being, and even lives, of those exposed to the drug. Here are some of the ministerial replies:[34]

Earl Howe, Minister of State, Ministry of Defence, 22 November 2017: *There is no established evidence of prophylactic drugs having long-term side effects causing mental health issues.*

Lord O'Shaughnessy, Parliamentary Under-Secretary of State, Health, 27 November 2017: *It has not been established that such adverse reactions may be permanent.* On 19 December, he was still of the opinion that mefloquine was *a safe... form of malaria prevention.*

And when pressed if he should consider suicide as a permanent adverse reaction, on 18 January 2018, Lord O'Shaughnessy blandly offered the evasion: *the risk of suicide would not be considered to be [a] permanent adverse reaction.* Two months later, he elaborated: *suicide is a possible outcome of suicide ideation, rather than... an adverse reaction to [mefloquine].*

Such sophistry simply demeans our Parliament.

So what was going on? Why were our politicians and national institutions so resolute in their defence of a drug that had inflicted so much harm? Did the pharmaceutical industry have a particular influence in certain quarters and did they just want the story to be quietly managed out? Lawsuits were now pending across the globe and the very week that Lord O'Shaughnessy was performing his parliamentary verbal gymnastics, *The Sunday Times* was reporting that his government had quietly paid off a former soldier from the Royal Artillery whose career and life had been wrecked by the use of Lariam.[35]

And remember that quote from Roche themselves back in 2007? "Science had advanced; more effective antimalarials with better side effect profiles were now available, and these were generally used."[36] The best tactic for Roche and the MoD would be to play this long and slow. That would save their money and protect their reputations. Meanwhile, the wreckage of these other David Kellys in helmets and body armour could just be written off as collateral damage.

But this couldn't be our British political system, not in the mother of Parliaments? Surely our MPs were better than that; they always learned lessons and any mistakes they made were honest human errors. We should be reassured by the government's track record in these matters, shouldn't we? They had 'learned' from the 1990s and the First Gulf War and its mysterious drug-induced syndrome and the embarrassment of defence ministers with rather unhealthy interests in big pharma.

The Minster for Armed Forces (Nicholas Soames) had, in 1996, assured the House of Commons of the concern of the MoD for serving personnel and veterans damaged by chemicals. (That promise now sounds rather hollow.) Soames had also been required to make an apology for misleading Parliament earlier about the matter but the blame was, quite cynically, passed to civil servants.[37] In the popular idiom, 'There was nothing to see here'. But, as reported in *The Independent*, there was an "intriguing piece of information" which Sir Nicholas did not wish to share with either the Commons or the Defence Select Committee.

At the time of the Gulf War, Soames was a non-executive director of the British arm of Hoffman La Roche. Roche had, according to *The Independent*, been involved in the supply of one of the nerve agent treatments provided to Coalition forces in the Gulf. Soames is quoted as saying "I had no idea it was even made by Roche. Plainly if I had I would have declared an interest."[38]

Nor, I suppose, should we draw any sinister conclusion from the fact that Andrew Lansley, after relinquishing the post of Health Secretary and being placed in the House of Lords thought it appropriate to take an appointment with Roche. Lansley claimed no conflict of interest arose, although he was in charge of Health while the Lariam scandal was at its height. Doctors clearly disagreed with Lansley. One said in the British Medical Journal:[39]

> *This is yet another example of the 'revolving doors' culture that is eroding confidence in our political system. The influence of big business on powerful politicians who in turn have influence over the legislature and policy making must be countered by much stricter controls.*

So if our Ministers are correct and they have no conflicts of interest and have acted with the probity expected of their offices of state, perhaps we should look elsewhere for an answer to the riddle of serial cover-ups involving all three British political parties in government over the past thirty years. As those concerned remain resolute in their determination not to stand up and argue the case publicly, it becomes essential to explore all credible possibilities. One particular avenue leads us down a dimly-lit path and back into the shadows of what was going on in 2006; just when Cameron Quinn took those rope reins from the porch of his Scottish Borders cottage and climbed the stairs to the spare room in the attic.

———

It is now beyond doubt that on a night in June 2006 three inmates at Guantanamo Bay had been tortured to death, and almost certainly during interrogation. We also know that on arrival at the base, detainees were required to ingest doses of Lariam/WR 142 490. The disturbing and highly plausible rationale for this practice remains the neuropsychiatric effects that the drug would induce on the prisoners.[40] But it would appear that it is not only the United States government that was implicated in this abuse.

Staff Sergeant Hickman, the whistle-blower from Guantanamo, makes a particularly shocking claim about British involvement, with the alleged presence of British intelligence officers at the Gitmo interrogations.[41] Hickman also tells us that on 9 June, when the three deaths occurred, a British national, Shaker Aamer, claims that he was also taken from his Guantanamo cell to an undisclosed location and, for about two and a half hours, subjected to tortures, including beatings, choking and having his eyes gouged and exposed to intense light and heat. All of these details were formally recorded by Aamer's US attorney, Zachary Katznelson, in a signed declaration which was approved for Public Filing by the US Department of Defense on 19 September 2006.[42]

Katznelson concludes his signed affidavit with the statement "I declare under penalty of perjury under the laws of the United States that the foregoing is true to the best of my knowledge and belief." Are we really to believe that the Blair government, including the Attorney General, would have been unaware of what Katznelson was claiming? The radar of the Security Services must have picked this story up even if there were some doubts about its veracity.

However, the Security Services and the Blair government would certainly have known what was happening, meanwhile, on the British Indian Ocean Territory of Diego Garcia, part of a remote archipelago whose native Chagos population had been forcibly evacuated in the 1960s. Like Cuba, Diego Garcia is an island hosting a strategic US military base where activities, such as torture, would be conveniently remote from any domestic oversight. The territory has been described by some as 'a legal black hole'.[43]

Over the past decade, it has emerged that Britain assisted the Americans in their rendition programme, providing tip-offs to US intelligence, and among the detainees secreted to Gitmo were seventeen British citizens or residents. The complicity of British intelligence and the degree of knowledge of the British government is well-cited in a BBC report dating from 2017.[44] At the time, the Blair regime was determined to hide the vital role Diego Garcia played in facilitating the movement of these men. Our government stated that the territory, which remains the responsibility of the Foreign and Commonwealth Office, was not involved in extraordinary rendition flights.

These assurances were ultimately acknowledged as false in 2008 by the then Foreign Secretary, David Milliband. Flight logs that might have assisted in determining who was coming and going from the island apparently became waterlogged and unavailable for scrutiny, adding to the suspicion that Diego Garcia may have been a site of torture as well as a transit post.[45] Perhaps the detainees were also being stuffed with Lariam/WR 142 490 on arrival.

What becomes abundantly clear is that when Jane was trying to find out what had killed her husband, our country was deeply implicated in illegal detentions and facilitating, and possibly conducting, acts of torture. In 2006, on top of the Kelly death, there was so much that the Blair/Bush alliance needed to suppress. If our government would lie about rendition and torture they would have few qualms in suppressing anything that might expose the part played by Lariam in the Gitmo/Diego Garcia regimes.

In the end, the columns of *The Independent* would confirm that British involvement in the rendition scandal would be concluded with millions paid to the detainees in order to keep the story out of the courts: "the sums had to be high enough to buy the victim's silence. They were tantamount to hush money."[46]

So, in 2006 was the subject of Lariam now as toxic in government circles as the drug itself has proved to be for so many who took it? Were the MoD and the Department of

Health told not to look too closely? Did General Dannatt get warned off and is this why the subject was off-limits to General Houghton as long as he was Chief of the Defence Staff? Somebody knew what was going on but no one with any moral courage or enough care for the welfare of our servicemen and women. We'd had the cock-crowing denials and the washing of feet. Now Pontius Pilate was busy washing his hands.

———

Some years later, and after we had uncovered so much more negligence and the glaring inconsistencies and untruths in various MoD positions, I did make one last approach to the Secretaries of State I had attempted to engage over the years, namely Fox, Hammond and Fallon, asking if they might revise their positions and consider meeting some of those damaged by their policies. In my files, I don't seem to be able to find any replies. But, of course, there was a well-known problem with the postal system in the Westminster area...

More than a decade after those bland assurances about the drug I had received from the army doctor in Freetown, the realisation was dawning that this looked like a major medical and political scandal. The MoD persisted in its defence of the drug while the Department of Health and the UK drug regulators turned a blind eye. (I was going to say 'Nelsonian blind eye' but Nelson was driven by the imperative for decisive action.)

We would need a new tack and in 2015, we found one—the House of Commons Defence Committee.

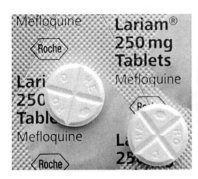

Double Jeopardy. Lariam
tablets and blister pack.
The fortnightly dose was
increased to weekly in 1991
(Photo by the author)

In Sierra Leone,
September 2003. About 40
Lariam pills consumed
by then
(Photo by the author)

Second World War Atabrine enforcement.
US Army 363<sup>rd</sup> Station Hospital.
(Kind permission Museum and Medical Arts Service)

**IMATT HQ and
Medical Centre,
Freetown, 2003.
(Photo by the author)**

**Sierra Leone
Army and
IMATT
Quarters,
Kenema.
(Photo by the
author)**

**Checking the
Sierra
Leone/Liberia
border.
(Photo by
author)**

**Dr Remington Nevin. Executive Director of the Quinism Foundation.**
**(Courtesy R Nevin)**

**Lt Col Ashley Croft conducting research at Lake Malawi.**
**(Courtesy A Croft)**

'Gassed' by John Singer Sargent. Soldiers damaged and
confused by chemical agents in the Great War. © IWM

Cameron Quinn in Kenya. Entering
Lariam's toxic vortex.
(Courtesy J Quinn)

Cameron Quinn in Iraq 2003.
Within three years he would
succumb to Lariam toxicity.
(Courtesy J Quinn)

The therapeutics of Alpine archaeology.
Clearing the mind in the Ecrins National
Park, South East France. (K Walsh)

Top Left: Jane and Cameron Quinn the night they were engaged in the Heywood Suite, Pennyhill Park Hotel, Bagshot. (J Quinn)

Above: Bea Coldwell. "Would you take this drug? Is this something you would ask your families to take?" The "unfair" question posed to Roche. (Courtesy B Coldwell)

Dave Rimmington five months after Sierra Leone. Smiles on the outside, dying inside. (Courtesy D Rimmington)

Dave Rimmington. Physical scars to add to the internal wounds of an attempted Lariam suicide (Courtesy D Rimmington)

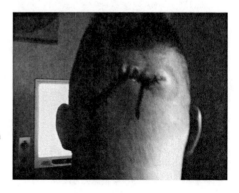

Assembling in Portcullis House to give our evidence to the Defence Select
Committee. December 2015. (UK Parliament Recordings)

Defence Select Committee Chairman Dr Julian Lewis questioning witnesses.
The Committee's seminal report described a lamentable failure by the MoD in
its duty of care. (Courtesy UK Parliament Recordings)

Jane Quinn today, Associate Professor in Veterinary Physiology, Charles Sturt University, Australia. (Courtesy J Quinn)

# Chapter 7

## Them That Ask No Questions

*We conclude that the MoD should designate Lariam as a 'drug of last resort'.*[1]

-House of Commons Defence Committee

Westminster is arguably the smartest and one of the most modern stations on the London Underground. As the tube train glides to a halt on the Jubilee Line, a sense of modernity is immediately apparent as the carriage doors neatly align with their glass, platform-edge counterparts. It had been some time since I had last alighted at Westminster and as I gained height through the steeply banked escalators towards street level, I guess like most infrequent visitors, I was struck by the austere, almost clinical, lines of the concrete and stainless steel architecture. With seemingly vast spaces for commuters at the heart of the metropolis, it seemed as though the place was trying to be an airport, and almost succeeding.

If I'd had time to linger in London, however, I would much prefer to have taken one more stop along the District or Circle Line to St James' Park station. There you can marvel at the Classical and Art Deco styles vying for attention in that wonderful Grade I Listed Building. Original enamels, timbers, wall tiles and the iconic 1920s Underground roundel are what I would choose to present to the travelling public and our overseas visitors. But this wasn't a day for lingering and I was soon emerging into daylight with the Elizabeth Tower of the Houses of Parliament rising high above me.

In tandem with the renovations of Westminster tube station, and a building for the new millennium, was the construction of Portcullis House, opened in 2001, and my destination on that drab and drizzly morning of 8 December 2015. Portcullis House provides offices and committee rooms for MPs that can no longer be provided within the now crowded Palace of Westminster. A street arcade to the left would take me towards Westminster Bridge and, following the pavement to the left once more, to the entrance on the Victoria Embankment.

As I joined the queue at the glass rotating doors for the security check, I heard the quarter chimes from the smaller bells nestled close to Big Ben in the Bell Tower (Big Ben only strikes the hour). I glanced at my watch and confirmed what I already knew: I was in plenty of time, adhering to an obsession with punctuality that doesn't always endear me to friends and family.

Portcullis House is an interesting construction. Externally, the seven storeys, stone pillars, steel struts and roof lines present a unique structure but one that mediates between the neo-Gothic of the Houses of Parliament and the Victorian and Edwardian facades of the Embankment and Westminster. It also offers strong hints of Britain's industrial past. Once you have negotiated the security procedures (definitely trying to be an airport), you come into an internal courtyard, or atrium, with a glass roof at second floor level. This is surrounded by what looks like a two-storey cloister, with the upper level containing the committee rooms where at

11.30, with three other panel members, I would be giving evidence about the MoD's use of Lariam to the Defence Select Committee.

On a typically dull winter's day in London, the atrium, where MPs can meet constituents and others in a more informal setting, was struggling to achieve best effect. Whatever Roman had originally come up with this airy design might not have been too impressed. Winter sun in the city can be at a premium and I recalled the saying that sunlight is the best disinfectant. The Lariam scandal was certainly going to need a lot of sunlight.

There's an old army saying that time spent on reconnaissance is seldom wasted and, as I knew it would probably be a little while before the other witnesses arrived, I went to the upper level and found the Wilson Room where we were due to convene. As there was a meeting underway I didn't look inside but I had already watched some committee proceedings on the Parliament website so I knew what the layout would be and how our evidence would be heard. I then located a corner room with a coffee machine, got out my notes and waited for the others to arrive.

First was Trixie Foster. We had never met before but she had joined our group a few years earlier. Trixie was someone who had experienced service family life and had never lost the sense of care for our people that was for so long at the heart of army life. She was a tenacious researcher and she had amassed much of the detail that we would be putting before the Defence Committee. She was also a close friend of Ellen Duncan, the wife of Major General Alastair Duncan, who was currently languishing in a secure mental hospital. Ellen would be joining us in the Wilson Room but, as she was not giving oral evidence herself, would be joining Bea and others in the public seating. Ellen had, however, sent the Committee a written statement and what it contained alone should have shamed the Secretary of State.

Alastair Duncan had served with great distinction and was one of the most decorated officers of his generation. His leadership in Northern Ireland, Bosnia and Sierra Leone saw him awarded respectively an OBE, the DSO and a CBE. Ellen wrote:[2]

*(Alastair's) military medical notes record that Lariam had an adverse effect on him when it was prescribed in late 2000 prior to deployment as a brigadier to Sierra Leone. Nevertheless his notes show that for some reason he continued to take the drug for the following 6 months. He was subsequently twice issued with medical tags warning against the use of Lariam in 2002 and 2004, when as a major general he would have been about to visit training in Kenya and Belize.*

*My husband and I were told by the doctor then in charge of the military mental health assessment programme that "we don't believe in neurotoxins." This was accompanied by dismissive and derogatory remarks about ex Service personnel merely having an eye to the main chance. This doctor also remarked "oh what do they know?" when I mentioned American research on the effects of blast related brain injury and military trauma. He subsequently referred my husband to another psychiatrist whose insensitive questioning included "how does it feel to kill?" This caused such distress that a Quantitative EEG of his brain by a private consultant later that day showed massive disturbance.*

*(He) has had 3 periods of detention in secure units run by the Somerset Partnership NHS Foundation Trust, one for 7 weeks in 2013 and two, effectively one, which started in January 2015, all a result of aggressive outbursts. Unlike his private consultants, the Trust has made no attempt to deal with the case holistically. The blast injury and the possibility of PTSD and Lariam damage have been completely ignored and instead he has been treated as an elderly dementia patient throughout.*

*Despite my many requests he has not been seen by an endocrinologist or a neurotoxicologist and the views of a well-respected psychopharmacologist and psychiatrist have been ignored. As a result the NHS has never carried out the appropriate tests. Since January he has been in a short term facility and since May in the extra care area, which is effectively a corridor and a small exercise yard. His only treatment has been medication with different psychotropic drugs, approximately 20 to date in varying combinations.*

*I am certain that it is these drugs that have changed him from a physically fit active man on admission, albeit with Complex PTSD and an underlying brain condition, into his present shuffling, neurotic, frightened state. This is a much more serious version of the condition which similar psychotropic medication caused during his treatment in 2013. That his present state is largely drug induced is evident from the lack of any significant change between his 2013 and 2015 MRIs.*

*Lariam is a most insidious form of friendly fire.*

Within a year Ellen was a widow. In July 2016 Major General Duncan died in Northampton General Hospital, abandoned and ignored by the MoD. No compelling evidence or indications to be found here?

While Trixie and I were comparing notes, we were joined by Dr Remington Nevin. Remington had served as a doctor in the US Army, including operational deployment to Afghanistan. He was currently a consulting physician epidemiologist and he has since qualified as a Doctor of Public Health at Johns Hopkins University where he studied the mental health effects of Lariam and other anti-malarial toxicity. He is probably the leading authority on the subject in North America and one of the world's best informed researchers into both the science and the marketing of Lariam /WR 142 490. He is now the Executive Director of the Quinism Foundation, a US not-for-profit charitable organisation supporting education and research on chronic quinoline encephalopathy and other medical conditions caused by poisoning, or intoxication, by mefloquine, tafenoquine, chloroquine and related quinoline drugs.

Remington had just arrived from Heathrow having flown overnight solely for the purpose of presenting evidence to the Committee. Shortly before the session convened, we were joined outside the Wilson Room by our fourth panellist, Dr Ashley Croft, now a Harley Street consultant public health physician and medical epidemiologist. With a special interest in infectious diseases and tropical medicine, he had served in the British Army for over 25 years as a medical officer. During that time he carried out considerable research into Lariam and its effects. Again, I had never met either Remington or Ashley but Bea, Jane and I had become quite well acquainted with them through many telephone calls and email exchanges.

The Defence Committee is one of a range of Parliamentary Select Committees composed of about a dozen House of Commons backbenchers. They are cross-party bodies and scrutinise the activities of government departments and their ministers, especially in areas of policy and where there may be a particular matter of public concern. I first wrote to the Chair of the Defence Committee (then Rory Stewart) in August 2014 asking that he consider an investigation. In July 2014 there had been an Early Day Motion in Parliament (ignored by the government) calling on the MoD to immediately cease prescribing Lariam to UK personnel in its charge and to conduct a full review of its use.[3]

Mr Stewart accepted that important questions were being raised but decided that the Committee had insufficient time to pursue the subject in the life of that Parliament. Therefore, we had to wait until the 2015 General Election the following June before trying once more. This time we gained very positive traction from the incoming Chair, Dr Julian Lewis, a most independently minded and enquiring MP, with a charm and integrity that is too seldom found in politicians and almost entirely absent from those charged with the nation's defence. Years later Dr Lewis told me that he had also been alerted to the dangers of Lariam by his friend and once Chairman of CND, the American-born Marjorie Thompson. She had been horrified by the drug's side-effects, especially among US service personnel. Someone else who cared and wanted something done. Thank you, Marjorie.

The drive for an inquiry was also boosted by the arrival of a new MP in the House, Johnny Mercer, who had unexpectedly won the Plymouth Moor View seat. It was his displeasure at how his cohort of military personnel and veterans were treated by the governments of the day that drove him into politics.[4] The 34-year old former Royal Artillery captain seemed the perfect advocate for damaged veterans. He was elected to the Defence Committee and supported our calls for an inquiry. Then something rather peculiar and a little disturbing happened.

In late-August, Mr Mercer posted a short video on social media which Bea, Jane and I feared might scupper the Lariam inquiry even before it had got underway. He informed his viewers that he had just had returned from "a really important meeting with the MoD" about Lariam.[5] In London he had met a senior minister in the MoD (although it is not clear who that was), the Surgeon General and representatives of Public Health England. Now he appeared to be endorsing an MoD line, presumably set by the Secretary of State, Sir Michael Fallon, which "made clear" to Mr Mercer that Lariam was carefully and properly prescribed and that the drug was "very, very rarely used".

This unexpected (and unconvincing) reassurance was followed by a comment that there was "still a conversation to be had" but, it seemed, that "was for the future". Yet again, the MoD was peddling the "nothing to see here" fallacy. As would be exposed (and was well known within the MoD), it was quite untrue that Lariam was being prescribed either properly or safely. Equally, the MoD's own documents showed that Lariam's use was very far from rare. At that very time, it remained the default antimalarial drug for British Army personnel deploying to sub-Saharan Africa.[6]

Perhaps a Secretary of State for Defence whose CV included a conviction for drink-driving might be expected to adopt such a casual attitude towards the effects of a psychotropic drug.[7] But here he was, presiding over a department that was either deliberately misleading the public and a newly-elected MP, or was recklessly incompetent. Ultimately, Fallon's standards of personal conduct were, by his own admission, so low that he could not remain as a minister and he was eventually forced to resign in 2017.[8] Apparently, the Prime Minister, Theresa May, considered his being a sex pest as an indiscretion too far.

Thankfully, this attempt by the MoD to frustrate our efforts to have an inquiry was unsuccessful and clearly the other Defence Committee members were not quite so sanguine as Johnny Mercer. I have often wondered who set up the Mercer/MoD meeting of August 2015. It smacked entirely of a cynical attempt to confound, confuse or silence a new rogue MP who was to be treated with all the ministerial disdain and contempt reserved for junior officers or non-commissioned ranks. Now Fallon, his ministerial acolytes and the Surgeon General would at least have to provide some answers, if not necessarily truthful ones.

The title of this book takes its inspiration from Rudyard Kipling's poem *A Smuggler's Song*. Kipling presents a delightful and highly romanticised picture of smuggling in Georgian times and an invocation to a child not to be curious about the clandestine comings and goings of men and ponies at the dead of night. Many will be familiar with line 'Them that ask no questions...' The little girl is told:

*If you wake at midnight, and hear a horse's feet,*
*Don't go drawing back the blind, or looking in the street,*
*Them that ask no questions isn't told a lie.*
*Watch the wall, my darling, while the Gentlemen go by.*

The imperative for secrecy can lead to deceit and in exceptional circumstances, such as the defence of the realm, lies may prove to be an operational necessity. Unfortunately, some seemed to think that this could extend to cover-up of malfeasance and the protection of the reputations of those who had behaved illegally or immorally. Entering the Wilson Room, we would certainly be drawing back the blind and we were now in a world where no question should be met with a lie.

Giving evidence to a select committee can feel rather like attending court but there are some significant differences. The first is that evidence is not given under oath. This is to encourage witnesses to speak freely. However, to knowingly mislead a committee is a serious offence and would be considered a contempt of the House. In effect, it would be perjury. Another difference is the manner of questioning. It would be directed by the Chair, Dr Lewis, who would ask various Committee Members to lead on certain questions or areas of concern. The general approach was investigative rather than inquisitorial but we had been invited as witnesses because it was believed that we had important information to divulge. We would be expected to validate our evidence and each of us was able to present carefully researched and largely objective testimony.

On entering the Wilson Room, we were greeted informally by some of the Committee and their staff and reminded how the proceedings would evolve. These pleasant and relaxing preliminaries were welcome and I recalled how profoundly different it all seemed to my first Crown Court experience during the Troubles in Northern Ireland, many years earlier at the beginning of my army career. Then, as a teenager serving in the Ulster Defence Regiment, I had been a witness for the prosecution in a case against four so-called Loyalists who had committed a sectarian murder in my home town. My patrol had intercepted their getaway and I suspect they little realised how close they themselves came to the penetrative effects of 7.62mm bullets from my British Army standard issue Self-Loading Rifle as they threw away their sub-machine gun and sawn-off shotgun.

For the trial, we had to make our own way to the Courthouse on Belfast's Crumlin Road, and tucked into the waistbands of our suit trousers we each had a Browning 9mm pistol. When we checked in at the police security desk I was a little surprised that we were to take our weapons into the courtroom. The Browning is quite bulky and we had no holsters. The waistband seemed more discreet than a pocket but I am sure the judge noticed how my left forearm was preventing the pistol's exposure and keeping it secure while, standing in the witness box, my right hand held a bible and I took the oath. We were given no anonymity but anyway, at least two of the accused in the dock knew me.

Their life sentences were later followed up by a warning from Special Branch that I was now on a terrorist hit list. From that day I have had nothing but contempt for bullies, thugs or warlords wherever I have encountered them. That experience probably also cemented a determination not to be cowed by injustice or corruption. So I, too, know something about cowards and standing up to argue my case in public.

We took our seats together as a panel facing the Committee. They sat at a U-shaped table with Dr Lewis central. Not all of the Committee were present. Only seven attended and members would come and go as they had to deal with other parliamentary business. That's not uncommon and the Committee also had other evidence sessions with the MoD and Roche (UK). What did surprise me, though, was that two of the Committee, the Conservatives James Gray and Bob Stewart were absent from all sessions. With their former military profiles, and particularly that of Bob Stewart who shared with me and Alastair Duncan active service in Northern Ireland and Bosnia, I had thought they might have taken a closer personal interest. Perhaps they had more pressing engagements. I never heard from either. Yet a great service was done by the Committee whose members presented Parliament at its best and exemplified by the Chair and, I thought, Madeleine Moon, the Labour MP for Bridgend.

A full text of our evidence session is available,[9] but here I only need to cover a few key matters. We were all agreed that the MoD was not aware of, or was deliberately ignoring, the scientific evidence available from the peer-reviewed literature published in Europe and North America. In fact some of this evidence was even coming from British military medical officers.[10] In this context, Dr Croft presented two important observations. The first was that the MoD had been taking advice from medical professionals who had serious conflicts of interests, including those who received funds from the manufacturer of Lariam, Roche. He was referring in particular to a civilian, Dr Ron Behrens, a consultant adviser on tropical medicines to the Ministry of Defence.[11,12]

Dr Behrens was also a member of Public Health England's Advisory Committee on Malaria Prevention, a body which likewise included Group Captain Green from the Surgeon General's Department. According to his own published papers in the BMJ and 'Tropical Medicine and International Health', Dr Behrens had received financial support from Roche (UK).[13,14] The second observation was that a clinical trial of Lariam conducted by the MoD on soldiers exercising in Kenya in 1995 was followed by the suicide of one of those men. As we have already seen, the MoD concealed the details of that study, and the consumption of Lariam, from the coroner investigating the death.

In his evidence, Dr Nevin focused on a particularly important aspect of Lariam toxicity (or quinism as he now defines it); the prodromal nature of many of the drug's side effects. Adverse reactions may range from psychosis to paranoia, and even ostensibly mild reactions such as restlessness or confusion have to be considered as prodromal to a more serious event. That means that these side effects may be warnings, perhaps the only warning, of a much more serious event, which might possibly even lead to suicide. Therefore, the only safe response for anyone experiencing any of these prodromal symptoms, even simply restlessness, is to mandate immediate discontinuation of the drug and to prescribe an alternative therapy.

Dr Nevin explained that this particular characteristic of that class of drugs had been known for more than seventy years, and it was something that Roche had been aware of since at least 2002. These prodromal symptoms simply make Lariam quite unsafe in the military environment. Anxiety, restlessness and confusion are routinely experienced during military operations. Indeed, training exercises are constructed with the intent of allowing soldiers to experience and work through them. As it would be impossible to determine if such reactions were triggered by the drug or the military environment, the only safe option must be to assume Lariam toxicity. Lariam consumption was, by its own definition, incompatible with the safe and effective prosecution of military operations.

Dr Nevin also explained that many of the side effects of Lariam toxicity mimic or could be confused with PTSD. Thus many American service personnel were being diagnosed with and treated for PTSD when they were more plausibly suffering from the chronic effects of mefloquine toxicity. This was just what we had encountered in General Duncan's case. And Trixie Foster made a penetrating observation about how research into mefloquine toxicity was absent from the agendas of one of the key investigative bodies commissioned by the MoD. She said:[15]

*The MOD relies a lot on the King's Centre for Military Health Research to submit papers on PTSD and alcohol. Since 1998 to 2015, over 425 publications have been done and 85% have been either written or co-authored by Professor Neil Greenberg and Professor Sir Simon Wessely. Only two, as far as I could see, by Dominic Murphy, have mentioned mefloquine—nothing [sic]. I have been in contact with Professor Neil Greenberg and had an email back to say that pharmaceutical research is not on their to-do list. So they are not even considering the idea that mefloquine or any other vaccinations have anything to do with this.*

Not on their to-do list. This chimed with a disappointing and rather patronising response I had received from Professor Wessely when I had raised a similar question.

For my part, I was able to inform the Committee that the drug was routinely issued without any prescribing process. In many instances, the tempo of military deployments would make prescribing impossible within the context of emergency or short notice deployments. The army needed a drug with a side-effect profile that was safe to issue at speed. I also explained that, contrary to civilian best practice, and in contravention of operational orders, military doctors were not reporting adverse events to the UK drug regulators.

This requirement had been explained in the Dannatt-directed letter to Jane Quinn of 2006 in which the then Wing Commander Green had said "Adverse events are required to be reported by military Medical Officers to the MHRA in common with standard United Kingdom medical practice."[16] That process simply requires a doctor to complete a Yellow Card which is passed to the MHRA in order that our drug regulators can better understand the risks presented by some products.

Through a Freedom of Information request, I had discovered that the Yellow Card process was, in fact, being largely ignored, denying the MHRA of the data relating to hundreds, if not thousands, of adverse reactions to Lariam.[17] It would seem that not one of at least five military doctors dealing with my illness thought to use the Yellow Card system. More disturbing is that, while during the years 2008, 2009 and 2010 when there appeared to have been just one Yellow Card completed, a Parliamentary Question raised by Madeleine Moon revealed that there had been no fewer than 157 referrals for mental health assessments for military personnel who had taken Lariam.[18]

We were in the Wilson Room for two hours. No doubt sitting behind us among Bea, Ellen Duncan and other Lariam survivors, were some note-takers from the MoD. After Dr Lewis had called 'order' to close the session and we chatted with some of the Committee and their staff, I thought about whose desks our evidence might be passing over that afternoon. I did even have some sympathy for the MoD officers who would be pressured by ministers and senior officers to come up with some fig leaf for a very naked Emperor. But not too much sympathy. If they couldn't find the moral courage to present the truth they would be no better than Fallon, Dannatt, Ainsworth and their ilk.

———

In January 2016 it was the MoD's turn to present a panel for questioning by the Committee.[19] That team was headed by Mark Lancaster, the Minister for Defence Personnel, Welfare and Veterans. He was accompanied by the Surgeon General, Surgeon Vice-Admiral Alasdair Walker, the Medical Director of the Defence Medical Services, Brigadier Timothy Hodgetts, and Surgeon Captain John Sharpley, Defence Consultant in Psychiatry. They looked very smart in their service uniforms and the Admiral, with his white beard, seemed to be affecting a salty seadog persona. (After his evidence, the less charitable suggested Captain Birds Eye.) I watched the proceedings live on a computer link and after calling the session to order the Chair, Dr Lewis, made this explosive opening statement. He said:

*I understand that the Minister wants to make a brief statement to open. Before I ask him to do that, I would like to say that this inquiry was announced last September, so the Ministry has known about our interest in this subject for several months. Therefore, it was a little disconcerting to receive what is entitled an "ad hoc statistical bulletin" relating to the subject of this investigation only at four minutes to 10 this morning. That is not an acceptable timescale. If you are going to give us information that is, in your opinion, germane to our inquiry, it should be given to us with a reasonable amount of notice before the relevant hearing. It is a mixed blessing to receive information so close to an inquiry hearing that we can't make proper use of it.*

*I hope that message will be taken back to whoever was responsible for this bad timing, especially as there is a sentence in the document that states: "This bulletin has been developed in support of the House of Commons Defence Committee... inquiry into Mefloquine use in the armed forces and to provide Official Statistics to meet the continued public interest in the number of UK armed forces who have been prescribed Mefloquine." As I say, had we received this even a week ago, it might have been helpful. It is not very helpful to get it on the very verge of conducting a public evidence session.*

*Having got us off on that particular, and not very pleasant, opening, I invite the Minister to say what he wishes to put forward.*

The contempt for the inquiry demonstrated by Michael Fallon's department was simply breath-taking. On the very morning that the MoD was to present its oral evidence, they presented their 'Ad Hoc Statistical Bulletin'.[20] This paper attempted to suggest that Lariam was rarely prescribed during operations in Afghanistan between the years 2007 and 2014. It was little wonder that Mr Lancaster and his team did not want to allow the Committee any time to scrutinise the bulletin before they were submitted to questioning. It claimed that only 536 personnel had been given Lariam during that period in Afghanistan. However, closer appraisal exposes either a shambles of record keeping or appalling levels of deceit: take your pick.

According to the Bulletin, almost 13,000 personnel were known to have been given antimalarial drugs in that theatre of operations but the MoD didn't know what drug they had been issued. Even worse, more than half of those sent to Afghanistan over those seven years (a total of 131,000) may or may not have been given chemoprophylaxis: the MoD simply didn't know if they were ever given antimalarials, never mind which one. Furthermore, the Ad Hoc Statistical Bulletin is entirely silent upon why anyone serving in Afghanistan would have been given Lariam.

According to the ACMP guidelines (which the MoD claimed to follow and were set by, among others, Dr Behrens and Group Captain Green), no one in Afghanistan should ever have been given Lariam. The ACMP recommendations for

Afghanistan are quite clear.[21] They say "There is a risk of malaria below 2000m from May to November (C+P (Chloroquine plus Proguanil)). There is low to no risk in areas above 2000m (BA (bite avoidance) only)." What the MoD will admit is that from 2007 until 2015 *a minimum* of 17,368 personnel were prescribed Lariam. The real figure is likely to be very much larger.

As I watched the session, among the curious and evasive responses to the MPs' questions there were two that I found almost mind-numbing, encompassing medical complacency, negligence and a clear attempt to mislead the Committee.[22] They were answers to questions about the side effects of the drug (one from John Spellar and the other from Ruth Smeeth). The Surgeon General made the astonishing claim "There is no evidence that I can find any place that Mefloquine impairs function." Really? The senior clinician in the Armed Forces who agreed that he was "the person who signs off the policy and therefore I have the final responsibility" could find no evidence, *any place*, that Lariam would impair function.

Apart from all the peer-reviewed articles available to him, Admiral Walker seemed to be quite ignorant of the common side effects reported by the manufacturers themselves in the pamphlets provided to prescribers and patients. And are we to be believe that the Surgeon General was unaware of evidence presented to the Committee only two months earlier by Dr Frances Nichol, Head of Drug Safety Quality at Roche (UK)?

Dr Nichol had stated quite clearly that common side effects included dizziness, nausea, bad dreams, insomnia and depression. She had also said that the drug's leaflets had been "updated primarily to pull out the preponderance of what we have classified as neuropsychiatric effects."[23] The positions of Dr Nichol and the Surgeon General were quite incompatible. It is difficult to characterise Admiral Walker as anything but utterly incompetent or simply mendacious.

But Walker was continuing something of an MoD tradition in misleading Parliament about Lariam. In 2014 a similarly bizarre statement was made in the House of Lords by Lord Astor of Hever, then Parliamentary Under-Secretary of State at the MoD. Lord Astor, in an answer to a question tabled by Baroness Corston declared:

*As with all prescriptions the Ministry of Defence follows the drug manufacturer's advice which stipulates that Mefloquine (commercially known as Lariam) should not be taken if you are carrying out complex tasks such as driving.*[24]

Astor was displaying, at best, very lazy research as to what the manufacturers actually said about driving. There was no such stipulation: they advised caution. Anyway, did he really believe that those taking Lariam were not to conduct essential but routine tasks such as driving? In Sierra Leone that would have confined the whole force to barracks. Just how out of touch with reality, or even basic common sense, could a defence minister be? Failing to check any of the facts, in one sentence he had misled Parliament on three points. Even at this late stage, he should be required to withdraw his statement. He might also do a major public service and withdraw to his pile in Kent.

The other response that I found especially worrying was one offered by the Royal Navy psychiatrist, Surgeon Captain Sharpley. Supported by Brigadier Hodgetts, Captain Sharpley correctly suggested to the Committee that a range of side effects, such as disturbed sleep or stress, could be attributable to factors within the operational or geographical setting, such as helicopter noise or the tempo of events. It was simply not possible to determine if the drug or the environment were the cause. But they both seemed to be blissfully ignorant of the uniquely prodromal nature of Lariam's side effects. As stated by the manufacturers, the presence of any of these side effects mandated the immediate discontinuance of the drug and the transfer to a safer medication. Did Sharpley and Hodgetts not know that? Or were they taking their line from ill-informed and unqualified ministers such as Lord Astor? These were supposed to be expert witnesses but they were clearly unfamiliar with, or withholding, the essential details of the drug's characteristics. And I wasn't the only one worried about the integrity of the testimony being offered to the Committee that day.

Dr Nevin and Dr Croft were so alarmed by the quality of the evidence presented by this panel that they felt impelled to respond in some detail to the Committee. In an utterly damning critique, they co-authored a paper titled 'Joint scientific response to oral evidence from the Ministry of Defence, given on 12th January 2016,' exposing to the Committee, in forensic detail, just how misleading these four witnesses had been.[25] They explained that the evidence presented was variously wrong, false, contrived or specious, that it contradicted UK military expert papers, was vague and presented by doctors who were unfamiliar with the prescribing processes for the drug. Like me, they were also disturbed that important government papers, essential to the inquiry, appeared to have been lost, as admitted by the Surgeon General.

There are two particular charges made by Drs Croft and Nevin, apparently unchallenged by the MoD, which are hugely damaging to the reputation and integrity of the MoD and the Defence Medical Services. The first is that the medical witnesses from the Royal Navy and the Army failed to comply with GMC guidance for witnesses at such inquiries. None of them had any expert knowledge in travel medicine, far less Lariam toxicity. According to Croft and Nevin:

> *In its current guidance to doctors... the General Medical Council states: "You must always be honest about your experience [and] qualifications...You must make clear the limits of your competence and knowledge when giving evidence or acting as a witness." When giving evidence to the Defence Committee on 12th January 2016 the three medical witnesses did not comply with the GMC's guidance, as set out in Good Medical Practice. The three doctors did not make clear to the Defence Committee, at the start of their oral evidence, that their competence and knowledge in respect of malaria was severely limited. It would appear therefore that... the medical witnesses for the MoD did not fulfil their duties as set out in the GMC's 2013 guidance document, Good Medical Practice.*

Throughout their testimony, the panel presented evidence far beyond their competence, or even experience. The dangers are obvious and exemplified by a gross error of judgement by Brigadier Hodgetts. He ventured into terrain which took him far beyond his qualifications as an accident and emergency physician in discussing, in a questionable manner, the effects of alcohol in combination with drugs such as Lariam. In this instance, Hodgetts was either unaware of, or withheld, the fact that a paper he was citing was industry-sponsored, in fact by Roche. As Dr Nevin says, "It was improper of Dr Hodgetts to quote this study to the Committee, without making it clear that the study was funded by Roche."

The second is a charge levelled at Captain Sharpley, but which he obviously shares with many others, in that he was appearing to subordinate his prime responsibility towards his patients to an unethical support to his employer, the MoD, and their Lariam policies.

I tried to raise these matters with the GMC in 2016, with little effect. This was their response:[26]

*There is no suggestion when they are introduced or being questioned by the Inquiry that they were being treated as expert witnesses in the case or that the evidence that they gave was being used for the purpose of formulating an expert view.*

It seems utterly bizarre that the GMC should believe that these three doctors were lay professional witnesses, and highly unlikely that they were not considered as experts by the Committee members. Even if they were not experts, the GMC conceded:

*Lay witnesses are of course bound by the same principles outlined in Good Medical Practice as expert witnesses. All witnesses should be open and honest about the*

*evidence that they give and they should be clear (about)*
*the limits of their competence and knowledge.*

The GMC may have formed the opinion that these three doctors were fit to practice. In the Army we know all about closing ranks. My view is that they were quite unfit to hold the Queen's Commission.

———

There was one other evidence session where again, unfortunately, the Committee was certainly deliberately misled, something that only became apparent to us in 2016, after the inquiry had been concluded and the Committee had moved on to other work. Roche (UK) was invited to attend the Committee on 10 November 2015 where they were represented by Dr Frances Nichol, Head of Drug Safety Quality, and Mr Mike Kindell, Lead, Established Products. Their oral evidence had been preceded by an anonymous written statement, dated November 2015. Its title was 'Memorandum submitted by Roche Products Ltd' and it addressed topics such as Lariam's licencing, effectiveness, safety and side-effects, and comparisons with other antimalarial drugs.[27]

Curiously, when I checked the document's properties on my computer, it appeared that it had not been written by Dr Nichol. The originator seemed to be a Sarah Buckley who, we would learn later, was the Roche (UK) lead for Public Affairs. The interest of Public Affairs in this matter may be unremarkable except that the document was grossly misleading and was withholding essential safety information from the Committee.

The Memorandum stated that Roche monitored published scientific and medical studies on the effects of Lariam, looking for new and significant safety information relevant to Lariam, in order to keep their benefit-risk assessments up to date. They claimed to factor this evidence into their assessments of the drug's safety. Towards the end of 2016, we discovered this was quite untrue. For over a decade, and at the height of the Lariam scandal, Roche (UK) had been withholding the vitally important prodromal nature of Lariam's side effects from both British patients and prescribers. Lariam product papers that I had found online referring to the prodromal warnings since 2002 had been produced by the company's US affiliate. The company, I discovered, was marketing its drugs with different warnings across the globe. The prodromal warnings were not published by Roche in UK patient or doctor leaflets until 2013.

The Roche memorandum also contained this statement:

*A study cited in the Lariam SPC (Overbosch et al) explored overall frequency of adverse events and efficacy of chemoprophylaxis to another anti-malarial (atovaquone-proguanil). Results indicated that Lariam and atovaquone-proguanil are similarly effective for malaria prophylaxis in non-immune travellers.*

It is true as far as it goes but it neglects to say that, as we saw in the previous chapter, atovaquone-proguanil (malarone) is much safer, especially regarding neuropsychiatric adverse events. Nor did it mention that, since at least as early as 2007, more effective antimalarials with better side effect profiles were now available, and these were, in the global context, generally used.[28]

Mr Kindell seemed to have little to offer the Committee and it fell mostly to Dr Nichol to defend Roche and Lariam/WR 142 490.[29] Dr Nichol explained that her background was as a GP but that she had not seen a patient for fifteen years. She did eventually admit that the risk of neuropsychiatric effects were twice as high in Lariam compared with malarone, but neither she nor Mr Kindell ever mentioned the word prodromal. Perhaps they didn't understand its importance.

Roche might have been expected to do better than offer only witnesses who, from their testimony, clearly knew nothing about the reality of the sales practice for the drug on the High Street, far less what was going on in the MoD. Dr Nichol stated that since 2013 all patients were being provided with a Patient Alert Card as well as the standard information leaflet. She also said that Lariam was "not an over-the-counter drug. It is not a drug that is being given out by pharmacists." She claimed it was being provided through a one-on-one setting with qualified physicians who knew how to ask and elicit the appropriate responses from their patients in an individual setting. What she said was simply untrue. Cal Watt, Bea and I all tested the system in England and Scotland. Outlets across the country, such as Boots and Superdrug, were selling this stuff over-the-counter without a physician in sight.

While listening to Dr Nichol give her evidence, it became increasingly clear, and with hindsight certain, that Roche was hiding something. As it turned out they were hiding a lot. Mike Kindell was clearly uncomfortable. He said that Roche "had just started to get in touch" with the MoD after the most recent articles about the drug came out in the press. When pressed further he backtracked, saying "We haven't contacted the Ministry of Defence as a body, but we will have contacted all the general practitioners who work within the Ministry of Defence." Dr Nichol added "We have reached out to the MoD, and we haven't yet had a meeting." Reached out? They needed to do more than reach out.

Remember the SSgt Bales case of multiple homicides in Afghanistan in 2012 and the Roche "periodic update report"? Roche knew about that event almost immediately after it happened and the company was now telling Parliament that they monitored the effects of Lariam, for new and significant safety information, in order to keep their benefit-risk assessments up to date. What could more significant than mass murder? Why was the MoD not informed? Dr Nichol didn't think she was allowed to speak about individual cases for legal reasons.

———

When it was published in May 2016, the Defence Committee's report proved to be a shocking indictment of the MoD and its practices.[30] They formally recorded that the MoD had shown a "lamentable weakness in its Duty of Care" towards service personnel and made the unequivocal recommendation that Lariam should be designated as a drug of last resort. And there was much else in the report that brought shame on a series of defence ministers implicated in this national disgrace. But there was something else that neither the MoD nor Roche wanted to declare to the Defence Committee and which they had managed to keep suppressed.

In January 2014, the European Medicines Agency published their report which concluded that there was now enough evidence from the available drug safety reports, the published literature and a recent US Food and Drug Administration assessment report to support a causal relationship between Lariam and the occurrence of long lasting and even persistent neuropsychiatric side effects. Furthermore, there was a strong suspicion that Lariam could cause different kinds of permanent brain damage.[31]

I didn't discover the existence of this 36-page document until after the Committee published its report. It couldn't be found through any online search and I had eventually obtained a copy from my contact in Ireland. Didn't this count as *compelling evidence (or indications) produced from the body of global scientific evidence regarding the toxicity of mefloquine?* And how come Fallon, Soubry *et al* didn't know about it; or did they? Why was this document so difficult to find? It certainly demolished the integrity of the Surgeon General—*There is no evidence that I can find any place that Mefloquine impairs function.* Them that ask no questions...

Somewhere, there was a rat giving off a very nasty smell. We now started some very deep research and discovered that an especially unpleasant odour was emanating from Welwyn Garden City, the home of Roche Pharmaceuticals (UK).

# Chapter 8

## See How Dumb They Lie

*Knocks and footsteps round the house—whistles after dark*
*You've no call for running till the house-dogs bark.*
*Trusty's here, and Pincher's here, and see how dumb they*
*lie.*
*They don't fret to follow when the Gentlemen go by!*

*-Rudyard Kipling, A Smugglers Song*

Watchdogs can be invaluable but not, if like Kipling's *Trusty*
and *Pincher*, they have been trained not to bark. Why did
Roche not bark after the Bales murders in Afghanistan? And
how could it be that a pharmaceutical giant like Roche could
market drugs across the world with such differing information
leaflets? When I was serving in Sierra Leone I had Americans
and Canadians in my team. We all took Lariam and my medic
could be relied upon to provide tablets if someone ran short
or mislaid their own supply in the jungle.

Presumably, we were all consuming the same product.
But according to Roche, the drug warnings needed to be
different depending upon whether you were American or
British. Seemingly, side effects for my US Navy SEAL medic
and US Marine Corps captain would be prodromal. But not
for me and my British comrades. And what about the
Canadians?

It might be naïve to except absolute uniformity in drug literature across international legal jurisdictions, but this should not absolve a company from providing essential warnings about hazards that clearly are no respecters of nationalities. In this respect, Lariam toxicity is rather analogous to the Volkswagen emissions scandal exposed by the United States Environmental Protection Agency in 2015. VW had used software in their vehicles to cheat federal fuel emissions tests and were thus selling cars emitting nitrogen oxides at many levels above the legal limit.[1]

Not surprisingly, after the story broke, European nations determined that what poisoned in the USA would be equally toxic in their jurisdictions and multiple legal actions followed.[2] A coherent, unequivocal warning is essential and a bit more effective than 'reaching out'. No wonder Roche like such euphemisms.

I was stunned when I discovered that for years Roche had been withholding the prodromal warning. I found that out when I was provided with copies of Roche's Summary of Product Characteristics (SPCs) and Patient Information Leaflets (PILs) for Lariam in the US and UK over a twenty year period and had an opportunity to make comparisons. I got those documents from a contact overseas: Roche refused to provide me with any copies. The evidence is stark.

That Roche knew of, and was concerned by, the prodromal side effects of Lariam, is clear in a letter sent to all doctors in the United States in 2002.[3] Addressed as a 'Dear Doctor', it alerted American prescribers to "Important changes and additions to the prescribing information" and explained that both the prescribing information for doctors (the SPC) and the PILs (the leaflet accompanying each prescription to the patient) were to be updated with immediate effect. The letter, signed by the Medical Science Leader for Roche Laboratories, contained this warning:

*During prophylactic use, if psychiatric symptoms such as acute anxiety, depression, restlessness or confusion occur, these may be considered prodromal to a more serious event. In these cases, the drug must be discontinued and an alternative medication should be substituted.*

It would take another eleven years before Roche in the UK provided this upgrade to their warnings. Hence, as late as 2013, British consumers were simply being advised that if they were experiencing any of the side effects that should now have mandated immediate discontinuance of the drug "You should consult a doctor immediately before taking your next tablet."[4] Back in 2003, that is exactly what I did and I now discovered that the SPC upon which my British Army doctors were then reliant stated:

*Patients should be advised to obtain medical advice before the next weekly dose of Lariam, if any concerning or neuropsychiatric symptoms develop. Discontinuation of Lariam should be considered, particularly if neuropsychiatric reactions occur. The need for alternative antimalarial therapy or prophylaxis can then be evaluated.[5]*

Nothing here about prodromal side effects. And the change to an alternative, safer drug, remained entirely discretionary. Doctors could continue to ascribe side effects to the environment and not the drug. Hence, Roche UK chose to expose all its customers, military and civilian alike, to the risk of long term and possibly permanent neuropsychiatric damage or even suicide. That all changed during 2013 when Roche UK recognised that it had to bring the warnings of the hazards of Lariam toxicity into line with those provided in the United States. The SPC would now include a boxed special warning, in bold text, about neuropsychiatric adverse events and what the proper and only safe response should be. The side effects *had* to be regarded as prodromal and Lariam would have to be replaced by alternative malaria prevention medication.[6]

What was it that ultimately caused the UK warnings to change in 2013? There were probably three factors at play. The first is that we can only assume that Roche was concerned about Lariam's connection with the Bales case. Perhaps someone within the company was worried; they had every reason to be. The second is that 2013 was the year when the 'Lariam Scandal' was re-emerging in the British national press, and was now emblazoned as exactly that across the front pages.[7]

Lariam had also been the subject of an investigation by the Irish broadcaster, RTÉ, in a Prime Time documentary shown in May 2013. The Irish Army had an alarming rate of suicides among its contingents of United Nations peacekeepers serving in sub-Saharan Africa, all of whom were required to take the drug.[8] And there is a third, equally worrying, aspect to this belated pharmaceutical epiphany at Welwyn.

During 2012 and 2013, Roche had been subjected to inspections by the UK regulator, the MHRA, during which critical deficiencies had been found in the company's pharmacovigilance system.[9] It is almost certain that those publicly exposed shortcomings would have prompted an internal audit of the quality of the product warnings of all of their drugs, including Lariam. There would have been some very hasting housekeeping in Welwyn.

The conclusion seems quite simple. Product safety information had been governed by perceived company vulnerability to litigation in differing international jurisdictions, rather than by the hazards known to be inherent within the drug itself. The alternative is that the Roche outfit in Welwyn had just been grossly negligent over many years. It was hard to tell. Given the especially idiosyncratic manner in which Roche had managed to bring the product to the UK market in 1989, I decided it was time to look more closely at the details of the UK licence and also the nature of the transatlantic relationships between the British and American branches of the company, and also their respective regulatory bodies. When we look at the responsibilities of the various Roche affiliates around the globe, Roche in the UK begins to look very vulnerable.

One of the acknowledged characteristics of Lariam/mefloquine, and since 2013 also stated in bold text in the UK SPC, is its long half-life. This means that it takes a long time for the body to be clear of the drug. There is, rather like radioactive decay, a long time for the drug to continue to cause adverse reactions and, as we now know, any damage caused may be permanent. When the drug was first marketed, the toxicity risk for users was somewhat mitigated by the fact that those staying in malarial areas for more than three weeks would reduce to a fortnightly dose, rather than continue to take the pill on a weekly basis.

Through a Freedom of Information request[10] I discovered that the fortnightly regime was abandoned in 1991 when the UK regulator agreed to a request from Roche that long-term users should continue with the weekly schedule. That decision was founded mainly on an American paper published in January 1991 (Lobel *et al* 1991).[11] The Lobel paper reported a study conducted among US Peace Corps Volunteers which concluded that a weekly regime was necessary to afford long-term protection.

But there were major flaws in that study, acknowledged by the lead author, Dr Hans Lobel himself, during testimony he gave as an expert witness in later court proceedings concerning Lariam in the USA in 2002.[12] The study was neither randomised nor had it used a double-blind placebo. Another major shortcoming was that the cohort being studied may not even have been complying with the requirement to take the drug on a fortnightly basis. Thus there was no credible scientific basis on which to recommend an increase in dosage. Furthermore, Lobel characterised Lariam as a very safe compound and described those with contrary views as "anti-mefloquine activists".[13]

This is rather disturbing as Dr Lobel had been in charge of malaria surveillance at the US CDC from 1966 until retiring in 2000. It seems fair to assume that his profile and position within the CDC would have influenced the decision of the UK drug regulators to accede to the Roche request to vary their licence (and substantially increase their profits) and effectively double the usage for long-term travellers. Equally disturbing was that the same application to vary the licence to permit increased dosing was accompanied by a series of additional warnings about the drug's side effects and their duration.

While Dr Lobel was defending the drug in court, it seems that the American Food and Drug Administration were not quite so relaxed about Roche and how its adverse events were being recorded. Hoffman-La Roche Inc in New Jersey received multiple inspections in December 2002 and January 2003, causing the FDA to raise a formal report, cataloguing what are quite clearly some serious deficiencies within the company, including a number related to Lariam.[14]

If this American dog wasn't barking, it was certainly growling. The report opened by stating that "Establishment and maintenance of adverse reports has not provided for accurate reports" and went on to say that "correspondence between the Drug Safety Department and adverse event reporters was not maintained in an orderly manner." Papers were often unsigned and there appeared to be no proper auditing of important telephone conversations. Perhaps most damning is the paragraph which reads:

*The firm has not established procedures for receipt and surveillance of complaints and inquiries within the Roche Pharmaceutical Service Center. There were no provisions for providing a mailing address should a consumer or other complainant request one. In addition, there was no established Drug Safety procedure for consolidation and reporting of duplicate adverse event reports.*

With hindsight, I might not have expected any better from Roche, but it was what I read in the Summary of Findings attached to the FDA report that both shocked and angered me. Among the Drug Safety personnel from whom the inspectors "obtained information" was a Dr Martin Huber, Vice President, Global Safety Risk Management. The summary explains:

*Dr Huber... described the [redacted] person global organization which has reported to him since 12/01. He stated that Welwyn, Great Britain, was the central site for all affiliates and had its own medical evaluation group and associated drug safety personnel. Welwyn was responsible for entering data from the affiliates onto the Advent software system. Dr M Huber stated that the smaller affiliates relied on Welwyn for investigation and follow up to adverse drug experiences.*

*According to Dr M Huber, Welwyn maintained a core data sheet for each Roche product which incorporated all approved product insert information on products marketed around the world. Welwyn had the responsibility to upgrade, if necessary, the seriousness assigned to all adverse event cases by all affiliates. He stated that Basel, Switzerland, which had about [redacted] medical evaluation personnel, was responsible for the Advent software itself and also for some Advent system entries.*

*All clinical study adverse events were reportedly handled out of Basel. Dr M Huber stated that, by written procedure, literature searches for adverse experiences were a Welwyn responsibility.*

This looked just as arcane as the legal black hole at Gitmo, and probably just as intentional. And Welwyn, the very affiliate that was the global hub of the Roche reporting system, seemed the most tardy in responding to the medical and patient reports that would have been (or should have been) flooding in from across the world. It took them more than a decade to provide the essential warnings to UK users. Was that negligence or a deliberate business decision?

When I read the FDA report my mind then went back to something I had seen in the Roche 1991 application to adjust their licence in the UK. The opening paragraph had given an assurance to the British regulators that the company was taking a holistic, global view of their products, presumably in part because they were relying on American data in their quest to have the prophylactic dose for their product increased. They wished to "vary the licence particulars in accordance with our present day knowledge." And they declared:

*An international task force within F Hoffmann-La Roche Ltd has been established to harmonise all package insert/data sheet statements world-wide[15]*

Was that a deliberate deceit or a failed promise? It certainly failed me and countless others. The Roche dogs didn't bark but some of their cats were going to get very fat on the cream.

There was also another international mechanism that seemed to be failing those reliant upon safe administration of the drug in the UK. I was passed a copy of a US Department of Defense letter which was responding to questions that had been raised about malaria and Lariam use by Congressman

John McHugh, the Chairman of the Subcommittee on Military Personnel of the House Armed Services Committee in 2002.[16] The Department of Defense acknowledged that while mefloquine remained a mainstay antimalarial in the USA, scientific studies had raised concerns regarding the side effect profile of the drug and that "Recent peer-reviewed reports show adverse event rates at levels much higher than previously reported." But what really attracted my attention was the following paragraph:

> *DoD is part of the Interagency Working Group for Antimalarial Chemotherapy which is comprised of representatives from the Department of State, the Peace Corps, CDC, FDA, the United Kingdom, the Netherlands, and Germany. The subject matter experts within this Group meet periodically to exchange information and make recommendations regarding antimalarial medication. Mefloquine was the subject of a recent Working Group meeting on April 16, 2002. The results of the meeting are summarized in the enclosed document.*

So someone from the United Kingdom was participating in a US-led international grouping which met regularly to discuss antimalarial chemotherapy. It seems reasonable to assume that our representative would have been made aware of the developing literature on Lariam and the pending increased warnings that the US would be requiring from Roche, as well as the growing concern within the US Armed Forces about mefloquine's toxicity. Presumably the Roche 'Dear Doctor' letter of 2002 and the subsequent changes to the American SPCs and PILs would have been aired at these meetings. And presumably the UK representative was advised when the US Armed Forces were to relegate Lariam to a drug of last resort, while the American Special Forces Command would ban its use entirely.[17,18]

And surely all this information, especially if UK attendance was facilitated by public funds, should have been making its way into the MoD and the Department of Health. Would none of this be considered as *compelling evidence (or indications) produced from the body of global scientific evidence regarding the toxicity of mefloquine?* And what about Roche? Was none of this helping to inform the "international task force within F Hoffmann-La Roche Ltd… established to harmonise all package insert/data sheet statements world-wide."

It was difficult to determine who was representing the United Kingdom at these American meetings. I couldn't find any minutes or agendas for the Interagency Working Group but I did get hold of what looks like a fax distribution list of attendees being invited to participate in an 'Expert Meeting On Malaria Chemoprophylaxis', on 29-30 January 2003 being held by the US CDC.[19] The only UK expert on the list is Dr Ron Behrens, who was a member of Public Health England's ACMP and an adviser to the MoD. The 'Expert Meeting' and the 'Interagency Working Group' may have been separate forums but it seems most unlikely that, even if they were, they did not share their discussions or findings.

Then in 2017, Roche provided another public statement about Lariam's marketing in the UK which seemed very difficult to reconcile with the tangled web of realities that we were beginning to uncover. Interviewed by Cal Watt in 2016 in the Roche site at Welwyn, Dr Frances Nichol said:[20]

*Since 2013 the MHRA, and working together with Roche, strengthened our label for Lariam, and specifically calling out the neuropsychiatric events; and we believe it is very important that prescribers and patients are made aware of that information from the outset so that they know how to respond should anybody be concerned that they might be having a change in their mental state.*

I agree entirely that prescribers and patients should be made aware of vital safety information from the outset. So why had Roche so obviously put so many patients at risk, for so long, by doing the opposite of what their Head of Drug Safety Quality was publicly presenting as company policy? We needed to speak directly to Roche, and the regulator, the MHRA. Had the MHRA simply been watching the wall as the Roche gentlemen went by?

——

Sunday, 9 April 2017, was overcast in Yorkshire as I picked up Bea Coldwell and we set off down the A1 towards Hertfordshire and Welwyn Garden City. There we would be meeting Trixie Foster to prepare for a conference the next day with Roche at their UK headquarters. It was a long drive and on the way we went over what we had learned from Roche over the past year. I was surprised that they had agreed to meet us but we were not so naïve as to discard the notion that Roche were probably keen to establish just exactly what we knew about them and if we posed any threat. It was a glorious late afternoon as we checked in to our hotel, very convenient for the Roche site at Shire Park, about a mile off. Trixie had arrived from the West Country by train and while they were settling in I did a quick recce of the route.

I soon found Falcon Way and the entrance to the Roche domain. It all looked very modern and clean, even clinical, but the high walls, lighting and access controls rather took me back to my time in Berlin during the Cold War. Perhaps this is how Big Pharma protects itself, but it was all a little too Check Point Charlie and East Berlin for my liking.

The hotel was fine but we decided to treat ourselves to supper at a nearby restaurant in the countryside. There we were able to go over the agenda for the meeting and sort out who would take the lead on various topics. Roche had agreed to set up a video link so we were going to be joined by Jane Quinn from Australia and Remington Nevin from the USA. The meeting had been agreed in principle by Roche over a year earlier in February 2016 when Bea had begun requesting information from Dr Frances Nichol.

We were particularly keen to see a copy of a transcript of the Roche meeting that had apparently been arranged with the MoD, and also to learn why Roche had been unaware of how Lariam was being provided so easily 'over the counter' by High Street outlets such as Boots. But Dr Nichol didn't seem to want to 'reach out' to us. She was unable, or unwilling, to answer some very basic questions and decided that we must deal with her colleague at Roche, Sarah Buckley. The Roche UK Head of Drug Safety Quality was apparently passing responsibility for detailed answers on safety to the Public Affairs Officer.

Trixie had received a similar response in October 2016 when she emailed Dr Nichol. It was quite illuminating for us to learn that this was a public affairs matter but, of course, we

225

had found out that it was Sarah Buckley, from public affairs, who had probably drafted the anonymous statement sent to the Defence Committee in 2015. Bea had passed me Sarah Buckley's email address and during 2016 I had asked to her clarify the Roche position on a number of points. Top of my priorities was to determine exactly when UK prescribers were first notified about the prodromal nature of Lariam side effects and how that was passed was to them.

Ms Buckley responded that the SPC was updated with that information in 2013 but would not provide any copies of the SPC other than the most current, 2016, version. Much later I would find out why Roche was so coy about their earlier literature. I was also given a copy of a letter sent to the Surgeon General by Dr Nichol in October 2016.[21] That short missive stressed the importance of proper prescribing but made no mention whatsoever of prodromal side effects, the vital element in safely managing the drug once prescribed. The letter did mention a meeting between Dr Nichol and Brigadier Hodgetts but Roche was unwilling to give us any details of exactly what was covered. (Brigadier Hodgetts and his staff did have a meeting with Roche before the MoD gave their evidence to the Defence Committee in January 2016. Who attended from Roche remains secret and there was no recorded discussion of prodromal side effects.[22]) We reviewed what we had gleaned over a couple more drinks in the hotel bar and speculated on what Roche might say before calling it a night.

Submitting to my slight obsession with punctuality, in the morning I was checked out in advance of the others and going over my notes in the lobby for a final time before we started the short drive to Falcon Way and the Roche site. At the entrance we were directed to a car park and, as I locked the car, I was wondering if Bea was only half-joking when she said "I wonder if they'll put a bug in it?" I smiled as I knew that one her favourite books was John le Carré's *The Constant Gardner*. I'd read it during my first tour in Sierra Leone and that dark narrative of dirty pharma and corruption was gripping as I turned the pages by the light of my head torch during the dark African nights.

In those days, I took the tale with a pinch of salt but having learned so much over the years, I don't think le Carré was that far from reality. Back then, I knew nothing of MKULTRA, WRAIR, or Diego Garcia, or how British Service Chiefs and Surgeon Generals had been behaving. Yet even on the 10th April 2017, I still had some optimism that right might eventually be done.

A short walk took us to the main lobby where we were greeted by one of our hosts, Simon Rivers, who was the Roche UK Medical Leader for Lariam. Mr Rivers had been our main contact in setting up the meeting and after cordially shaking hands he arranged for our details to be recorded by a receptionist. I'm not sure what I had been expecting and perhaps I am a little old fashioned, but my first impressions were not enhanced by the absence of a jacket and a tieless white shirt with rather too many buttons undone, nor by the Laurel and Hardy cufflinks at his wrists. Dress code at the company appeared somewhat relaxed and I recalled that we had all been a little surprised by the outfit chosen by Dr Nichol when she had given her oral evidence to the Defence Committee.

While we were waiting to pass through the internal security barriers in this pharmaceutical world of polished reflective surfaces and glass partitions, I asked Simon Rivers to confirm who would be attending the meeting. He said, as Roche had already told us, that we would be joined by Sarah Buckley, and by Dr Rav Seeruthun, their UK Medical Director, and Sonja Rollenhagen, Franchise Leader. We were disappointed that Dr Nichol would not be present and when I pressed Mr Rivers, he stated that she had left the company "in order to spend more time with her family." It sounded like more euphemisms. I chose not to take it any further.

I didn't notice it at the time, but during the preliminaries and as the live connections to Australia and the US were being set up, Bea asked if she might visit their washroom. It was only a few yards away but she was escorted by Simon Rivers who waited outside and then accompanied her back into the meeting room. Quite why 'escorting', if deemed necessary, could not have been done by one of the females struck Bea as odd, and the incident, if unintended, felt rather creepy.

When the proceedings got underway, it was apparent that the Roche lead lay with Dr Seeruthun. After welcoming us, he requested that the proceedings should be held under Chatham House rules. Chatham House is the home of the Royal Institute of International Affairs, an independent and entirely non-aligned body whose purpose is to facilitate open debates and private discussions in the world of politics. There is actually only one 'Chatham House Rule' that I am aware of and it is often misunderstood as meaning that what is discussed is to remain in confidence; in other words, 'what's said here is to remain within these four walls'. The Chatham House website is quite clear, however, and explains that the rule:

*is now used throughout the world as an aid to free discussion of sensitive issues. It provides a way for speakers to openly discuss their views in private while allowing the topic and nature of the debate to be made public and contribute to a broader conversation.* [23]

From our point of view, we were interested in discussing matters that ought to be in the public domain. I don't think anything we discussed could have properly been characterised as 'sensitive', no matter how embarrassing or uncomfortable they might prove for Roche. While it would be impossible not to identify Roche as the host and participant in what was essentially a bilateral event, in the spirit of what Dr Seeruthun was asking, I was content to proceed on the understanding that some comments might only be attributed to Roche without identifying any specific individual.

It was, still, rather irritating and I felt we had been ambushed with these conditions (even if they were not properly understood by the other side) well past the eleventh hour. Did they think that after all the trouble we had gone to, we would simply walk away? Only while researching this book did I learn that Dr Seeruthun also had party political associations and had recently been a parliamentary candidate in a general election. Did this colour his approach? Either way, it would have been courteous if it had been declared. Respecting his request, however, I will only summarise the meeting without attributing Roche staff names to comments.

Jane and Remington Nevin took the lead for us on the medico/scientific picture. Roche should have been in little doubt that they were now on the losing side of the academic research argument. And, again, Remington Nevin stressed the prodromal nature of Lariam's side effects. Unfortunately, at this stage we were still completely unaware of the EMA report of 2014 and the confirmation that there was sufficient evidence to satisfy European regulators of a causal link between Lariam use and the onset of long-term or even permanent neuropsychiatric damage. Having withheld this key information from the Defence Committee, it will come as no surprise that Roche made no mention of it during our meeting. But there remained three other important areas I wanted to explore.

The first was the US Interagency Working Group and/or the Expert Meeting on Malaria Chemoprophylaxis hosted by the US CDC in January 2003. Roche claimed that they had no records of any such meetings. Experience has taught me that having no records of meetings does not mean that the organisation was unaware of them or that they did not have any representatives attending them. Perhaps Roche was entirely ignorant of the Interagency Working Group. We decided to leave it at that.

The next issue was the statement made by Roche in the United States about the central role played by Welwyn in collecting and disseminating the data about adverse events. I read out the quotes from Dr Huber as presented in the FDA report of 2003. Assuming that Dr Huber was being truthful in his testimony, why had it taken so long for Roche in the UK to recognise the dangers of prodromal side effects? How was it that the global hub for collating all adverse event data and for the updating of warnings, had failed to revise the warnings in its own host country. The response was complacent and utterly unconvincing. Roche said that the eleven year delay was caused by 'glass walls' between the respective offices on the Welwyn site responsible for the data management and those for updating the UK PILs and SPCs. There were certainly a lot of glass walls in their buildings. It was just a pity that no one seemed to be able to see through them!

My third point was to ask why Roche had failed in their promise to harmonise all package insert/data sheet statements world-wide. Our hosts seemed unsettled by this statement and I agreed that this was something they could take away and come back to us with a follow up answer. Two months later, Roche said in an email that they were unaware of any promise regarding harmonising information leaflets. As I had explained to them, the promise was made in their own application to varying their UK Lariam licence.[24]

Roche did, however, go to great lengths to explain the responsibilities that they shared with the UK regulator, the MHRA. This was an area that Dr Nichol had discussed in her evidence to the Defence Committee and tying down who was ultimately responsible for the PIL and SPC deficiencies was clearly not going to be resolved at our meeting. But Roche did make an interesting and important suggestion. It would be much more beneficial if we were to have a tripartite meeting between us, Roche and the MHRA, perhaps in the MHRA's offices in London. Would we like to set up the meeting? Roche would be happy to attend. We seemed to be making at least a little progress and we agreed to take this on.

Then, before the meeting closed, Bea looked at each of the Roche team in turn and asked "Would you take this drug? Is this something you would ask your families to take?" Apparently that was deemed an unfair question and they wouldn't answer. It struck me as the most important and appropriate question raised during the whole the session. The

Roche reply was political, evasive and represented to us an utter failure of confidence in their own product. But it was their livelihood. The meeting was closed as, I recall, Dr Seeruthun had a more pressing engagement. But we had probably got as far as we could.

I was also personally very keen to rise from the table. I had been sat opposite one of the Roche team who had, throughout, sat in a most inelegant manner. Perhaps these days it is my fault for noticing, but Roche could either improve their office etiquette or invest in some modesty screens for their tables. Another reason, I guess, for wanting Chatham House rules. I wasn't going to mention it, but as we went back to the car Bea told us of her escort to the washroom before the meeting had convened. I then felt somewhat liberated as both Trixie and Bea laughed at my own discomfiture. They had indeed been aware of it and complimented me on my attempts not to notice. "It was certainly not very Lucie Clayton," smiled Trixie, revealing her rather traditionalist approach. Not to be outdone, Bea guffawed something about *Basic Instinct*!

I did actually check the car after we dropped Trixie off at Welwyn station. I didn't expect to find anything but I had learned not to trust Roche. And some old habits are hard to kick.

———

In July the three of us met once more, this time in London. Largely through Trixie's efforts, we had managed to get a meeting with the MHRA at their offices in Buckingham Palace Road, again with live connections to Jane and

Remington Nevin. The MHRA was represented by Dr June Raine, the Director of Vigilance and Risk Management of Medicines, supported by members of the Benefit/Risk Management Group, Dr Phil Bryan and Mrs Sarah Morgan. This time there was no suggestion of any Chatham House Rule. But in the meantime, apparently advised by their legal branch, Roche had withdrawn from the meeting. I thought that was, at best, shabby, and represented another outfit that was not prepared to argue their case in public. Something was definitely making Roche feel uncomfortable.

We did make some progress and, following the meeting, the SPCs and PILs were probably going to be about as good as they could be. A further matter that was explored was whether firearms were considered as complex or dangerous machinery and, therefore, deserving of a higher profile in the drug literature. That subject has still to be resolved but I suspect that the MHRA now have it noted. There will certainly be no excuse if future quinoline drugs are marketed without fully informed, comprehensive and appropriate warnings.

But once again, there was no mention of the 2014 EMA Report. With hindsight this looks distinctly odd. Before taking up her appointment with the MHRA, Dr Raine had worked for the EMA. In fact she had been the head of the EMA Pharmacovigilance Risk Assessment Committee and she had chaired the very committee meeting in October 2013 that had called for the investigation resulting in the subsequent report. Perhaps she thought we knew about it but it remained largely out of the public gaze and, as late as 2019, apparently unknown to defence ministers.

I did press Dr Raine about the failure by Roche, and by implication the MHRA, to have the prodromal warning inserted in the Lariam SPC. Here, the MHRA were rather defensive and we left without a clear explanation. However, I persisted and continued to write to Dr Raine in pursuit of an answer. Eventually, in February 2018 I received a letter with an astonishing admission.[25] Dr Raine advised me that the historical SPCs could be viewed in something called the ABPI Data Sheet Compendium. She pointed out, as we already knew, that the prodromal warning was inserted into the UK SPC in 2013. But she also revealed that Roche had been aware of the prodromal nature of Lariam side effects as early as the initial UK SPC from 1990. But the prodromal warning had been removed in 1996, which would have been the time that the drug was becoming the preferred antimalarial within the MoD.

Little wonder that Roche UK didn't want us to see the historic copies of the SPC. They had known all along about the prodromal side effects but had decided to withdraw that essential safety net in 1996. Many would have to pay for that decision, including Cameron Quinn and Alastair Duncan. And little wonder that over the coming couple of years Roche would abandon their interest in the drug.

———

There was one other interesting matter that we were also able to partially resolve in 2017. Just who was attending those Interagency Working Group meetings in the USA back in the 2000s? After our meeting with Roche, I asked Public Health England if they could let me know how the UK was represented and how the information from those meetings was then shared with interested parties in this country. I also asked if I might be provided with minutes from the Working Group meeting known to have been held on 16 April 2002. They confirmed that the meeting was attended by a member of PHE's ACMP, but declined to say exactly who that individual was. It also appeared that Public Health England did not retain any minutes of the meeting, which struck me as rather poor practice.[26] But they did provide an excerpt of a few notes relating to mefloquine taken by the UK representative, and they included these observations from the United States CDC and FDA:

*CDC reviewed efficacy and AE.*

*FDA MEDIWATCH REPORT*
*Global surveillance system for AE (all drugs). Includes reports in literature, from Medical and Nursing personnel, self-reporting, and drug companies.*
*Mefloquine use steadily increased until 2000 when Malarone introduced. Cumulative reports of CNS AE are:*

*1996 882 52% neuropsychiatric*
*2002 2463 64% neuropsychiatric*
*Major symptoms (in order): dizzy, anxiety, depression, insomnia, headache, hallucination. Few reports of suicide with confirmed association.*

*Presentation discussing impact on compliance of adverse publicity [sic], and strategies to deal with negative impacts.*

*NB: USA seems to be currently facing "mefloquine AE" problems similar to those seen in UK 5 years ago. UK position defended including rationale for apparent movement away from mefloquine recommendation in 1997 UK guidelines.*

Public Health England declined to explain how these observations were addressed or shared within the British medical community.

In our own way we had achieved something. But why did we have to bark when the professional watchdogs continued to sleep?

# Chapter 9
## Anatomy of Suicide

*Suicide is Painless.*

*-Johnny Mandel and Mike Altman*

Unless you can afford the services of a very expensive end-of-life clinic in Switzerland, and especially with the development of cleaner auto-engines, suicide is rarely painless. The haunting verses from *Suicide is Painless,* the theme song of the 1970 film *MASH,* are very seductive but they were produced essentially for the cinema and perhaps an audience that, in general, did not need to ponder too closely the real impacts of suicide. Lariam probably deserves its own poetry to add to the canon of death and remembrance of war, but that would be far beyond my meagre literary talents.

I wonder how Wilfred Owen or Robert Graves might have portrayed Lariam, with its invisible sirens luring the unsuspecting to their deaths. I'm not sure that even in the world of commercial art and entertainment something like suicide should be reduced to the 'take it or leave it' option of Mandel and Altman. And Lariam certainly wasn't offered under those terms by the MoD. Those serving their country just didn't have that choice.

Sadly, since 1996, when Roche UK decided that the prodromal warning could be withdrawn, countless numbers of service personnel were put at a huge additional risk. The restlessness, confusion and anxiety that should have alerted doctors to the hazards of the drug were just considered to be part of the background battle noise: just like Captain Sharpley had explained, erroneously, to the Defence Committee in 2016. Decisions have consequences, and the consequences of the actions of drug companies like Roche, and those of our drug regulators, must be faced. And, of course, they should have been anticipated. Multiple attempted and completed suicides were but one consequence of those bad decisions. It's time to take a closer look at what drives someone to try to kill him or herself when they do succumb to the siren songs of Lariam toxicity.

I first met Dave Rimmington in May 2018. We arranged to meet for a coffee at Durham railway station. I was coming home from Newcastle University and Dave had been doing some consultancy work for Durham. Dave is a former sergeant major with a full military career behind him and he is one of those veterans who represents the very best of the Army. As we often say in the infantry, I would gladly have shared a trench with him. He was clearly the sort who would have been prepared to fix bayonets, set his helmet at a jaunty angle and do Her Majesty's bidding.

Over the past couple of years, I have got to know him well. I watch with admiration his work at the coalface trying to get the National Health Service to recognise what it is that has damaged so many of our former colleagues. He gets things done. Most critically, he has pulled many veterans back from the brink. Unlike ministers and officers who lacked the moral courage to get their hands dirty, he has put his hands out and saved others from the noose, the overdose or the high-speed train. But Dave has also been there himself and I asked if he would be prepared to share his story. Like Jane's, it deserves to be told in his own words. It's raw, it's a soldier's story, and this is what he says.

———

Intro:

"24888514!" That's not the number of soldiers who've taken mefloquine and suffered its adverse effects. No! This was my Regimental Number. Like Lariam, you'll never erase it from your head. It comes imprinted in your brain from early conditioning in basic training. For me, that was 1990, and twenty four long and difficult years later, I reached for an early window of opportunity in desperation and somehow threw myself over the finishing line and into civvy street. This was even after selection to Warrant Officer Class One and potential commissioning to the dark side and life in the Officers' Mess.

My first and 'lasting' experience with Lariam occurred in Sierra Leone, with 1 PARA Battle Group, in May 2000. An African rebel Army, known as the *Revolutionary United Front (*RUF)' took control of Kambia, Sierra Leone, and blocked access from the capital city of Freetown, and all routes to Lungi International Airport, following brutal escalations in the country's civil war.

The diamond funded RUF had already claimed some 50,000 lives and displaced approximately two million people during their eleven-year reign of terror. A RUF militia group, known as the 'Westside Boys', were notorious for recruiting children into its ranks and routinely carried out drug-crazed rituals, rapes and beatings. The 'Westside Boys' were well known for their brutality and leaving their calling card by amputating the hands of their victims with machetes.

With the RUF's continued advance on the capital city, the United Nations Mission in Sierra Leone (UNAMSIL) had to evacuate and prepare for a total withdrawal of personnel. In response to the deterioration in West Africa, the British government's emergency cabinet committee, COBRA, concluded that rapid military intervention was needed and ordered the UK spearhead stand-by formation to deploy immediately. 1 PARA Battle Group (BG), reinforced by D Company 2 PARA, the specialist Pathfinder Platoon and ten members of 13 Air Assault Support Regiment, instantly departed the UK Air Movements Centre at South Cerney, in Gloucestershire, before arriving in Dakar, Senegal. There, the soldiers made their final preparations on Dakar runway and transferred into RAF Hercules C-130s to fly the final tactical bound into Sierra Leone and quickly secure Lungi Airport.

This was the first operational deployment conducted by the newly formed 16 Air Assault Brigade, that had only formed over one month ago. 1 PARA BG had been given the mission to conduct a Non-Combatant Evacuation Operation (NEO) in support of the UNAMSIL mission and to protect civilians caught up in the country's civil war. The operation was known as OP PALLISER.

Within a week, British forces evacuated approximately 500 entitled persons from Sierra Leone, with almost 300 leaving in the first two days of the Operation. Since the evacuation was largely complete, the British government turned its attention to four British United Nations Military

Observers (UNMOs) being held as hostages by the RUF, as the British mission expanded and facilitated their escape.

In theatre:

About a week into the deployment, I finally received anti-malarial drugs to protect me from this deadly tropical disease. Back in South Cerney, rumour had it that soldiers were picking up their anti-malaria medication, Lariam, from a light plywood storage box as they were processed before deployment. Unfortunately, we were the last members to arrive that day and they had run out of the drug. We ambled over to the tables and joined the short queue to be processed. "Here you go"; as a Para Sergeant dropped a jungle hat on the table. "What size?" he said. Eh? I thought. What size of what? "Oi, What size jungle boots?" he elaborated. "Err, size 10 medium Sarn't."

This Sergeant just growled, "Grab some stuff from the boxes and move down" as he pointed to a box of sweat rags and sun cream. We moved down the table, gave our Regimental details, and then went to the guys breaking out ammo boxes. "Here you go," one of them said as he slid several bandoliers of 5.56 ammo at me. "Grab that and head over there for an 'Int' (Intelligence) brief!" as he pointed towards the side of the hangar, with the usual openhanded 'Brecon point'. [s]

So, eight days into the Sierra Leone deployment, I had just finished sentry duty and was walking back across our compound to the area where we were sleeping. Just as I got

---

[s] A bit of military slang, the Brecon point is a field signal taught at the British Army's battle school in the Brecon Beacons in Wales.

there, I was tossed a couple of packets of Lariam by a lad from 1 PARA who was passing by. He'd just dished them out to the rest of the blokes that never got any in South Cerney, and I saw packets had been placed on the top of ponchos,[t] where people were sleeping or absent on other duties.

While others stood about, opening their packets of Lariam, I sussed out, purely by asking around, that it was only one tablet a week. I'd never heard of a weekly tablet before but trusted my mates knew what they were doing, and, let's face it, you wouldn't expect your own Army to prescribe any harm. By this stage, I'd have done anything to stop being eaten by insects and mosquitos anyway, so I palmed the first tablet that afternoon, which later became known as Lariam night.

Within hours of taking the first 250mg Lariam tablet, I wasn't feeling right. I was feeling dizzy and nauseous. When I got up or looked at the floor, I had a sense of spinning. A kind of ground rush feeling and intermittent mild headaches. Unsuspectingly I thought I'd picked up a tropical virus or bacteria from the rough living conditions or maybe I was just dehydrated with constant heat and humidity.

That evening I didn't sleep and was restless throughout. In the morning I felt even worse! I remember the bouts of 'ground rush and vertigo' getting worse and struggling to stay on my feet. I couldn't eat in fear of vomiting and becoming even more dehydrated. During the course of the deployment, not eating wasn't a bad thing. I'd somehow dipped out with the same ration pack menu, and I was getting pretty tired of eating corned beef hash every day. Eating this and smoking a

---

[t] Waterproofs used to make one-man bivouacs.

dodgy local brand of 555 cigarettes, I was starting to get acid reflux and was choking on my stomach acid at night.

During the day, I was struggling to concentrate on tasks, listen to conversations, or take instructions. When I was writing notes from our daily briefings, I'd lose my focus on what I was writing and had occasional blurring. I'd also developed a constant jaw cracking like a temporomandibular joint (TMJ) disorder? Maybe, I was just feeling tired? "Oh well, just 'crack on', you'll be alright," I thought to myself. How wrong I was!

I'd never experienced anxiety or any kind of mental health problems before. These symptoms were only for the weak but, honestly, I had never even heard of anxiety before! But here I was on Ops, having growing attacks of hypervigilance and strange thoughts; panicking that I was never going to get home from Sierra Leone alive.

It never crossed my mind that I might be experiencing adverse symptoms from Lariam. We certainly weren't informed of any bad side effects and I can't recall seeing any drug instructions inside the packets. Who even reads those anyway? I don't suffer from these kinds of things!

Knowing I had been exposed for eight days without any malaria prevention, I took another 250mg tablet three days later, believing this would boost my immunity or get rid of how I was feeling. I used to take loaded doses of Lemsip when I had the flu and thought this would have the same principle of making me better. Big mistake!

Whilst on guard duty outside our location, I remember seeing several partially clothed, hungry Sierra Leonean children, raiding the rubbish from the burn pit approximately twenty five metres away. These kids appeared desperately hungry and as I watched on, they were dabbing their tiny fingers into disused tea whitener from our ration packs to get out every edible morsel. Whilst guarding my post, a 'fighting-age' Sierra Leonean youth came from behind an adjacent hut, with a two-metre long wooden stick and proceeded to 'beat the shit' out of these kids who were only after a bit of food.

I could hear bones cracking and their screams of pain, as these poor kids were being attacked right before my eyes. Blood was oozing from their arms and I could hear their sobs, as they fled in pain. I desperately wanted to intervene; I was raging! But I couldn't bring myself to get involved. My task was to protect our location, not get involved in some local domestic punishment. After the children had fled, the Sierra Leonean youth turned to me with a big smile, laughing, knowing full well I couldn't do anything about it. He then reached down and picked up the half-empty packets of tea whitener the children were feeding on and began dabbing his fingers in before walking away, smiling to himself.

I was so enraged like never before, I wanted to drop a magazine of rounds into this evil youth, and visualised bayonetting him to death. This just wasn't like me. I had such an unusual feeling of mixed guilt, fear and aggression. I kept running the scenario over in my head, over and over again, as if it wasn't real, and I couldn't make any sense of it...the situation became a bit of a blur in my mind. Was I going to kill this youth? Little did I know that these unusual aggressive and intrusive thoughts of bayonetting and killing this evil youth were the prodromal paranoia, anxiety, and hypervigilance of Lariam.

On many occasions, it felt like this deployment wasn't real and that I'd wake up at home, but the cycle of thinking "I shouldn't be here, I shouldn't be here" just wouldn't leave me. Every guard duty felt like forever and every passing local looked out of place as if they were observing our position to attack (*'being dicked'*)[u] which just elevated my anxiety and fear in 'standby mode'.

Each dawn and dusk, we continued to 'Stand to' [v] and I remember the feeling of helplessness and feelings of lost reality as we patrolled down the drainage ditch and peeled off into our firing positions. My fire position had been disturbed by red ants, from where I'd been 'digging in' previously, and I remember lying in this swarm of red ants, struggling to maintain composure while being bitten to death. On another occasion, during last light, a dark topped snake with silver-ish underbelly (*black mamba*) passed over the top of my rifle barrel. A small head popped from the side of the concrete protection on my left of arc and initially I thought it was just another lizard. As it flicked its tongue out, it was mildly entertaining. Certainly more interesting than observing the ground to my front, over the top of my weapon sights. But then its head became longer and longer. It lifted its neck slightly to slither over the rifle's muzzle and continued on its way. Must have been a good 'six-footer' and I couldn't help keep thinking how lucky I'd been that this deadly snake didn't put me on the menu.

On 17 May 2000, we received a set of orders telling us that tonight would be the most dangerous night of our lives. We were advised to write our 'goodbye letters' as an

---

[u] Another bit of slang, commonly used in Northern Ireland, to describe low-level enemy intelligence gathering.

[v] At 'stand to' everyone is deployed ready for any enemy attack.

impending attack of a thousand *plus* RUF fighters were closing in on our position and intended to use the internal rivers and streams to get up close to our location. I was issued a stretcher in anticipation of recovering our injured forces. On this night, just a few miles away, the RUF, dressed in UN Uniforms, engaged the Pathfinder Platoon in what was later known as the 'Battle of Lungi Loi'. That night was so long…and tiring, my thoughts were racing constantly and I was twitchy with panic.

By the morning, we were finally stood down. Drained, tired and feeling low, the content of my Bergen backpack was later emptied into a black bin liner and filled to the brim with hand grenades, three and five-second grenade fuses, 7.62 belted machine gun ammunition and 5.56 rifle rounds to provide the Pathfinders with a much-needed ammo resupply. The Bergen was a solid metal weight and could hardly be dragged, let alone lifted.

Shattered from the long night of adrenalin and fear, I recall seeing an injured enemy rebel later that day. It looked like he'd been shot in the leg, and he had both his feet and wrists tied together. He was on the floor being kicked and beaten by some UN Nigerian soldiers (UNAMSIL) in front of our location and was deliberately being paraded in front of us, like some kind of trophy prize, as they made him crab walk down the track. After gaining our attention, a soft-top British Land Rover whizzed by and bundled the rebel prisoner into the back of the vehicle and rapidly took him away.

I remember patrolling over to the foreign United Nations locations close to Lungi Airport, to see if we could trade some rations with the local Jordanian or Nigerian soldiers, just to help break up the uncomfortable routine. As I moved through the close palm trees on the outer rim of the Airport, I caught a glance of two young boys (looked about 8 years old) in the far distance observing us. Once they'd noticed I'd seen them they disappeared into the trees; clumsily carrying what looked to be an oversize AK 47 assault rifle on such a small body. I kept thinking, I'd unnecessarily put myself in danger, and kept replaying the consequences of shooting and killing these children that were a similar age to my children at home. I then began doubting that I'd seen them, convincing myself that I'd been dreaming or hallucinating.

One evening I finally got to sleep and remember an extremely vivid dream; that my deceased Grandad had come to visit me and had woken me up for a chat. It was so 'life-like' and real. He was sat at the end of my makeshift bed/shelter I'd built from a metal pallet crate used for water. He was alive at the foot of where I was lying. He was just having a casual chat and I recall him telling me about his dogs, Piddles and Squibs. This dream felt so real, I expected to see him again the following morning whilst awake! I physically checked around our compound in the morning to see if there were any signs my Grandad had been here.

Another night, my mate, Phil, was sleeping in the area next to me and woke up screaming, shouting "get it off me!" I was lying restlessly awake and went to see if he was ok. He was flapping and told me he'd been pinned down by a massive spider on his chest (*Had to laugh*). We searched the area for the 'real' spider, before shaking our kit out and packing everything away. We both sat on our Bergens all night in disbelief at what had happened.

Tired and depressed for the remainder of the night, I recall chatting with Phil about the circulating stories that Lariam gave you funky dreams. Several of the Para lads had remarked about how late we'd got our anti-malaria tablets and I remember some of them saying "there's probably going to be trouble over this." I remember another lad from 1 PARA, saying "fuck that (*Lariam*), I've got the French stuff, I wouldn't touch Lariam." He went on to tell us that they normally took antimalarials three weeks before deploying, so we were probably too late for it to be effective anyway.

Later in the deployment, there was talk of a soldier with us who had woken in the night, took his rifle and shot himself in the forearm. The Unit treated this as a negligent discharge but I later understood from his disciplinary hearing he was having Lariam dreams.

Despite the continued feeling of nausea, unexplained bouts of dizziness, insomnia, night sweats, vivid dreams and mental symptoms, there was no way I would report sick whilst in theatre. I wasn't going to let my teammates down or get labelled as being 'weak', 'a biff' or 'malingerer'. So I just 'cracked on'.

With the dominance of 1 PARA BG in Sierra Leone, many foreign citizens saw the British Army as their saviours and opted to stay in Sierra Leone. 1 PARA BG was ordered back to the United Kingdom at the end of May to resume its UK spearhead role, while HMS Ocean, the amphibious assault ship, had arrived off the coast. We'd operated with minimal support, equipment and preparedness and were finally relieved by 42 Commando, Royal Marines.

On return:

Despite feeling so relieved I'd made it home from Africa alive, things still weren't right. I had fever-like sweats the whole time. I was constantly soaking wet, especially at night and couldn't stop thinking about the deployment. I was stuck in 'Standby Mode' and feared that any confrontation would spark a split second 'zero to kill' escalation. I'd lost a grip on reality and felt invincible.

The first days at home, I went into the town of Colchester but remained on edge throughout. I was hypervigilant and paranoid about being attacked or watched. Black people stood out everywhere I went, I could feel my stomach sink and heart pound. It was as if I was seeing everything in slow-motion as I focused on the target and everything else became blurred. I'd felt sick to my stomach; my fists would clench, and I would instantly play out in my mind how I would kill him when he attacked while looking for routes of escape and cover. The night sweats and strange moods continued, and my girlfriend became increasingly concerned that something wasn't right. She can recall me telling her about my 'trip-like' dreams and remembers me explaining a realistic snake dream I had.

I was also starting to think I may have contracted malaria or another tropical disease and reported to the Medical Centre to have a blood test for malaria after about two days being back. Despite explaining my physical symptoms of sweating profusely, pinpointed foot/leg rash and just not feeling right, the medic paid no attention. The malaria blood test came back negative, so what was the reason for me feeling like this? Surely some 'alarm bells' should be ringing? I'd half-expected some form of medical screening for those that had returned from Op PALLISER, but we received nothing.

I completed the course of Lariam for the next 4-5 weeks after returning home, and continued to experience all the bad effects of the drug. My mood would change in a split second and I became increasingly enraged, frustrated and violent at home. I had continual thoughts of a frenzied killing and naturally became more aggressive, exploding over the smallest of things. It was like a switch was being flicked that allowed me to explode over nothing. I struggled to think rationally, and processing information became slow, with frequent brain zaps, forgetting what I was talking about or the word to say.

These outward-facing feelings of aggression soon reverted inwards towards me, as I noticed self-destructive tendencies and then had unwanted thoughts of taking my own life. As my mental state deteriorated, it took a massive effort to report my symptoms to a doctor at Colchester Garrison Medical Reception Centre knowing this could potentially end my career, my reputation and brand me as a mental case.

With what I saw as great courage and feeling really embarrassed, I struggled to describe and verbalise the difficult and intrusive symptoms to the doctor stemming from my time in Sierra Leone. I just didn't know what words to use to describe what I was feeling, but as I tripped over my words the doctor abruptly stopped me and dismissed my concerns:

*Look! You haven't got malaria and you don't have PTSD; you didn't see any action! There's nothing wrong with you, stop wasting my time!*

The doctor left me feeling extremely stupid, embarrassed and rejected. The medical consultation was concluded in less than five minutes and his unprofessional remarks had left me doubting myself. He was right, I hadn't seen any 'contacts' or "action" as he put it, but why do I have these unwanted symptoms? Was I just being weak or over-sensitive? "Nothing was wrong with me" and I "don't have PTSD"? I was starting to think I had a lucky escape that the doctor hadn't acknowledged my mental health symptoms which could have cost me my career. That was the last time I visited the Medical Centre in Colchester, and the last time I raised these issues with anyone! I'd just crack on, keep silent and mask my symptoms somehow.

Suicide:

Months after my return from Ops, I was posted to an All Arms Training role and quickly learned to suppress my symptoms by becoming a workaholic. I had become a completely different monster at home. The strategy of working every hour I could, kept me away from my family, but it kept them, and others, safe. I desperately needed to rebuild my damaged self-esteem and prove to myself that I wasn't just being weak or some sort of mental case. Working as a Section Commander, and acting Platoon Sergeant was extremely rewarding, requiring controlled aggression and gusto.

The pace distracted me from unwanted thoughts, even though I was dying inside. It was easy to disguise and I portrayed myself as a robust, alert and switched on soldier. I'd always go that extra mile for my peers and would get the very best from my soldiers. So much so, that it was recognised with winning the Commanding Officer's Section Commander's trophy a couple of times during my appointment and later promotion to Sergeant, which would result in returning me to the same Field Force Unit I had served with in Sierra Leone.

I often thought I'd have made a great actor by the way I was able to mask my persona. I demonstrated bags of confidence, portraying the perception I was strong in my skills with an abundance of potential, and everyone bought it. The last few years had changed me from a smiley, fun and 'top-bloke' on the outside, to a seriously fake, dark, deceptive, and dangerous monster. I was petrified of what I might do if my trigger was flicked.

The change of employment, from a high tempo Training Regiment to a more relaxed Field Force Unit was no longer sufficient to release aggression or manage my unwanted thoughts of suicide ideation. I desperately needed the same fix to continue suppressing my symptoms and tried even harder to self-medicate. Throwing myself deeper and deeper into being a workaholic was a proven technique and had kept me alive and others safe, since Sierra Leone. But in reality, burying my symptoms away was finally starting to show. It was like this huge Bergen on my back was so full; it was bursting at the seams.

Adding to the struggle of keeping a lid on my symptoms was a new obstructive and vindictive Sergeant Major. In such a short time in the Unit, I was 'delivering the goods', and more! My workhorse ethos and military profile hadn't gone unnoticed and had already received the kudos from Regimental Headquarters and the remaining Chain of Command. However, this 'absolute throbber' went out of his way to devalue his Troop's work, belittle people in front of others and showed very little empathy or leadership to his troops.

The old me would have taken his unhelpful rebukes with a pinch of salt. He was the Sergeant Major, after all; he can do what he wants. I'd have just 'sucked it up', 'cracked on' and taken his abuse on the chin. But the changed 'Lariam me' perceived his behaviour as an added stressor that would tilt my anxiety and mood to its limit. My stress cups were already overflowing with good stressors and Lariam symptoms, so the slightest addition to the cup would inevitably cause it to overspill the edges and flick that trigger *(apparently, there is a PTSD Stress Cup Theory)*. In time, even my subordinates started seeing through the cracks and my immediate boss became concerned with my change in mood and unusual output.

It was March 2004 and this weekend was the same as any other. I'd avoid my family, and as usual, distracted myself with doing additional military work from home. An old mate, Edd, had come back up to Colchester from his Commando Unit, in Plymouth, to visit me and have a few beers just like old times (before Lariam). I was so chuffed to get out of the house, let off some steam, and have a good catch up with my best mate. He was a 'top bloke' to be around. He had the infectious personality that inspired you to compete and do even better in your career. We'd had several beers and had a great laugh, talking about the things we used to do when we both served together in Colchester previously. I finished the evening with a kebab to eat on my way home, but Edd had a better offer of a young lady he'd got speaking to at the end of the night, so we parted ways.

The next morning there was no real hangover, but my wife, Louise, was infuriated with me for getting back home past 02:00 am. She wasn't speaking to me and it was easy to see that my children sensed there was an atmosphere again. The kids had become used to 'stepping on eggshells' around me, just in case I exploded out of nowhere. My stressor cup was already overflowing, and I was exhausted hanging on to my symptoms for so long. I'd fought so hard covering this up, but I was at absolute breaking point. I couldn't talk to anyone about it, not my wife, my mates or my family—they wouldn't understand. I'd undoubtedly never ask for medical help again!

I was completely numb and the thoughts of ending my life were strong. I cooked a Sunday dinner as a peace offering to my wife and family but ate my dinner alone. My oldest son was out at the local skate park with his friends, and my other 8-year-old son, Shane, was playing a game, with my 3-year-old daughter in her bedroom. I took a glance at my kids, as I walked slowly up the stairs. The unwanted suicide ideation came back again tenfold, repeatedly telling me to "Do it! Do it! Kill yourself!"

Within a split second, as I walked into my bedroom and closed the door, my thoughts became actions. Without thinking, and in moments, I had grabbed a coax cable to make a noose, secured it inside the cupboard, passed it over the top of the door and hanged myself. The last thing I can remember was sliding down the door, with the noose tightening around my neck. My vision dimmed with patches and dots flashing in my eyes as the pressure in my head grew. I could feel a warm pulsating buzzing in my ears getting louder and louder and louder, and then…nothing!

At some stage later, Shane and Ella had finished playing together, came out of their bedroom and walked into where I was hanging. There was an almighty cry, as Shane sprinted down the stairs in a panic, crying "Dad's turned blue! Dad's turned blue!" Ella was only 3 at the time, so she just followed Shane around, but he was distraught in what he had just found.

My wife knew something wasn't right by the sheer panic in Shane's voice. She ran up the stairs, pushing Ella out of the way to get to me quickly. When she found me, I was deep blue and purple. A large wound was developing on the back of my head and there was blood all over the carpet. She tried to release the cable from around my neck, but it had tightened too much and had become pinned in the cupboard by my body weight.

In her frantic panic, she told Shane to go next door to get help while she called for an ambulance. The neighbour came quickly and saw the terror that was unfolding. Louise was taking instructions from the 999 despatchers while the neighbour looked for a knife to cut me down. I dropped to the ground and the cable was removed from around my neck.

In tears, Louise sent Shane and Ella into the bedroom to stay out of the way. The neighbour tried to revive me when I finally responded with faint grunting sounds. She asked Shane what had happened, and he said, "Dad was walking up and down the landing talking to himself, then he went into his bedroom."

Louise was overcome with despair. She never expected to find herself in this position, especially with someone so close to her. She was desperately upset, scared and angry. How could I ever do this to her? And what about the kids? They'd be left without a dad! What image of this terror would be left in their minds?

The paramedics finally came to takeover and carried me to the ambulance. As they did, a small crowd had gathered outside our army married quarter and people were talking about what they thought had gone on. I was then rushed to A&E as quick as they could.

My wife telephoned my mum, who obviously thought it was a prank call. As soon as they learned it was life-threatening, they jumped in the car from Lincolnshire and set off to Colchester hospital. My parents didn't say a lot; I don't think they wanted to make the situation worse, or probably didn't know what to say. She also called my mate Edd. She wasn't sure why, but he was the last person, other than my family, that I had been in contact with. Edd was massively shocked by the news, it was completely out of character and didn't know what to say.

The welfare team and my immediate boss were called in to look after my children while my wife went to the hospital waiting to hear if I'd survived. In typical military fashion, they were confused as to why I'd attempted suicide but were already talking about posting me away, as I probably wouldn't want to be reminded of what happened.

Louise was met at the hospital by the police and made a statement of what happened. They retained the cable as evidence in case it later became a crime scene. After her statement, she called her father. He was strong and gave her the reassurance she needed, while her mother and sister were both crying in the background. They were all understandably upset. They never thought I could do something like this. There were certainly no signs, no inclination of mental illness either; I appeared so strong.

The doctors tried to sedate and ventilated me, and my wife could hear me from the corridor as I struggled. I'd become so combative in intensive care that they had to administer even more medication to try and sedate me quickly.

Both my parents and my wife's sister, Kerry, had arrived at the hospital by now. Kerry was too afraid to see me and had to be encouraged to go in by my mum. Louise and Kerry were still crying while I lay motionless on the bed. They tried asking me stupid questions to see if my brain could respond but there was nothing.

After three days sedation in Colchester General Hospital's Intensive Care Unit, I recall the utter panic and confusion I experienced as I flitted in and out of unconsciousness. My first thoughts were 'Shit, where am I? I'm late for work!', but I quickly realised I couldn't move. I recalled a period of violent vomiting whilst I was helplessly sedated, as doctors forced pipes down my throat. I seem to remember hearing my Mum's voice close to me saying "you silly, silly boy!"

My neck and head were screaming in pain with the most horrendous headache I'd ever experienced. I was so weak and couldn't comprehend what I had done. Where did that come from? Did I actually just 'snap' and act on these suicidal thoughts? It was surreal. I was petrified I would do it again. I didn't want to die; I just wanted the pain to stop and someone to believe how I had been feeling. But this realisation very quickly reverted to deep feelings of guilt, shame and embarrassment. Now everyone would know I'd attempted to kill myself. My soldiers, the Sergeants' Mess and all the military families that lived in my area. I'd be the laughingstock of the Unit, and my reputation was in tatters.

The hanging resulted in a soft tissue neck injury, a pressure wound on the back of my head and further brain damage by asphyxia. I severely struggled to hold a conversation and would completely forget what I was saying or the words to use. I'd forget where I was and couldn't look anyone in the eye, not even my family, with the shame, guilt and embarrassment I was experiencing. I'd lost three days of my life and had been bedridden to the extent my strength, coordination and general function was significantly impaired. I'd been fitted with a catheter and had wires and oxygen tubes fitted everywhere. I felt that my life really was over and that just made matters ten times worse. Yet, I was extremely lucky to still be alive.

At home, my family were visited daily as a 'welfare case' and they took Louise to and from the hospital. They tried to keep everything as normal as possible, school, nursery etc., but there were lots of tears, concerns, what-ifs and what will happen now? My oldest brother was rapidly flown back from Kenya where he was serving and assisted my Unit with the welfare arrangements.

Days later, my wife was informed they would be taking the tube out and that I was finally awake. They talked about my readiness to come home in a few days, but my family felt this was too soon. As expected, there was no intervention, no recovery time, no follow-up, nothing! My wife was informed that I'd told the doctors this was something I wouldn't try again, and they deemed me as low risk. If only I'd been better managed from the very start of reporting my symptoms. Things wouldn't have been left to fester and Louise, Shane and Ella would have been spared all of these horrors.


Life with:

I'd quickly assumed the default mode of covering everything up again to protect myself from the added pain and embarrassment I'd now inflicted on myself. I told the military psychiatrists or doctors exactly what I thought they wanted to hear to make out my suicide attempt was completely out of character and that I was no longer at risk. Despite the concealment, I had to adopt several coping and management strategies to disguise my disabilities and retain some form of mental/physical function. After all, I had quickly gone from being a capable contender for an RSM and having a fully mapped out military career, to becoming an absolute Unit welfare case, with a destroyed career and a shattered family.

As time went on, it was clear that my cognitive and physical issues from neurotoxicity continued. My working memory was slow to process information and I found communicating challenging. I'd struggle to take instructions, lose words or sentences when talking. I couldn't recall more than 4 or 5 digits or retain key information, as my working memory went blank with panic. Even now, sometimes when I read, or am concentrating on a task, it feels like it's happening in slow motion and my vision blurs in and out. I've lost my sense of taste and smell, and massively struggle to hear in social situations, especially with ambient noises or as a result of tinnitus screaming in my left ear. I've got a sizable head scar that serves as a constant reminder to me and my family that I tried to take my life. It becomes a talking point with unknowing work associates, and I've noticed strangers pointing or staring.

Emotionless, sad and empty, I still push my family away. I struggle to show any love or affection and avoid social situations where possible in case I become dangerously aggressive. I'm still petrified what I might do.

Hypervigilance springs into action every time I'm on my own in a public place or shopping. It makes me feel sick, even though I know I'm safe. My chest aches, my heart pounds and

I feel my arms and shoulders tense ready to fight. Occasional bouts of dizziness remain when looking directly up, and the suppressed acid reflux from Sierra Leone resulted in grade 2 *oesophagitis* and continued medication.

The continued bouts of severe depression, shame and guilt have not gone away, and it frequently spirals me back into that 'dark place' and life on anti-depressants. I rarely have an unbroken night's sleep and dreams can feel extremely real. Worst of all, the intrusive thoughts and suicide ideation have not gone away. They are with me every day, poking and prodding me to attempt suicide again. Whilst working, I once stayed at a hotel in Manchester. The suicide ideation started, and I physically sized up the bed drape material against the back of the bathroom door in a surreal attempt to hang myself again. As I came close to putting the ligature around my neck, the painful memories, and suffering I had put myself, and family through, came flooding back.

I still find it a struggle to communicate these intrusive thoughts and seriously fear the risk of losing my wife, family and home as a result. I can't imagine how they would react if I told them about these awful thoughts I get. In January 2018, I left my job to help my mental state which was getting too much to bear. Later that evening, I went to the woods with my dog with the sole intent of not returning home and hanging myself. However, after an emotional breakdown close to the selected tree, I was unable to leave my dog running lost in the countryside, whilst hanging from the tree.

Further attempts to take my life have been planned, but these have been met with police intervention, as my wife has spotted the signs in time or I've managed to use my protective factors.

Treatments:

I've had to tell the same story over, and over again and have been seen by Combat Stress, psychiatrists, therapists, tropical medicine experts, brain trauma professionals, disbelieving GPs and nosey doctor receptionists. I've been subjected to immense delays, ineffective treatment and denial by those that are designed to help you with your medical care. Each time, as I had to dig up the past, it would destroy another piece of me, so I resorted to writing it all down to prevent or avoid the pain. This is a recommended 'top tip' and it's a really useful strategy.

Veterans UK / Tribunal:

There was no doubt both my body and mind had taken a kicking from 24 years of military service. The physical damage to my limbs and joints, while chronic, were much easier to accept. If I thought I wouldn't get a few knocks and bruises on the way, it would've been extremely naïve. However, I couldn't accept the acquired brain damage sustained from Lariam, and this uncomfortable truth continued to be brushed under the carpet by the Ministry of Defence department called Veterans UK. But the adverse and permanent symptoms of this neurotoxic anti-malaria drug were well known and were the root cause for my injuries. I decided to approach Veterans UK to see if I could make a war pension claim.

The long drawn out War Pension process was never driven by financial gain, nor apportioning blame. That boat had long sailed, and I knew it was tangled in a deep-rooted web of lies, cover-ups and impunity. But it was imperative that I finally receive real acknowledgement for my brain

261

injuries. Not just for personal closure, but to label the neurotoxic effects of this drug, so that all Veterans can finally have this condition acknowledged properly and follow the appropriate treatment pathway that they all deserve. This wasn't "PTSD", mental health or, as the MOD call it, "adjustment disorder". It was Mefloquine Toxicity or Chronic Quinoline Encephalopathy, known as 'Quinism' for short.

In July 2019, on a sunny day in Birmingham, I finally had my day at Her Majesty's Courts and Tribunal Service to contest Veterans UK's denial of this condition. Anxiety and unwanted thoughts were racing all over the place, even though I was being held together by a friend and a representative from the British Legion who were allowed to accompany me. But I still felt like a young soldier on CO's Orders ready for a custodial sentence.

The tribunal members introduced themselves. Miss Mark, the senior judge spoke first, followed by the medical member, Dr Frampton, and finally the military member, who introduced himself as Giles Orpen-Smellie. He added that he was the 'Regimental Second-in-Command' for 1 PARA Battlegroup for OP PALLISER and had deployed to Sierra Leone with me. I couldn't believe my luck! Only 800 soldiers deployed on this unique and rapid Op and even fewer of these were officers. What were the chances of that?

My case was read before the court, and all tribunal panel members quickly concluded that my 'mental health problems' had resulted from the neuropsychiatric symptoms of mefloquine (Lariam). The military member, Colonel Orpen-Smellie, added that he fully supported my submitted evidence and had no doubt that this was the root cause of my mental health. He also added that he had to deal with an "aftermath

262

of issues" in the Regiment after using this anti-malaria drug so could empathise where I was coming from and reassured me that I was not alone.

Finally, I'd been acknowledged. The Tribunal members hadn't brushed me aside and this came as a huge relief. For years, I had been rejected and left to struggle on my own, but not this time. I'd finally been listened to and that was a massive weight off my shoulders.

The Judge reprimanded the Veterans UK representative for the weak handling and response to my case before closing the session. Veterans UK had not acknowledged the root cause of these service-related injuries during my appeal. Unfortunately, due to some technicalities, I had to withdraw from the Tribunal process and was advised by the Court to pursue an alternative War Pensions route. And so it goes on. But after nearly twenty years, I at last heard the system say that it wasn't me. It was those tablets tossed to me in the steaming heat of Sierra Leone, long ago, one May afternoon.

——

Consequences. This is what happens when someone has to pay for the shortcuts, negligence and greed that characterise the Lariam scandal. With soldiers' black humour, it is possible to describe Dave as one of the lucky ones. Not unscathed, but a survivor. Kipling could probably have found the right words but I'm afraid I struggle. Dave has come through it but at immense personal cost. I was the friend who was with him at the tribunal. Whatever he was feeling inside, he held himself with great dignity and I wished that some of our generals and our Roche hosts from Welwyn could have listened to his testimony. It was a humbling and chastening experience.

There are others who tragically, like Cameron Quinn, are not found in time. What happens next? Does anyone ask any questions? Jane tried. And how she tried. In England and Wales, we have coroners' inquests. As the suicide count mounted, we would find another dog that didn't bark.

# Chapter 10
## Not an Interested Person

*We have a zero tolerance policy towards suicide.*

*-Kate Davies, NHS Director of Armed Forces*
*Commissioning, 2017*

On 8 November 2015, after I had given my oral evidence to
the Defence Select Committee in Portcullis House, I felt
confident that no one could now be left in any doubt about
how dangerous Lariam/WR 142 490 was. Dr Nevin had
stressed that, even according to the MoD's own figures, "over
a third of service members prescribed Lariam will experience
such prodromal symptoms as vivid dreams, nightmares and
insomnia, which the current Lariam SPC indicates are cause
to immediately discontinue the medication."[1]

In other words, they could become potential candidates
for suicide ideation or even completed suicide. Dr Croft had
even informed Parliament that during the early Army trials in
the 1990s one soldier had committed suicide. As we travelled
back to Yorkshire on the train that evening, Bea and I went
over the events of the day. It had gone well, but as we left the
train, and went our separate ways at Northallerton station, we
had no idea of a tragedy that had just unfolded in North Wales.

Even as we had been talking to the MPs in the Wilson
Room, another family was swirling in the emotional vortex
that Jane had experienced in Scotland almost a decade earlier.

A life had been ripped from this world. A living being had become a body, the soul departed, and now the corpse was an object for the official post-mortem processes and the focus of grief for the bewildered next of kin. The story didn't break until the following weekend, but it is still chilling for me to reflect that on Sunday, 6 November, as I was rehearsing what I would say to the Defence Committee, a veteran was setting upon the course of suicide. This time the rope did its bidding and, unlike Dave, there was no one to find her.

The death of Kate Fell-Crook made the Welsh and national press on Saturday, 12 November. From the various media accounts, it appeared that she had hanged herself in her home and was reportedly the first female British veteran suffering from PTSD to have taken her own life.[2,3,4] She was 35 years old and had left the Army in 2014 after fifteen years of exemplary service. Exactly what drove her to suicide, and leave a young daughter, will probably never be determined. She was certainly struggling with her mental state and had, it would seem, been formally diagnosed with PTSD. Apparently, like General Duncan, she had been sectioned under the Mental Health Act, but only for a short while.

Just what might have caused her to have PTSD was not explained in the newspapers, nor was it clear who had made that diagnosis. What is obvious to me, however, is that it would have been most unusual for PTSD to have resulted from her Army service. While she did spend some time in Northern Ireland, the security situation by then was largely benign and her role as a clerk would probably have kept her away from any traumatic stress. The press reports did state that her time in Northern Ireland was ended when she suffered a bout of depression but what really caught my eye was a photograph of Kate in uniform with a caption explaining that she had also served in Sierra Leone. According to *The Daily Mail*, she spent some time on a training mission in West Africa before she was posted to Northern Ireland.[5]

This would have put Kate in Sierra Leone in the mid-2000s, and at a time when Lariam was the default antimalarial for military personnel. And we have seen just how casually it was issued. The sequencing of her postings may also prove highly significant. If Kate had been taking Lariam before she began to experience depression, the drug is clearly a plausible cause for her illness. Such causal links are expressed in multiple case studies contained in the EMA Report of 2014 (the one the government is so reluctant to acknowledge). Of course, if she had been experiencing depression before her work in Sierra Leone she most certainly should not have been taking Lariam. The SPC in 2005 warned that patients with a history of depression should not be prescribed Lariam as a prophylaxis.[6] So had she taken it?

I was anxious to find out but this presented me with a tricky moral dilemma. I've often had to deal with the recovery and repatriation of the fallen. I've also helped bereaved families as they tried to navigate the rites of burial and the memorial of their loved-ones. I've broken the news to distraught parents and once had to help carry the body of a young UN-translator colleague into her devastated family's home. I think, therefore, that I understand as well as most what they go through and this was not a time for insensitive intrusion into the grieving of Kate's next-of-kin. But didn't they have a right to know what might have driven their daughter to such an awful end? I decided on two courses of action. The first was to write a letter of condolence to Kate's father. I also alerted him to the known effects of Lariam and its implication in so many other tragedies. It was a particularly difficult letter to compose and I can only hope it was of some solace.

As I knew there would have to be an inquest, I later contacted the Denbighshire Coroner to ask if it had been held and if the details had been made public. I explained that I was particularly interested in knowing if the Coroner was informed as to what anti-malarial prophylaxis Kate had been given during her military service in Sierra Leone, pointing out that the Ministry of Defence's preferred anti-malarial at that time was Lariam/mefloquine, and that it had been implicated in other suicides. In October 2016 I was told by the PA to the Coroner for North Wales (East and Central) that a date had still to be set for a final hearing but that my concerns had been passed to the Coroner.

As time passed, I checked again and in March 2017 was advised that no date had been set but that I would be notified when it was fixed. All remained quiet until January 2018 when I read a local press report that the inquest had been concluded and that "Coroner xxxx xxxxxxx recorded a conclusion of suicide on 35-year-old Kate Fell-Crook who was found hanging in her home…in December 2015."[7] The article went on to say that the state of her mental health had been considered and it was reported that a pathologist found she had three times the driving limit for alcohol in her blood. There had also been indications of the consumption of therapeutic drugs of a potentially fatal range. But nothing at all about Lariam. Had it been considered, and if not, why? I emailed the PA on 10 January 2018 asking:

*Could you… please let me know if the coroner investigated which anti-malarial Ms Fell-Crook was given for her service in Sierra Leone in the 2000s? The anti-malarial of choice issued to military personnel at that time was Lariam/Mefloquine and the drug has a range of serious adverse side-effects which mimic conditions such as PTSD. The drug has also been implicated in multiple episodes of suicide ideation and suicide. If the coroner was unaware of this I would be very grateful if you could pass this on to him as I feel it should have helped to inform his decision.*

Two days later I received this reply:

*Mr Marriott*
*My apologies firstly for the omission in notifying you of the scheduled inquest date when my office had previously indicated that they would do so. This was an oversight on my part and I regret any inconvenience or [sic] disappoint which this may have caused to you.*
*With regard to your specific enquiry I confirm that I considered all evidence which was put before me, then in accordance with my role made determinations as to which matters were relevant to the death. In this instance, I received substantial evidence relating to Miss Fell-Crook's mental health and I am satisfied both as to the sufficiency of enquiry and the conclusion which was reached.*

*Kind Regards*
*xxxx x xxxxxxx*

*Crwner E.M. Gogledd Cymru (Dwyrain a Chanol)/H.M.*
*Coroner North Wales (East and Central)*

I didn't think this really answered the question. Had he examined the evidence which I had put before him? I asked him to confirm whether or not the use of the anti-malarial drug Lariam/mefloquine was considered as a possible contributory factor. The reply I received was:

*Mr Marriott,*
*I write to advise you that Mr xxxxxxx is currently on annual leave. I will pass your email to him upon his return.*

*Kind regards.*
*xxxxx xxxxxx*
*Cynorthwydd Personol Crwner E.M. Gogledd Cymru (Dwyrain a Chanol)/Personal Assistant to H.M. Coroner North Wales (East and Central)*

I heard nothing more from the coroner or his office and can only conclude that either by accident or by design, Lariam had not been considered. If it had been, and formally dismissed as a potential factor influencing the death, why not say so? Meanwhile, another tragedy much closer to home was unfolding.

Chris Small, like Dave Rimmington, had served with the Royal Logistic Corps in Sierra Leone. He had also seen operational service in the Balkans, Iraq and Afghanistan. After more than twenty years' service, which had clearly taken their toll, Chris separated from his wife Mandy and son

Jamie and was working as a chef in County Durham. In December 2015, just around the time we learned of Kate's suicide, Chris put up a post on Facebook. It read:

*Who do I speak to if I think I have taken Lariam. I am having terrible mood swings and panic attacks.*

The post was picked up Dave Rimmington, Bea and many others who tried to direct him to the help he needed. Sadly, sometimes you cannot tell just how desperate people are and quite how close to the edge they have moved. He was hardly half an hour's drive away from me but I didn't pick up the vital warning signs. The next we heard was that he had hanged himself. He was alone in his house near Bishop Auckland. We were too late for Chris but this time surely we could get a coroner to think about the possible role of Lariam in this suicide.

There is, after all, a duty laid on coroners to raise what is called a 'Regulation 28 Report to Prevent Deaths' if they consider that any agency or government department should be alerted to a matter that may have contributed to a death and where future preventative action could be taken.[8] With that in mind, I sent what I hoped would be seen as a helpful email to the County Durham Coroner. It read:

*Dear Sir or Madam,*
*I have learned through social media that a Mr Chris Small of Darlington is believed to have recently taken his own life. I understand that he was a military veteran and that he had been posting about the effects he was suffering from mefloquine/Lariam toxicity. I do not personally use*

*social media but have attached a couple of screen shots to confirm the case. I have been told that Mr Small took mefloquine/Lariam while serving with the army in Sierra Leone around the year 2000. You may be aware of a recent investigation into the Ministry of Defence's use of this anti-malarial drug by the Parliamentary Defence Committee. It published its report earlier this year and is available at this link. I gave evidence, both written and oral, to that committee.*

http://www.publications.parliament.uk/pa/cm201516/cm select/cmdfence/567/56702.htm

*Mefloquine/Lariam has been implicated in a number of acts of violence, suicide ideation and suicide. It has affected individuals this way both when taking the drug as a prophylaxis and years after the course of medication has ended. Of course, never having met Mr Small, I have no appreciation of the scale of factors that may have caused his death. However, I would like to draw your attention to the possibility of mefloquine/Lariam as a contributory factor. I suspect that he may have been one of a number of individuals suffering from mefloquine/ Lariam-related ill-health that has not been recognised for what it is.*

*I live close to Darlington and would be happy to assist should you wish to have more detail. I can certainly direct you to creditable, peer-reviewed medical publications by internationally recognised experts in the field who would substantiate the hazard profile of the drug.*

*Do please let me know if I can be of assistance.*

And this was the initial and, I thought, very positive response.

*Dear Mr Marriott,*
*Thank you for today's email. I am forwarding this to my investigating officer.*

*Yours faithfully,*
*xxxxxx xxxxxxx.xx.x*
*HM Senior Coroner*
*County Durham and Darlington*

I kept an eye on the local press and was then really surprised and disappointed when I read in the *Northern Echo* less than two months later that the inquest had been concluded.[9] Suicide had been confirmed and the only cause suggested by the journalist covering the inquest was evidence of a number debts Chris had been unable to pay. Again, there appeared to have been no consideration of the possible impact that Lariam may have had.

Bea also saw the article. Straightaway, she telephoned the coroner's office and had a conversation which seemed to indicate that the Lariam details had somehow been mislaid. Perhaps there had been a genuine mistake and an internal breakdown in communications. Bea followed up her phone call with this email.

*Dear xxxx*
*Thank you so much for your time this morning, and your interest in my questions about the involvement of Lariam (Mefloquine) in Chris Small's suicide. Chris came to one*

*of our group's Facebook pages (Mindfields for Service Personnel) on 16 December 2015 asking how he could find out whether he had been given Lariam, and reporting mood swings. We all advised him, but contact was then lost until we heard of his suicide last November. Sadly, suicide ideation and completed suicide are well-known side-effects of Lariam toxicity, and I believe that he is yet another of its victims.*

*Our group, the International Mefloquine Veterans' Alliance, www.imvalliance.org, works globally to raise awareness of this problem. Our doctors write extensively on the subject, and if you are interested, it would be well worth having a look at Dr Remington Nevin's website. Remington is an ex-US Army epidemiologist who specialises in the subject of Lariam toxicity, and flew to London to give evidence to the Defence Select Committee's enquiry into the MoD's use of the drug.*

*https://www.publications.parliament.uk/pa/cm201516/c mselect/cmdfence/567/567.pdf*

*Remington's website is here:*

*http://www.remingtonnevin.com/home/home.html*

*As I said on the telephone, this is a growing problem as around 20,000 service personnel have been given this drug since 2007. Since around 42% of those taking it suffer "moderate to severe neuropsychiatric side-effects", which are often permanent, you can see the scale of the problem. I would be really grateful if you could pass on this information to all other Coroners and ask them to be alert to the issue when dealing with military and ex-military suicides.*

*Please feel free to contact me if you have any questions; if I can't answer them myself, I will put you in touch with an expert. My mobile number is xxxxx xxxxxxx.*

But then things quickly turned much cooler and it looked as though the whole matter was being closed down in the coroner's officer. I pressed the Senior Coroner for some clarification and got a fairly terse response. He simply said he and his officers did consider my earlier email as part of their investigation. He also added that "There was no reference to it at the inquest hearing." I didn't find this at all satisfactory and tried one more email to him:

*Dear Mr xxxxxxx,*

*Thank you, but I would ask that you provide some clarification. In your original response to the details I sent alerting you to the possible implication of the anti-malarial drug Lariam in Mr Small's death, you said, "I am forwarding this to my investigating officer". Could you please tell me:*

*To which investigating officer did you pass those details? I would prefer to have the name but would accept that individual's appointment.*

*Exactly why did you pass those details to your investigating officer?*

*What were your expectations of anyone receiving those details?*

*I would also be grateful if you would explain exactly how you and your officers considered my earlier email. Specifically:*

> *Did you ask the Ministry of Defence if Mr Small had ever taken Lariam as part of his military duties?*
> *Did you ask any medical experts in malaria prevention for their opinions on the possibility of Lariam as a causative factor in suicide?*
> *Did you examine either the Summary of Product Characteristics or the Patient Information Leaflet for Lariam? If so, which ones did you access?*
> *Did you study any of the peer-reviewed publications about the adverse events associated with Lariam and its association with symptoms that could be confounded with, or mistaken for, PTSD?*

*Finally, I note that you say there was no reference to Lariam at the inquest. Did it require the presence of a third party to raise the matter? If so, given that I had drawn this to your attention, and had offered my help to you, would it not have been advisable to invite me to attend the inquest?*

*Thank you for your assistance and I look forward to your reply.*

I felt that these were important questions and that there was a strong public interest in having them answered. Dave, who was one Chris's army mates, has supported his widow, Mandy, over the past few years and he has assured me that Mandy would like some answers too. This was the final response from the coroner, clearly intended to shut down the topic for good.

*Thank you for today's email. I do not wish to become involved in correspondence with you in this matter. You are not a properly interested person for the purposes of the inquest and therefore I neither can nor will provide you with any further information.*

So I was "not a properly interested person." Perhaps technically he may have been correct but I remain unconvinced that a coroner should not have been taking a closer interest in medications plausibly implicated in suicides. Isn't that the point of Regulation 28? In fact, if we fast-forward to 2020, another coroner did exactly that and in a case where a suicide was almost certainly driven by the side effects of an anti-malarial drug. But before we look at that I, and others like Mandy, remained very interested persons.

There was, at best, an information gap between coroners operating within the Ministry of Justice, and bodies such as the Ministry of Defence and the Department of Health. And there was a bit of a national pattern beginning to appear. Bea had noticed the same lack of curiosity with other veteran and even serving suicides. There had been the case of a Royal Navy nurse, Laura Hyde, who was found dead in her home in Plymouth in 2016.[10] Again, her inquest apparently made no mention of anti-malarial drugs even though she had recently served in Sierra Leone.

Bea took this up with two MPs who should have had a very special interest in the matter, Johnny Mercer (then still a member of the Defence Select Committee), and Oliver

Colville, the member for Plymouth Sutton and Devonport. She got no response from Johnny Mercer and no follow-up from Mr Colville. It looked as though they weren't particularly interested persons either. But a logical next step for us was to somehow try to close that gap in the information loop and we got a chance in 2017. Trixie Foster had managed to get us another meeting in London, this time with the MoD and the NHS.

———

By a quirk of fate, we seemed to be assembled on the first anniversary of Laura Hyde's death and close to the Cenotaph in Whitehall. It was late on a very hot August afternoon as we were ushered into a meeting room in Richmond House, headquarters of the Department of Health, and just a stone's throw from Portcullis House. We were joined by a trauma specialist, Mandy Bostwick, who had a particular interest in brain injury and was setting up a charity to provide residential support for damaged victims. The meeting was hosted and co-chaired by the Chief of Defence People, Lieutenant General Richard Nugee (it seems the MoD doesn't have personnel anymore) and Kate Davies, NHS Director of Armed Forces Commissioning.

It wasn't quite the Black Hole of Calcutta, but the meeting room was hardly big enough for the dozen or so attendees and it seemed odd that the Department of Health could muster no more than two small plastic cups of water to share among all the attendees. My antennae were picking up some discouraging vibes.

While much of the meeting was given over to Mandy Bostwick's work (an area in which Trixie, Bea and I could offer little of value), the latter part of the session gave us the chance to present some of our major concerns directly to these two government departments. But we were also trying to offer some solutions. Our headline appeal to General Nugee and Ms Davies was that Lariam toxicity be formally recognised. That was surely the logical and vital next step flowing from the Defence Committee's Report. At this stage no one on our side of the table was aware of the EMA Report of 2014 which had been withheld from the Defence Select Committee. But surely Kate Davies must have been aware of the Report, although she made no mention of it. Was the Chief of Defence People also so poorly informed? Both of them seemed to think that Lariam neurotoxicity was still a largely speculative matter. Either the quality of their staff briefings and preparation for the meeting was insufficient or we were being duped.

We now moved into some specifics and started with the potentially lethal Lariam/weapons cocktail. Depending on which copy of Roche's PIL or SPC you read, there are plenty of warnings about operating complex, dangerous or hazardous machinery while consuming Lariam. (That was the subject that got Lord Astor into his muddle when he told Parliament that Lariam wasn't used by personnel driving vehicles.) Trixie asked if General Nugee could explain why firearms were not considered to fall within the definition of complex machinery. Of course, he could not, and the matter was inexplicably excluded from the minutes of the meeting.

Knowing what Sgt Bales had done in Afghanistan (and remember the bar brawl in Nairobi involving Sgt Murray in the 1990s), the MoD remained content to avoid this inconvenient problem. A soldier with a rifle in the heat of the jungle, a tank commander in Iraq, the captain of a Trident submarine... taking Lariam? This wasn't the first time this matter had been presented to Service Chiefs. It had been placed in front of the Chief of Defence Staff, General Houghton, in 2015 and he duly ignored it.[11]

Now it was my turn and I asked General Nugee for his help with a number of matters. Surely it was time for a proper investigation within the MoD to determine what had gone wrong. Why had there been no inquiry? And why had no one from the MoD invited any of its veterans to explain to them what had really happened? That would, of course, have exposed the MoD to at least legal rebuke and probably thousands of claims for compensation. Maybe the MoD lawyers had been whispering in the General's ear. I could just picture one in impish form sitting on his shoulder.

But what I really wanted to drive home that day was the disconnect between the English and Welsh coroners and the MoD and the Department of Health. I gave them Chris Small's story which really encapsulated the whole problem. It would have been at that point in the meeting when Kate Davies offered the utterly crass comment that her department, as would be repeated in the minutes, had "a zero-tolerance strategy towards suicide." I was sitting at one end of our side of the table and I recall looking at the rest of our team and thinking "Did I really hear that properly?" Their expressions confirmed that I had, as did a particularly acerbic and terse riposte from Bea.

I thought to myself, "the next time one of us is trying pull someone back from the edge, I hardly think *that* is going to be top on the list of our reassurances— Don't do it! The NHS has a zero-tolerance strategy." For God's sake! But if I am being unfair and doing the NHS Director of Armed Forces Commissioning a disservice, how many Lariam suicides or attempted suicides has her organisation ever investigated as a part of this zero-tolerance?

The General was a little more circumspect with his words, but only a little. He pleaded that the MoD had no means of collecting data on veteran suicides. It is true that it would be impossible to collect all the numbers, not least because some veterans no longer advertise their service backgrounds, or 'self-identify' in the current idiom. They just get lost to the system. But I felt his response was both lazy and highly misleading. MoD Public Information staff are embedded in headquarters across the country, and their purpose is to collect and pass on to Whitehall news relating to the Armed Forces, whether it be positive or negative. Bad news is usually staffed to ministers and service chiefs well before they may choke on their toast and marmalade over the morning newspaper. I suggested that the MoD, the Department of Health and the Ministry of Justice might together address the problem, perhaps demonstrating some joined-up government. This idea didn't make it into the minutes either.

That week, Whitehall was closing down for the summer but as we dispersed we thought we had made some good progress. General Nugee and Ms Davies had apparently made some important commitments. Summer leave would probably cause a bit of delay in receiving the minutes (three weeks as it happened) but that was nothing in this campaign. When they did appear, the minutes were simply extraordinary.[12] They did offer some hope but my heart sank and my anger mounted once again. They looked as though they had been compiled by someone on work experience and I will save some embarrassment for the MoD and the NHS by not repeating them in full here.

I quickly noted that no one had even troubled to check how to spell our names. Such little matters of etiquette are hardly important when people's lives are at stake but these were minutes that were supposed to be of a standard acceptable to a three-star general and presented to the general public. They were, unfortunately, simply a list of bulleted points, incoherently expressed, with important terms conflated and key points excluded. It even looked as though they had been drafted by someone who was not even present at the meeting. This particular bullet point illustrates the utterly casual approach to what should have been a vitally important meeting:

*MoD provided further information on the discharge process and which scales were used. [Not sure what this refers to]—this is where Rachel describe the scales used on discharge. [sic]*

No, I have no idea either what this refers to. But the minutes did commit the government to a number of actions. I am reproducing them *exactly* as presented.

*1. MOD to determine whether it agrees with the statement that there is a link between neuro-toxicology (from Lariam) and mental health: MOD representatives from today will discuss with Surgeon General's area.*

*2. MOD to look at the possibility of how we can move forward a research study into the link between neuro-toxicology and mental health if such a link is proven.*

*3. International research piece around neurotoxicity and mental health a possibility to raise through 5eyes IUS/CA/AUS/NZ collaborations and potentially exploit US research.*

*4. NHS England/MOD to revise the commissioning documents to make reference to the neuro-toxicology and mental health issues once they have been acknowledged.*

*5. To ensure that the Veterans' Gateway refers any callers on Lariam to the MOD SPOCC that was implemented in September 2016. To look at ensuring the Gateway/SPOC are not credit limited when called through the criminal justice system.*

*6. To commission the Kings Study through phase 4 Longitudinal data cohort to tack those Iraq and Afghanistan deployees who took Lariam, and their control group and monitor their mental and physical health and wellbeing outcomes.*

Not particularly well expressed but the meaning can be understood. Point 5 regarding the Veterans' Gateway would have been easy to fix and was probably actioned. (The MOD SPOC (only one 'C') is a single point of contact for veterans using a MoD telephone help line. It simply directs them towards other agencies such as the NHS, GPs or charities).

We did try one other tack with a little nudge to the Ministry of Justice. In September 2017 we asked them if they could provide statistics for suicides by both serving armed forces personnel and veterans since 1985. We also asked if they might break down these figures into each coroner's area of jurisdiction. The response we received was very telling:[13]

*The MoJ does not hold any information in the scope of your request. No information on serving armed forces personnel or veterans are collected in the annual returns which coroners submit to the MoJ. This is because there is no legal or business requirement for the MoJ to collect or publish this.*

*You may wish to contact individual coroners' offices as they may hold some of the information you requested.*

Years have passed by and I can confidently state that the essential five points from the Richmond House meeting have been largely ignored. My confidence is based on the action or, more accurately, the lack of action and interest shown by the Ministry of Defence, and especially the newly appointed Minister for Defence People and Veterans, one Johnny Mercer, to address them. To make any progress, Mercer and the MoD would have had to recognise the fundamental point that Lariam had caused long-term damage to a significant number of service personnel, many now veterans—and, sadly, a number of them were now dead.

They would have to accept the conclusions presented in the 2014 EMA Report and come clean about when the MoD first knew about it. This is something that Mr Mercer repeatedly refused to do during his tenure as a minister. My own conclusion is that he was silenced with a ministerial appointment and, in true 'Yes Minister' style, had been house-trained.[w]

He would be allowed a lot of latitude on his pet projects but he wasn't to say anything about Lariam. He refused to meet me and nor would he answer my questions. His style was that of the politician climbing the greasy pole; to get someone else to send unnamed, never mind unsigned, letters on his behalf. He abandoned the Lariam victims: I would like to invite him to explain why.

When he was first appointed as a minister in 2019, I wrote to congratulate him and also alerted him to the EMA Report, giving him the document's full publication details. Here is an extract from my letter:

*My second issue relates to an important document, a European Medicines Agency Report of 31 January 2014, which concluded that there was a causal relationship between Lariam use and the occurrence of long-lasting and even persistent neuropsychiatric side-effects. I suspect that, like me, at the time of the Defence Committee inquiry you were unaware of this document. It remains difficult to access even though the EMA was based in London and its findings would have been transmitted, along with the increased warnings of the drug's potential toxicity, to the Department of Health.*

*We must assume that both Roche and the Surgeon General knew of this report when they presented evidence*

---

[w] Yes Minister was a popular BBC TV series from the 1980s satirically showing how the 'system' and civil servants could manipulate a vain and self-important government minister.

*to the Committee. If so, the fidelity of the MoD's evidence is clearly in doubt, suggesting that they knowingly misled Parliament. The report draws on a number of case studies and will, no doubt, be central to establishing a causal link between Lariam use and permanent neurologic damage in pending legal cases. Earlier this month questions were tabled in the Lords about the report and the responses by Baroness Blackwood and Earl Howe were, at best, evasive.*

*It would be most helpful if you could obtain from the MoD recognition of the report and their acceptance of its conclusion and recommendations. The report has been suppressed for too long and both the MoD and the Department of Health should be required to declare when they became aware of it.*

I received an anonymous non-reply from the Headquarters of the Joint Medical Group with nothing about endorsement of the EMA's conclusions, nor as to what was known or presented to the Defence Committee by the Roche and MoD witnesses. I tried twice more in 2019 to get Mr Mercer to answer. This is part of a letter I sent to him in October:

*As I said in my earlier letter, I suspect that, like me, at the time of the Defence Committee inquiry you were unaware of this document. Could I ask you please to confirm when the Ministry of Defence and the Department of Health each became aware of this report? I would be grateful for a precise date but a month and year would be sufficient. I would even be satisfied with a not before and not after date range, but I believe it would be reasonable that such a range should not be greater than six months.*

He refused to answer. He wouldn't engage and I must be driven to the conclusion that he was unwilling to tackle the wider MoD cover up. Why? He even publicly denied any knowledge of the EMA Report when questioned about it during his personal re-election campaign during the 2019 general election. On *Johnny Mercer Live,* a Facebook session, Dave Rimmington asked him when the MoD was first aware of the Report and had this information been presented to the Defence Select Committee.[14] This was his response:

*Oh my God! Dave, I have no idea. Can you email that to me? That's a really complicated question and when I get back, if I get back, on 12 December, I'll answer that for you. That's quite a complicated question.*

Complicated? The question wasn't complicated. It could hardly have been simpler. It was, however, uncomfortable and he didn't want to give the answer. Dave did email the question to him in early 2020 when Mr Mercer was back in his ministerial office. Dave was similarly treated to one of those anonymous non-answer letters from the Headquarters of the Joint Medical Group.

I had a look at Johnny Mercer's page on the Gov.UK website. It said "It was Johnny's displeasure at how his cohort of military personnel and veterans were treated by the governments of the day that drove him into politics." Find a mirror, Johnny. And by the way, thanks, General Nugee.

We now need to return to the key investigative milestone from 2020 when a coroner did consider the role of an antimalarial drug in a suicide.

In early August 2019, news began to break of the death of a Cambridge University student who had thrown herself out of a light aircraft while flying over the Indian Ocean island of Madagascar. The story was extensively covered by British and worldwide television networks and in the press media. As soon as I heard about it, my immediate suspicion was the involvement of Lariam.

Alana Cutland, aged 19, had been conducting some research on the island and, according to *The Times, The Daily Telegraph* and *The Sunday Telegraph* she was returning home early after a sudden deterioration in her mental health. She was in a bad way, apparently suffering from paranoia and experiencing hallucinations. It was reported that she had been taking both Lariam and Doxycycline antimalarials, and *The Daily Telegraph* stated that the local police had later discovered both medications among her luggage.[15,16,17] She had been about ten minutes into her flight in a small Cessna plane, with one other passenger, when, at about 3,500ft, she opened the door and, fighting off attempts by the pilot and her companion to save her, she jumped to her death. That was meant to be the first leg of her journey home.

Her body was eventually found and it fell to the Milton Keynes Coroner to hold an inquest. The Coroner's investigation ended on 30 April 2020 and it concluded that Alana had died from traumatic injuries following a fall from a plane. The Coroner also recorded that she had taken doxycycline as an antimalarial medication and it is believed that she suffered a psychotic/delirium event that led to her behaviour and death. Using Regulation 28, he reported the circumstances to the MHRA in order to prevent future deaths.[18]

I have no knowledge of any toxicology reports and I expect that the coroner will have been guided by prescribing records for Alana which may well have confirmed that she was prescribed doxycycline for her trip and she may well have experienced a bad reaction to it. But had she at some stage acquired Lariam during her stay in Madagascar? According to the media reports, the local police had found both drugs in her luggage. Perhaps those questions will never be resolved. The key point is that the Milton Keynes Coroner had done his job properly. The evidence presented to him suggested that an antimalarial drug had caused the psychotic reaction leading to Alana's death. The UK drug regulator was suitably alerted.

I am very grateful to the Milton Keynes coroner for not dismissing me as "Not an interested person". And yet even while researching this chapter in 2020 I came across yet another extraordinary example illustrating how our system for investing some deaths appears both arcane and unfit for purpose.

In September 2020, it was reported in the press that another veteran, Ashley Nickless, had committed suicide the previous November, hanging himself in his home in Conwy, North Wales. It was said that Corporal Nickless had been discharged from the Royal Marines two years earlier with a diagnosis of PTSD.[19] A local newspaper, The Daily Post, covering the inquest, said that a post-mortem examination had found traces of a drug to treat malaria in his system.

Apparently, Ashley Nickless had quite recently been to Sierra Leone and the Democratic Republic of Congo but there was no further clarification as to which drug he might have taken. He had also been experiencing panic attacks and nightmares. This story seemed to chime with so many others and I was more than intrigued to discover that the inquest had been the responsibility of the very same office for the investigation into Kate Fell-Crook's death a few years earlier.

Straightaway, I emailed the North Wales coroner's office but was ignored for two weeks. A hastener was sent on 15 October 2020 asking if the coroner could confirm which malaria drug treatment had been found and I was then subsequently telephoned by the PA to the coroner. Apparently Mr xxxx xxxxxxx was still the senior coroner but he was not available to speak nor, it seems, even able to reply to my emails. On that late-afternoon I did discuss the Ashley Nickless inquest with his PA and my notes of the conversation were that the details of the toxicology report would only be shared with 'interested persons' or those who attended the inquest. The coroner was aware of which drug had been taken but was not at liberty to share that information. Furthermore, no Regulation 28 Report had been raised. To ensure that my notes were correct, I sent a follow-up email on 17 October 2020 at 11:21 saying:

*Thank you very much for your assistance during our telephone conversation last Thursday. Just to summarise: I understand that you are unable to release the details of the toxicology report for Ashley Nickless and that those details could only be shared with interested parties or with those who attended the inquest.*

*The toxicology report did identify which anti-malarial drug was found, but this cannot be made public.*
*A Regulation 28 Report was not raised.*

The reply was simply this:

*Further to your email in relation to the case of Mr Nickless, I did not give any indication as to what was in the toxicology report as this is not information that I can share with you.*

I guess it is fair to assume that no Regulation 28 Report was raised.

I remain bemused and frustrated at the opaque nature of some of the investigations into suicides where anti-malarial drugs may have been implicated. Coroners are independent judicial office holders and provide a service to local authorities but it is the Ministry of Justice that holds responsibility for coroner law and policy: and it is probably at governmental level where action and reform are required. Perhaps coroners are constrained both in the scope of their investigations and in what they may share in the wider public interest. I had the problem set before the Ministry of Justice in 2018 and this was part of their response:[20]

*It is… not within the remit of the coroner to explore events that happened many years prior to the death, or to hear evidence of opinion from those who knew the deceased, except where this may be relevant to the factual questions… [of who has died, where and when they died, and how they died]. There may therefore be occasions where a coroner will decide that they do not need to consider some issues or pieces of evidence during the course of an inquest. This is a matter entirely for the coroner presiding over the inquest to decide in each individual case.*

*However, if someone believes that during the inquest there was "rejection of evidence and insufficiency of inquiry" (section 13 Coroners Act 1988) they may make an application to the Attorney General for a new coroner's investigation to be carried out. If the Attorney General agrees, he or she will make an application to the High Court. Permission will only be granted, however, if it would be in the interest of justice to do so and there is no time limit for these applications.*

*We strongly advise anyone considering pursuing this option to take independent legal advice before proceeding.*

So no encouragement there for the individual citizen to address the perceived problem (rather the opposite); and no desire from the Ministry of Justice to recognise that any problem even exists, far less resolve it.

I wonder what might have happened if there had been an appropriately informed inquest into the death of that soldier who killed himself after the British Army Lariam trial in Kenya all those years ago?[21]

# Chapter 11
## Picking Up the Pieces

*The thousands of abnormal births were an act of God.*

*-Chemie-Grünenthal, the company that created and marketed thalidomide[1]*

A fairly short drive away from my home lives another Lariam victim but for a number of reasons I will keep him anonymous. His mother made contact with our group, desperately worried about her son's mental health. He had regularly rehearsed suicide in his mind and his family life was now in shreds. Only a few years earlier he had been a non-commissioned officer, working with Special Forces in Afghanistan. Like so many others, he had been given Lariam in the very casual manner that was so characteristic of the Army Medical Services. And like so many others when trying to get some form of legal redress, he had discovered that the Ministry of Defence simply did not want to know.

I went to visit him at his mother's house and we probably spent the better part of two hours talking. Just him and me. I think it may have helped, not least because a relatively senior officer was prepared to listen to what he had to say. Someone was interested; someone who cared and understood. And like so many others trying to come to terms with what had been going through their minds, he was able to get some context. Not the absolute clarity that every archaeologist seeks from context, but a comprehension of things; and my mind went back to my early studies at York and that observation from Jennifer Wallace that the archaeologist "plays a vital political role in revealing what is… inescapable when the general trend is to evade responsibility."[2]

Much of the archaeologist's work involves the detailed recording of excavations. Our trenches are not simply dug in pursuit of the iconic remains buried underground or in search of the exotic find. Those are, of course, exciting and we all feel the thrill of discovery as the trowel exposes the mosaic floor of a Roman villa or the soil gives up an exquisite artefact hidden from human gaze for perhaps millennia. If you do visit an active site you are more likely, however, to see archaeologists engaged in the more mundane tasks of taking measurements and making scale drawings of their excavations. The trench walls and other sections we dig can tell us as much, and often more, about human settlement at that location than we might be able to infer from what we find at the bottom of the trench, no matter how important and precious that discovery may be.

If you have ever walked along a beach past some fields just above the high-tide level, you will probably have seen an opened cut of land, rather like a miniature cliff, possibly carved away by storms or spring tides. Below the grass you can usually see roots in the topsoil, and below that maybe different colours and textures as the soil profile changes the lower you look. Each level indicates a different and, in theory at least, an earlier geological process or event.

The geologist would quickly and rightly protest that I am being rather simplistic. The process will usually be much more complicated, and the same is true with the archaeological record. When we look at the profile drawn from the wall of an archaeological trench, we can be fairly confident that the upper layer is the most recent, and the general principle is that the lower you go, the older the deposit. But it is entirely possible that lower down we may encounter evidence of more recent human activity; perhaps, say, as a result of tunnelling, which now may be collapsed and filled in.

What is absolutely certain is that eventually, we can get down to the point at which human activity started on the site. We have reached what archaeologists call the 'natural', below which we will only encounter the geological record. All this means that we have to be forensic in our recording of the trench profile and very careful in what conclusions we draw from it. Each layer is drawn and described in an accompanying report, and given a unique context number. The simplest drawing will show layers, a bit like a cake.

But we are much more likely to have to deal with odd lenses or other shapes, representing all manner of things such as a collapsed structure, a pit or a trench, or maybe burnt charcoal or a rubbish pit. We can't simply date and interpret from top to bottom, and to help our investigations we try to create a matrix, rather like a flow chart, indicating what context may have preceded or followed from another, and what their relationships might be. I know that I am laying myself open to all sorts of charges about being too deterministic or reductive, but isn't there an analogy here with the mind and human experience? Of course, I'm starting to probe a discipline way beyond my area of expertise.

But as the 'experts' had apparently abandoned this young veteran (a label that does seem something of an oxymoron), the field was left to those former comrades who might want to help. And while we are talking about context, Lariam was recently described publicly as only a *safe-ish* drug by a leading psychiatrist, Professor Sir Simon Wessely. I think somewhat complacently, he said this to the House of Commons Defence Committee as late as 2018,[3] when asked about Lariam neurotoxicity:

*The nature of psychiatric diagnosis is that it is not etiological. You diagnose someone as having depression and then look at what the causes might be. We do not have a diagnosis of neurotoxic depression; we have a diagnosis of depression, and then we look to see whether it could be due to, for example, thyroid problems, marital problems, early life, and so on. Unlike in other bits of medicine, our diagnoses are descriptive, and then you go deep down to find out what the causes might be. Usually you find a multitude of causes.*

*On the Lariam question, we have data on anti-malarials, but we do not have data on specific ones, so it is difficult for us to address that. The best data comes from the Cochrane review. To summarise quite a complex piece of work, the first thing is that Lariam is a very good anti-malarial, and malaria kills. Secondly, it is a safe-ish drug. It does have an increased rate of adverse symptoms compared with some of the others. You are more likely to have bad dreams, depression, and so on. I think most people who have taken it will probably remember that. It is higher than other anti-malarials.*

*On the other hand, other drugs have different side-effects that Lariam is better on. I think it is a bit of an open verdict on that. We have not been able to look at what the long-term outcomes are, and nor has the Cochrane review. For that, we would need to link our data with some of the data on prescribing.*

Perhaps Professor Wessely was unfamiliar with the contents of the EMA Report and what side effects had actually been listed at that time by Roche. The Cochrane collaboraion he referred to provides an international library of independent, high-quality literature reviews of the evidence regarding pharmaceuticals.[4] Cochrane is without doubt an immensely important body, but its library seems to be very limited regarding papers on the *safe-ish* Lariam/mefloquine.[x] It strikes me as both clinically and intellectually limiting that the safety of our antimalarial programmes should be so reliant upon one institution. And I think it does a major disservice to Cochrane that it should be used as a medico get-of-jail-free card by those unwilling to give mefloquine toxicity the scrutiny it so vitally needs. Especially so, as Professor Wessely admitted that "We have not been able to look at what the long-term outcomes are." The EMA Report of 2014 would be a good place to start.

Returning to the young veteran, and with Professor Wessely's words in my mind, I just tried to piece together what had happened to him and help him try to navigate a way out of his mental minefield. (I've been in some real ones so I think I'm entitled to use the metaphor.) I believed what I was

---

[x] Safe-ish seems a little short of the MHRA standard of "as safe as possible" given on the NHS website page 'Medicines Information', 17 December 2020.

being told and it was perfectly plain to me that he was suffering a form of neurotoxicity caused by Lariam. He had actually been given the drug in Afghanistan after he had asked medics for some help to stop smoking. All he needed were some nicotine patches. They discovered that he had arrived without any antimalarial pills and he was simply issued with Lariam. All his subsequent problems were consistent with the literature (Cochrane excepted) and with what Dave Rimmington and Chris Small had experienced.

I guess that unless you are a doctor, you may need a dictionary to understand what Professor Wessely meant when he said "The nature of psychiatric diagnosis is that it is not etiological." My dictionary, using the English spelling of aetiology, says:[5]

n. **1** *Medicine: the cause or causes of a disease or condition.* **2**. *The investigation or attribution of cause or a reason.*

Whether intentional or not, when the elite patronise, objectivity becomes the first casualty. Personally, I would prefer to collect all the evidence and keep looking at it until I could find a reason or cause. Furthermore, it was interesting what Professor Wessely had said about looking for causes from early life while apparently being so sanguine about Lariam. And the MoD lawyers have latched on to that too. They now assert that our troubled young veteran's difficulties arose from problems during his childhood. And to compound their indecency, they have placed the onus on him to prove that he was given Lariam. How does he get access to records that the MoD has acknowledged they never kept? Such legal behaviour is an affront to the Military Covenant and should be a cause of eternal shame for the Secretary of State for Defence and his Veterans' Minister.

As we talked, and I tried to revive some confidence in the wider institution this man had once served, the low afternoon sun created something of a haze. He spoke softly, looking often at the floor, an injured soldier who couldn't come to terms with what had hurt him. At that moment I was taken back to one of the most haunting and arresting images of the First World War. A few weeks earlier I had been studying the commissioned art of the Great War and the painting was fresh in my mind. It is called *Gassed*, painted by John Singer Sargent.

It depicts a line of gassed soldiers, eyes bandaged, some still with rifles and helmets, being led to a dressing station. Men stripped of one of their vital senses, probably dumb and utterly confused by the effect of an insidious gaseous cloud. In the far distance, others are playing football, quite oblivious to the carnage around them. Now, here in this room, a century on from that scene, I was looking at the soldier in the middle of that line. But this one had served in Afghanistan in the Royal Artillery, the same regiment as the then Veterans' Minister, Johnny Mercer. He wasn't blinded; his mind was poisoned. I wrote to Mr Mercer describing this man's plight. It was in one of those letters that Mr Mercer couldn't find time to answer.

The pieces of that man's life have been picked up but he remains very brittle. When I discussed this book with his mother, this is what she said:

*At _____ 's medical discharge hearing they did indeed blame childhood issues. However, it was to say _____ had suffered sleepwalking problems as a child. I refuted that and was, as you point out often happens, patronised. The female medical officer even saying they did not rely on 3rd hand accounts. Excuse me! Remember the reason they were discharging _____ was something pulled out of a hat, non-rem sleep disorder. The MOD sent _____ to a London hospital for an overnight sleep observation.*

*We have yet to see those results and diagnosis. He was too ill to carry on with his military career and welcomed the discharge naively thinking he would then be able to seek much needed treatment. At that time we were totally unaware of mefloquine toxicity and the difficult journey we were embarking on. It was on a visit to the veterans centre in Catterick and overhearing other veterans joking about which straw "discharge reason" they each picked, I realised the MOD were drawing from a list of diagnoses that would not have any liability of care.*

*Among them, the non-rem sleep disorder but also anorexia, bulimia, attention deficit disorder and even schizophrenia. The veterans were laughing and joking but in among that bravado was such shame of the military they once felt part of. I would like this included and the fact these shameful discharge hearings left these guys unable to seek appropriate care.*

And later, she also asked if I would include something that probably only a mother could fully appreciate. It also shows how Lariam's shadow can be cast over multiple generations.

*The story I wish to share… is the moment when I knew just how bad _____'s injury was. One day, after a friend was discussing the moment his first born came into the world, _____ asked me where he was when his own son Jack was born. He was looking at me with such anguish. _____ had no recollection; none. It was so hard for me to have to tell him he was there at the birth. He and his partner brought the baby boy home the same day.*

*On getting home his partner said she was going for a lie down and left the three of us alone together. She so sweetly gave me this greatest of all gifts. I can't put into words how it felt to show my son how to gently change his new-born son's nappy, make up a bottle and feed him for the first time, to wind him and rock him to sleep. The bonds being formed were so magical. My grandson still feels them today and we get teased he is my favourite; he isn't but the magic of those bonds is strong. Only for _____ his memory of that day is gone completely. Mefloquine has robbed him and us of the very thing that binds us.*

_____'s local MP has helped and his mother is still there, every day. Each day is a little victory.

———

Our damaged veterans need help and across the United Kingdom we have developed a fine national tradition in looking after the wounded and their families. Our service charities don't just stop there and many reach out to those who have fallen on hard times, regardless of what has caused, in

301

some cases, utter destitution. Most people would probably be able to name three charities in the vanguard of those working hard to support ex-service men and women: The Royal British Legion, Combat Stress and Help for Heroes. And while I would be at the head of those saluting their work, you can probably sense there is a 'but' coming: there is, and I offer that caveat with a twinge of regret as I have a very strong family connection with the British Legion. Anyone of these organisations would be an immediate port of call for those who need help in picking up the pieces of their lives. But not one of them seems to recognise Lariam toxicity or quinism. It is almost as if everything about Lariam has been air-brushed out of the Armed Forces charity sector.

Over the past few years I have contacted many charities to see what they might be able to offer those who, like _____, needed help with Lariam. I could find nothing, but coincidentally, Combat Stress did number Professor Wessely among its trustees.[6] I recently checked the Combat Stress and Help for Heroes websites to see what might be there.[7,8]

I entered searches for both Lariam and mefloquine, to which Combat Stress responded "Your search yielded no results", while Help for Heroes gave "No results found". On the other hand, they offer plenty about PTSD. So while they want to help veterans with their mental health difficulties, much of the help they offer appears to follow the PTSD pathway, to the complete exclusion of Lariam. Why?

There is a bit more of a hint from responses I had from the British Legion, and I get the distinct impression that they regard the matter as rather too political. That hardly strikes me as a valid reason for ignoring Lariam and thus abandoning some of the very people they have been chartered to help. Gulf

War Syndrome was probably 'political' as was the exposure of British servicemen to the nuclear tests in the Pacific of the 1950s and 60s. In 2017, I asked the Legion to consider a campaign to have Lariam toxicity formally recognised and not confused with PTSD. In an email, they said:

*As we do not have sufficient medical expertise at the Legion to properly consider all the medical evidence and arguments, this is not something we are currently in a position to do. That being said, we do have links to a Medical Advisory Committee consisting of a number of medical experts in a range of different fields. The Legion would be happy to raise this matter with them in order to find out more, and would welcome links to any academic papers you feel should be considered by the group.*[9]

I sent an immediate reply suggesting a piece authored by Remington Nevin, titled 'Mefloquine and posttraumatic stress disorder'[10] and offering more help if required. I heard nothing more from them. However, if you enter an advanced search on the Royal British Legion website, you can now see a single entry for Lariam/mefloquine, but it's not at all easy to find. It won't tell you anything about the drug but it does, for those who do persevere, alert you to the Mefloquine Single Point of Contact in the MoD.[11] It's an utterly circular process, with concerned enquirers then being by directed by the MoD to see their GP. The Single Point of Contact helpfully also redirects veterans back to "useful links" such as Combat Stress, Help for Heroes and the Royal British Legion. So, you can only make progress as long as you are prepared to embrace PTSD.

Forget Lariam toxicity. It must have been like this just over a century ago with shell shock.

This all, unfortunately, suits the government because of the likely scale of the scandal it is not prepared to acknowledge. In Chapter 2, we saw that in the United States some consider Lariam as potentially being the 'Agent Orange' of this generation. On this side of the Atlantic, we might more properly suggest that the extent of the damage may easily surpass that of thalidomide, a drug whose very name is a byword for gross pharmaceutical negligence and corporate greed. America was protected from this particular public health tragedy because the FDA, resisting constant pressure from the manufacturers, refused to licence it, recognising that the scientific evidence did not suggest it was safe.[12] Thalidomide, extoled as a wonder drug, was launched by the German company Chemie-Grünenthal in 1957 as a sedative to help with insomnia and also as a remedy for morning sickness during pregnancy. As reported by *The Guardian,* it said to have maimed 20,000 babies, many born with the characteristic foreshortened limbs, and killed up to 80,000 people.[13]

The piece in *The Guardian* was published as late as 2014 and is a remarkable piece of journalism by Harold Evans. It is both as disturbing and revealing as the Joseph Hickman accounts of Guantanamo Bay, and the parallels with Lariam and Roche seem far from coincidental. As in the American research programmes after the Second World War, Chemie-Grünenthal, founded by former-Nazi Hermann Wirtz in 1946, was not particularly choosy about the ethics and backgrounds of its researchers.

As *The Guardian* exposes, they included other ex-Nazis; Dr Heinrich Mückter, who had conducted medical experiments on prisoners in Polish labour camps, and Dr Martin Staemmler, who had been involved in Hitler's racial hygiene and eugenics programmes. And what is especially relevant for those damaged by Lariam, is the extent to which government and legal institutions, notably in Germany, thwarted the attempts of thalidomide victims (the word survivor seems utterly inappropriate) to get justice and to have those responsible held to account. Apparently, Hermann Wirtz was even able to combine Nazism with a devout Catholic family tradition. Perhaps he would also have defended the Holocaust as "an act of God." As I wrote these paragraphs the horrible irony of this chapter's title hit the pit of my stomach but, somehow, I feel it must stand.

I have little doubt that the utterly dishonourable treatment of thalidomide casualties gives succour and encouragement to the phalanx of lawyers that have now been deployed by Roche and governments around the world to defend both Lariam and how it has been marketed and imposed on unsuspecting users.

Globally, hundreds of cases, perhaps thousands, have been raised and some have even had successful outcomes. But they are the exceptions and in every case awards appear to be have been made by either making them conditional upon non-disclosure or they have been settled without any acceptance of legal liability.[14,15] Unfortunately, in the United Kingdom, time and the law do not stand in favour of serving or veteran litigants, factors that have been ruthlessly and cynically exploited by the MoD.

Unless you wish to sacrifice your career, it is very difficult for a serving soldier to sue the MoD. To use the well-worn phrase, most will loyally soldier on. And when you retire, by the time you begin to uncover what has been going on, it is probably going to be too late. Medical negligence claims are subject to a particular piece of legislation known as the Limitation Act of 1980.[16] In essence, from the date of the act of medical negligence, or from the date an injured party actually became aware of that negligence, the claim must be raised within three years.

For many medical negligence cases, the use of a time bar is probably reasonable; it would be quite unfair to make an individual or institution vulnerable to legal claims many years after the alleged act of negligence. But both the circumstances of military service and the years of cover-up make the Lariam story something out of the ordinary. Of course, the honourable and decent course of action for the MoD would be to waive objections on the grounds of time limitation for Lariam cases. But they won't do that. And now that Parliament exposed the negligence in 2016, I suspect that many cases brought after 2019 will be ruled as time barred.

However, there still remains the question as what should happen to Roche. The company withheld the vitally important prodromal warning for many years. I suspect the MoD might also have a credible case against the company: I wonder what Andrew Lansley, that Health Secretary who went to work for Roche, would advise either party. And I have often given thought to what a human rights lawyer might make of Roche's behaviour. I don't have sufficient funds to explore that avenue, but aren't patients, including those in uniform, entitled to expect that medications will not, unreasonably, expose them to the risk of death or pain?

But there was one other avenue that I did follow, although at some financial cost. I had long since learned that any claim I might have against the MoD had been compromised by my desire to alert them to the problem through non-public means. I'd certainly been suspicious of their negligence for a great deal more than three years. But it was only in 2016 that I had discovered that Roche had been withholding the prodromal warning from UK medical practitioners. Roche had either deliberately or mistakenly failed to alert British doctors about the full nature of Lariam's side effects. Surely a case against Roche wasn't time barred? So it was that in October 2017 I asked a solicitor to consider a case.

Eventually, more than a year later, my solicitor gained advice from a barrister which was far from encouraging. The advice he gave seemed very poorly researched and much was superficial and largely irrelevant. I was particularly dismayed to have to pay a substantial fee to be advised that Roche "had deep pockets." And I certainly have little reason to believe that the quality of the legal advice I was being given was much better than the clumsy spelling and grammar which attempted to describe it.[17]

What disturbed me most, however, was that the barrister declared that, "in the interests of transparency... I was employed by Roche in the early 1990s to work as a pharmaceutical representative, a position I held for a little over 2 years. I had no dealings with Lariam although I was aware of it." Apparently, he didn't see this as constituting any conflict of interest. I'm not sure that I agree, but you can only fight so many battles at one time and I had to pay his fee.

I pressed my solicitor to engage another barrister who might more properly investigate my case and, in March 2020, we had an interesting meeting in her chambers in The Temple, in London. It seemed the case did, indeed, have considerable merit and was one that this barrister felt she would have been keen to argue in court. But the Limitation Act remained the hurdle that could not be cleared, and that continues to surprise me, not least because of a particular section of the Act which I felt had been specifically drafted to help people like me. This is what Section 32 has to say:

*where in the case of any action for which a period of limitation is prescribed by this Act, either—*

> *(a)the action is based upon the fraud of the defendant; or*
> *(b)any fact relevant to the plaintiff's right of action has been deliberately concealed from him by the defendant; or*
> *(c)the action is for relief from the consequences of a mistake;*

*the period of limitation shall not begin to run until the plaintiff has discovered the fraud, concealment or mistake (as the case may be) or could with reasonable diligence have discovered it.*

Didn't the withholding of the warnings by Roche fall into one of these categories? Apparently not in my case. The legal position was that there was no relief here for veterans. The courts, the lawyers explained, would have expected me to have considered Roche as a potential defendant as early as 2009, even though I had no evidence or suspicions that the company had behaved negligently. The fact that the Defence Select Committee and the MHRA had equally been unaware of Roche's behaviour was, they said, irrelevant. They even went so far as to state that any lawyer counselling me about a potential claim against the MoD in those earlier years of 2009/10 had actually been negligent in not advising me to consider a claim against Roche.

It was my fault that I had not discovered the fraud, concealment or mistake, and I had apparently not applied "reasonable diligence" to discover it. Again, this was an expensive lesson to learn but I had at least exhausted the legal route. It seems extraordinary what the lay person is expected to know and I hope that Section 32 may one day be revised. The bar set for the interpretation of *reasonable diligence* seems to be set at an almost unachievable level.

———

The law was unable to help me pick up the pieces. And there was one other little aside that irked me as I left The Temple after our conference in those chambers that March afternoon shortly before Covid-19 caused the country to come to a standstill. I reminded the lawyers that my primary objective was not a financial settlement but that Roche should be brought to justice and that our wider campaign be vindicated. My solicitor's response was disappointing but profoundly revealing. Such altruism, he declared, was unappealing and generally lacked credibility. Was this legal objectivity or commercial cynicism? I guess we have differing views of the world and I'm just not prepared to compromise mine. I rather doubt if such people would quite understand how and why Dave Rimmington and Chris Small's widow, Mandy, have tried to cope, not by just getting their own lives back on track but also looking out for others they have never even met.

Mandy's response to her husband's suicide, like Jane Quinn's, has been quite inspirational and humbling. Mandy knows something of forces life, having served herself for twelve years in the RAF Police. Chris's final operational tour had been in Afghanistan in 2012 and when he returned to the family home in Germany he was, in many ways, unrecognisable. Chris then decided to leave the Army and the family came back to England. Chris's changed behaviours then caused them to split, Mandy moving to Suffolk with their son, Jamie, while Chris lived in the North East. Not long after, Chris was dead.

Mandy's first task was obvious; but how does a mother explain to an eight-year old boy what his father has just done, never mind why. No one had diagnosed PTSD and it was left to the family to attempt to work out what had happened. But thankfully the Armed Forces charity, SSAFA, (the Soldiers, Sailors, Airmen and Families Association) stepped in to help with this devastating crisis. A wonderful caseworker, Sue Cross, was there to sort the paperwork, help with the funeral and reach out a hand to a little boy in need of both material and emotional support. This is where all our service charities are at their best. Of Sue, Mandy simply says, "I'm not sure what we would have done without her."

A particular strength of Mandy is that she seems remarkably positive about the future. I have yet to meet her but have read and seen a lot in the press and TV media. Her mantra is "Not getting over it but getting through it" and that strikes me as a rather profound mix of military experience (which I know a little bit about) and a strong maternal determination (of which I know nothing but which Jane had displayed all those years ago on that awful night in West Linton in the Scottish Borders). Helping Jamie navigate all the emotions of his father's suicide must remain a huge part of her life but what is especially inspiring is how mother and son have picked up their lives with so little rancour and a determination to look forward and to remember the best of Chris.

Mandy credits Jamie with a mature head on strong young shoulders. She has taught him that there is no shame in opening up or shedding tears. And with a generosity of spirit that is quite extraordinary, both Mandy and Jamie have now turned tragedy into opportunity for others in crisis. Mandy is now an active fund raiser and has used multiple media opportunities to talk about her own experience and help others. Who knows how many have stepped back from the edge after hearing her talk.

For those whose families may be ripped apart like hers, she can offer hope, illuminate a path through the dark days of mourning and find a way to shed the wrongly-assumed mantle of guilt. And as for Jamie? His response has been to help those who helped him when he needed it. As a nine-year-old, he organised a SSAFA Fun Day at his school. A target of £200 was smashed by a total reaching nearly £6,000. He has had awards from SSAFA but probably the greatest accolade is this from his mum:

*The fact that we have been able to turn the worst experience of our lives into a way of helping others makes us extremely proud. I couldn't be prouder of Jamie; he really is a very special young man.*

Dave Rimmington is equally remarkable and one of the few positive outcomes of the Lariam scandal is that it has reaffirmed the quality of so many of the people who serve their country. They are team people. They look out for their buddies and will always want to do that bit more if a mate is in trouble or distress. It's probably part of the battle ethos— we rely on each other and we would never abandon a fallen casualty. I suspect that the further you get away from Whitehall and the MoD, the stronger and more enduring those instincts tend to be.

Dave got help, just in time, and he is returning that help in spades. Again, there is no bitterness. He is rightly proud, if typically modest, about his military career, a family tradition carried on by his son, Troy. I suspect there are a great many who have benefited from a social media virtual arm-around-the-shoulder from a sergeant major who has been there and survived. We will never know the number, but he has probably saved quite a few lives with his skilful and empathetic use of the various apps that can now reach out and catch the next Chris Small before tragedy strikes.

But he has also, quietly, engaged some of the people who matter and who might be able to make a difference. This has taken him into universities across England where he has enlightened some senior academics and researchers about the effects and likely causes of veteran mental ill-health, acquired brain injury and other neurological disorders. The list of his actions would make an impressive citation and they include the courage to publicly expose so much of his own life that most of us would want to keep private. But Dave is focused on the greater good.

An outstanding but little appreciated work stream has been with the NHS in his home county of Lincolnshire. The local NHS Trust has now been apprised of Lariam toxicity and I think they probably 'get it' at the coalface. But the institutional barriers are still there and the wider system is still resistant to ideas such as Lariam screening for sick veterans. Even at individual Trust level, there remains a major disincentive to address Lariam toxicity because it attracts no funds. It's PTSD that gets you the money. It's PTSD that fits all the research agendas, and especially those funded by the government.

But Dave is still working away, going to the next level, Kate Davies, who you will recall runs the NHS Commissioning for the Armed Forces. Perhaps she may find room for Dave's ideas within her zero-tolerance suicide strategy. Or is Lariam toxicity just another act of God? I suppose our ministers would echo Chemie-Grünenthal and say "He works in mysterious ways, His wonder-drugs to perform."

I have reached the bottom of my Lariam trench and I can now put my trowel aside. I've tried to make sense of the contexts, the drawings and all the finds. When presenting our evidence, I often find that archaeologists place themselves in tension with other academics, such as historians; my own view is that it's always much better when we work in tandem and collaborate. There is also a perfectly valid counterargument that tension is healthy and can itself stimulate better intellectual inquiry. But it's not tension I face with the government and Lariam apologists; it's denial and deceit.

For my part, and to paraphrase Jennifer Wallace, I think I have revealed what is inescapable when the general trend has been to evade responsibility.

# Chapter 12
## Coming Out of the Fog

*Among the calamities of war may be justly numbered the diminution of the love of truth, by the falsehoods which interest dictates and credulity encourages.*

*-Samuel Johnson, The Idler, 1758*

The eighteenth-century literary critic and essayist Samuel Johnson made the acerbic observation that truth was one of the primary casualties of war, although others have coined similar phrases. With the Lariam/WR 142 490 story, it has proved to be an enduring axiom, with honesty and integrity shrouded by veils of pharmaceutical and political fog. Lariam has certainly made its own unique contribution to what soldiers and military theorists describe as "the fog of war", both in theatres of conflict such as Afghanistan and in the legacy of the effects it has left in many of its victims. It has also profoundly undermined British military doctrine.[1]

The fog of war has exercised strategists for centuries although that particular phrase was probably only first published in 1896 by the Victorian soldier and *Times* correspondent Sir Lonsdale Augustus Hale.[2] The general concept is, however, more commonly attributed to the Prussian Carl von Clauswitz in his seminal work 'On War'.[3] This is what he says:

*The great uncertainty of all data in war is a peculiar difficulty, because all action must, to a certain extent, be planned in a mere twilight, which in addition not infrequently—like the effect of a fog or moonshine—gives to things exaggerated dimensions and an unnatural appearance.*

With regards to the wider Lariam debate, this quote is particularly apposite and could probably stimulate a full academic conference on the use of medicines on the battlefield. But to close, I would like to look at how the Lariam wounded and fallen can, at last, be brought out of the fog. It is time for them to come home. We can, and must, move towards positive outcomes and to that end we will visit three different continents. To begin, we need go no further than East Anglia and the home of Mandy Small in Suffolk, and from there, one day perhaps, take a relatively short drive across the Midlands to the National Memorial Arboretum, near Lichfield, in Staffordshire.

In 2019, Mandy attended the national Service of Remembrance in Whitehall, joining thousands of the Armed Forces community making their silent tributes to the fallen as they marched past the Cenotaph. Remembrance Sunday is the most solemn and dignified day in our country's calendar. My own memories of it stretch back to before I was ten years old, watching my father lead the marching contingent of the town's Royal British Legion, then still swelled by many Great War Veterans. We remembered the dead, but the pennies and half-crowns we donated for our poppies were to help the surviving wounded and others who had fallen on hard times.

In those days of the 1960s, the war-blinded, maimed and disfigured from the Somme and Ypres were still there, on the streets, maybe selling matches in their fading drab suits, but they remained peripheral except, perhaps, on this one day. On the other 364 days of the year, many people often looked the other way. And entirely out of sight were the mentally scarred. What was this thing called 'shell shock', anyway?

Mandy must have experienced an extraordinary flux of emotions on that crisp November morning. She had served herself and would be honouring her lost colleagues from the Royal Air Force, but Mandy would surely have had Chris foremost in her mind and her heart during the march-past.

Except for the dates of the Great War, the only inscription on the Cenotaph reads 'The Glorious Dead'. That's all; and everything. This memorial had been built for a war when the general policy was that the fallen would not be repatriated. Unlike the memorials in towns and villages across the country, it has no names, and it has served as a focus for memory for those unable to visit the war graves and memorials in the battlefields across Europe and the world. This all raises a particular emotional and moral difficulty in remembering all of our war dead. Where is Chris in this personal and collective act of remembrance and where can Mandy take Jamie to reflect on his father's service and struggles with his war wounds?

The concept of memorialisation has developed significantly over the past 100 years, as can be clearly seen by the variety and scope of sculptures and gardens across the site of the National Memorial Arboretum.[4] The purpose of the Arboretum, officially opened in 2001, is to commemorate those who served or sacrificed for the nation. Of almost 400 memorials on the site, the largest is, appropriately, that for the Armed Forces. The monuments, floral tributes and 25,000 trees planted over the 150 acres of its grounds reflect upon the contributions made across British society, now embracing the emergency services and a host of other bodies, such as the Women's Land Army. This would surely be the perfect place for Mandy and Jamie to remember Chris and, with others like her, she is quietly working to encourage the creation of a suitable locus of memory for those who later died from their wounds. It should, of course, acknowledge suicide and help to dispel the awful stigma it leaves behind.

This strikes me as a perfect metaphor for bringing all those men and women out of a dark remembrance no-man's-land where they have been left too long. Let them now be brought back into the service family and remembered among their comrades with honour and dignity. I said earlier that suicide is not painless. It's not. It remains, socially, an uncomfortable topic and I suspect there are those who would resist such a memorial—but why? Only recently, did we find room, physically and conceptually, for a memorial to the First World War's 'Shot at Dawn'. For a century, that subject had divided opinion across the country and across generations.

British deaths in the Great War were in excess of 720,000 and another 1,662,000 were wounded. Among the millions who served, there were a little over 3,000 death sentences delivered by courts martial, ninety percent of which were actually commuted.[5] In total, there were, in fact, 346 executions; 'the Shot at Dawn'. Most were shot for desertion (266), while what was cited as 'cowardice' accounted for eighteen. Thirty seven were executed for the capital offence of murder.[6] I don't offer any value judgement but, as I said a

318

couple of times in the opening chapter, things are never quite what they may seem. They are often complex, nuanced and often highly subjective. Of course the teenager, frozen by terror and unable to go over the top in 1916 must be remembered. But it is now time to bring in the others and recognise that Chris Small, Kate Fell-Crook, Cameron Quinn and Alastair Duncan were casualties, often suffering from the most insidious forms of 'friendly fire'. Perhaps one day, I could join Mandy and Jamie at the memorial they need and deserve. I could also say sorry to Chris for missing his call in 2016. He was only about fifteen miles away.

———

Just over 3,000 miles away, on the other side of the Atlantic Ocean, is White River Junction, Vermont, home to the Quinism Foundation, a not-for-profit charitable organisation established on 1 January 2018. You will recall that it was set up by its Executive Director, Dr Remington Nevin, whose work I have regularly cited throughout this book. In Chapter 7 we saw that his testimony, both oral and written, was crucial in steering the Defence Select Committee towards its vital recommendation that Lariam be relegated to a drug of last resort. His credentials are probably unrivalled as an epidemiologist and expert consultant in the adverse effects of antimalarial drugs.

This former US Army doctor, with service in theatres such as Djibouti, Korea and Afghanistan, has continued to develop an impressive and globally recognised academic profile. His recent Doctorate in Public Health from Johns Hopkins University has proved especially empowering. Now he is in the vanguard of research into the illnesses caused by Lariam and similar drugs, a responsibility that has largely been abdicated by governments across the world.

Chapter 2 showed us how toxicity was being signalled, yet too often missed or simply ignored, in the earlier development of antimalarial drugs. Dr Nevin has now defined that toxicity, in a group of symptoms which typically present themselves, as 'quinism'. Thus medical science has been provided with a highly credible and immensely valuable clinical descriptor. The medical disorder arising from poisoning by mefloquine, tafenoquine, chloroquine and related quinoline drugs is quinism.

A vitally important element of Dr Nevin's work is that he has advanced both the debate and the lexicon of these illnesses, freeing them from the arbitrary constraints of the more convenient term of 'side effects'. Those made ill by these drugs are presenting symptoms, *not* side effects. To quote Dr Nevin, those who suffer from a range of conditions, such as dizziness, vertigo, visual disturbances, nightmares, cognitive dysfunction or suicidal thoughts, are often experiencing symptoms:

> *of poisoning by a class of drug that is neurotoxic and that injures brain and brainstem. This poisoning has a name: chronic quinoline encephalopathy—also known as quinism.*

Furthermore, as we have already seen, many of the symptoms of quinism can mimic those of several psychiatric and neurological disorders, including PTSD and traumatic brain injury.[7] The work of the Quinism Foundation is especially liberating on two fronts. From a personal perspective, I take great reassurance from having my own illness classified and recognised for what it is. I suspect this is something I share with Dave Rimmington and _____. And when the scales finally fall from the eyes of clinicians in the United Kingdom, perhaps those dealing with these quinoline-related injuries will feel that they will (perhaps must) begin to make etiological diagnoses. Meanwhile, the Quinism Foundation is taking the lead on the vitally important work that must logically proceed from the identification of what I am going to loosely describe as the Lariam disease. Here are some of the Foundation's objectives.

*Preparing healthcare organisations to identify those exposed to quinolines and screen for symptomatic quinoline exposure.*

*Advance the clinical diagnosis of chronic quinoline encephalopathy and other conditions caused by quinoline poisoning.*

*Facilitate research to enable clinicians to distinguish quinism from other disorders such as PTSD and Traumatic brain injury.*

*Identify risk factors for the disease.*

*Support research for effective treatments.*

These all remain absent from the research agendas in the United Kingdom. Why? The science is there. We deserve better and need something beyond the NHS 'zero tolerance to suicide' sound bite and its insertion into in-vogue business and management tools such as balanced score cards.

Thankfully, a sound research model has been established and it can only gain more traction as the fog eventually disperses.

———

In 2008, the year when, as a novice archaeologist, I first scraped a trowel over some Roman and Iron Age remains outside York, Jane Quinn took her young family to Australia, departing the land which Lloyd George wanted to make "a fit country for heroes to live in."[8] In one of life's bitter ironies, she quickly discovered that she had not left the horrors of Cameron's death back in the quiet village of West Linton in the Scottish Borders. Australian soldiers had, she learned, been just as badly affected by Lariam when they were called upon to serve abroad, and notably those in contingents deployed to East Timor. Worse, many had been duped into participation in trials in 1999-2000 of the next antimalarial quinoline, tafenoquine. Tafenoquine damage, unsurprisingly, proved remarkably similar to that caused by Lariam.[9,10]

What went on in East Timor could fill another book, as, indeed, might the use of Lariam by the Canadian Armed Forces in Somalia and Afghanistan. After the behaviour of our own service chiefs and ministers, no one could have blamed Jane if she had felt that she had had enough. But I guess a flame of Cameron still burned and, as we saw, she retains the 'Bydand' spirit. Of all those involved in the sordid Lariam tale, in many ways she must speak with the utmost authority. Not only had she earned that right on 11 March 2006, she was now carving out a career as a clinical neurotoxicologist. The extent of the support she has afforded damaged communities worldwide is clear from the evidence she has given to national legislatures and especially in testimony to the Canadian and Australian parliaments.[11,12]

But Jane hasn't stopped there. She has stepped in to help across a number of fronts. She is the scientific adviser to the Australian Quinoline Veterans Families Association and is also a member of the 'Open Arms' Neurocognitive Health Programme Steering Committee. Open Arms is Australia's leading provider of mental health assessment and counselling for their country's veterans and their families.[13] Unlike in Great Britain, and thanks to Jane, these bodies have their arms open for people who know about Lariam. It's not just about PTSD.

So let's give the last word to Jane. In her evidence to the Australian Parliament she reminded us that this is not about whether malaria is a deadly disease.[14] We know it is. Nor is it about whether new treatments are necessary. We know they are. But our story is very much about how new drugs should be developed and deployed. The extraordinary tafenoquine trials gave Australian soldiers a double-whammy of quinism yet that drug is slowly emerging into the world markets. Of tafenoquine, Jane said:

*The past is an issue, but the future also worries me greatly.*

That was in 2018 and she was worried about quinolines. (No one had yet heard of Covid-19.)

# Chapter Notes

## Chapter 1

1. The Royal Irish Rangers Regimental Association.
2. BBC News (2003).
3. Roche UK (2003).

## Chapter 2

1. The Lariam Legacy, BBC (2015).
2. MacLean, D, S (2014).
3. Public Health England (2014).
4. NHS UK Malaria Overview (2018).
5. World Health Organisation (2019a).
6. CDC (2018).
7. CDC (2018).
8. Rénia et al (2012).
9. Weina, P, A (1998).
10. Achan et al (2011).
11. Noon, G (2001).
12. Mefloquine: The anti-malarial drug investigation (2017).
13. National Museum, United States Army (2020).
14. Pages et al (2010).
15. Slim, W (2009).
16. National Museum, United States Army (2020).
17. National Museum, United States Army (2020).
18. Weina, P, A (1998).
19. Nevin, R, L (2019).
20. The Washington Post (1979).

21. Andrews, J, M (1963).

22. US Army (1945).

23. Rooney, D (2003).

24. Nevin, R, L (2019).

25. Masters, J (1979).

26. Pappas, M (2019).

27. Danchev, A and Todman, D (2001).

28. Owen, J and Walters, G (2004).

29. Owen, J and Walters, G (2004).

30. Pou et al (2012).

31. WRAIR (2018).

32 WRAIR (2020).

33. U.S. Food & Drug Administration (2020).

34. The New York Times (2020).

35. World Health Organisation (1983).

36. Croft, A, M (2007).

37. World Health Organisation (2001).

38. Trenholme et al (1975).

39. Clyde et al (1976).

40. Trenholme et al (1975).

41. Harcourt, B, E (2011).

42. Harcourt, B, E (2011).

43. CBS Baltimore (2014).

44. Croft, A, M (2007).

45. Croft, A, M (2007).

46. USAMMDA (2020).

47. MHRA (2017).

48. Croft, A, M (2007).

49. Overbosch et al (2001).

50. Stateville Correctional Center (2020).

51. Foucault, M (1991).

52. The Lake County Star (2020).

53. Encyclopaedia Britannica (2019).

54. Baatz, S (2008).

55. Comfort, N (2009).

**Chapter 3**

1. Ellis, C, J (2004).
2. World Health Organisation (2019b).
3. SPVA (2009).
4. WPA (2009).
5. Bathie, P (2020).
6. OED (2011).
7. Elsea, J, K and Else, D, H, (2017).
8. Hickman, J (2016).
9. The New York Times (2006).
10. Denbeaux et al (2011).
11. Nevin, R, L (2012a).
12. Denbeaux et al (2011).
13. Project MKULTRA, The CIA's program of Research in Behavioral Modification (1977).
14. Project MKULTRA, The CIA's program of Research in Behavioral Modification (1977)
15. Ghooi, R, B (2011).
16. Ketchum, J, S and Salem, H (2008).
17. The New Yorker (2012).
18. Ketchum, J, S (2006).
19. Voice of America (2001).

**Chapter 4**

1. Wallace, J (2004).
2. Croft, A, M (2007).

**Chapter 5**

1. Mefloquine: The anti-malarial drug investigation (2017).

2. Gov.UK (2015).

3. Galbraith S, N (2006).

4. Defence Medical Services (2004).

5 Terrell et al (2015).

6 Hansard (1997).

7. Mefloquine: The anti-malarial drug investigation (2017).

8. R v Ministry of Defence, ex parte Murray 1997.

9. Galbraith, S, N (2000a).

10. Galbraith, S, N (2000b).

11. Galbraith, S, N (2000a).

12. Galbraith, S, N (2000a).

13. Fraser, N (2000).

14. Eastwell, I, C (2006).

15. House of Commons (2001).

16. Quinn, J (2006).

17. Green, A, R (2006).

18. Braidwood, A (2015).

19. MHRA (2017a)

20. Croft, A, M (2016).

21. Dannatt, R (2010).

22. The Independent (2013).

23. Eastern Daily Press (2010).

24. Ministry of Defence (2016a).

25. Victoria Derbyshire BBC Two (2016).

**Chapter 6**

1. Andrew Marr Show (2011).

2. Roche US (2002).

3. Roche US (2003).

4. Marriott, A (2009).

5. WPA (2009).

6. Information Commissioner (2010).

7. Haig, W (2010).

8. Iraq Inquiry (2016).

9. Hutton Report (2004).

10. BBC News (2011).

11. The Guardian (2017).

12. Thames Valley Police (2017).

13. Goslett, M (2018).

14. Surgeon General (2009).

15. Surgeon General (2010).

16. Croft, A, M (2007).

17. The Observer (2000).

18. The Sunday Telegraph (2009).

19. Fox, L (2010).

20. Haig, W (2014).

21. Jones, K (2009).

22. Hansard (2012).

23. Fallon, M (2015).

24. Croft, A, M (2007).

25. Overbosch et al (2001).

26. HSCIC (2015).

27. Andersson et al (2008)

28. Nevin, R, L (2012b).

29. Irish Medicines Board (2013).

30. Time (2013).

31. Nevin, R, L (2015a).

32. EMA (2014).

33. EMA (2014).

34. They Work For You (2020).

35. The Sunday Times (2018).

36. Humer, F, B (2007).

37. Hansard (1996).

38. The Independent (1997).

39. BMJ (2015).

40. Nevin, R, L (2012a).

41. Hickman, J (2016).

42. Katznelson, Z, P (2006).

43. Harris, P (2015).

44. BBC News (2017a).

45. Harris, P (2015).

46. The Independent (2017).

**Chapter 7**

1. House of Commons (2016).

2. Duncan, E (2015).

3. House of Commons (2014).

4. Gov.UK (2020).

5. Mercer, J (2015).

6. Terrell et al (2015).

7. The Northern Echo (2017a).

8. BBC News (2017b).

9. Defence Committee (2015a).

10. Adshead, S (2014).

11. BBC News (2015).

12. Ministry of Defence (2016b).

13. Grabowski, P and Behrens, R, H (1996).

14. Behrens, R, H (1998).

15. Defence Committee (2015a).

16. Green, A, R (2006).

17. MHRA (2010).

18. Parliament UK (2014a).

19. Defence Committee (2016).

20. Ministry of Defence (2016c).

21. Public Health England (2014).

22. Defence Committee (2016).

23. Defence Committee (2015b).

24. Parliament UK (2014b).

25. Croft, A and Nevin, R (2016).

26. GMC (2016).

27. Roche UK (2015).

28. Humer, F, B (2007).

29. Defence Committee (2015b).

30. House of Commons (2016).

31. EMA (2014).


**Chapter 8**


1. EPA (2019).

2. BBC News (2020).

3. Roche US (2002).

4. Roche UK (2012).

5. Roche UK (2003).

6. Roche UK (2014).

7. The Independent (2013).

8. RTÉ (2013).

9. Monckton Chambers (2015).

10. MHRA (2017b).

11. Lobel et al (1991).

12. USA V Edward Mezvinsky (2002).

13. USA v Edward Mezvinsky (2002).

14. FDA (2003).

15. Roche UK (1991).

16. Winkenwerder, W (2002).

17. US Africa Command (2011).

18. House of Commons (2016).

19. CDC (2002).

20. Mefloquine: The anti-malarial drug investigation (2017).

21. Roche UK (2016).

22. Hodgetts, T (2016).

23. Chatham House (2020).

24. Roche UK (1991).

25. MHRA (2018).

26. Public Health England (2017).

## Chapter 10

1. Defence Committee (2015a).
2. The Daily Mail (2015).
3. Rhyl Journal (2015).
4. Rhyl Journal (2018).
5. The Daily Mail (2015).
6. Roche UK (2005).
7. Rhyl Journal (2018).
8. The Coroners (Investigations) Regulations (2013).
9. The Northern Echo (2017b).
10. Forces Net (2016).
11. Marriott, A, G (2015).
12. Ministry of Defence (2017).
13. Ministry of Justice (2017).
14. Johnny Mercer (2019).
15. The Times (2019).
16. The Daily Telegraph (2019).
17. The Sunday Telegraph (2019).
18. Milton Keynes Coroner (2020).
19. The Daily Post (2020).
20. Ministry of Justice (2018).
21. Croft, A, M (2016).

## Chapter 11

1. The Guardian (2014).
2. Wallace, J (2004).
3. Defence Committee (2018).
4. Cochrane (2020).
5. OED (2011).
6. Combat Stress (2017).
7. Combat Stress (2020).
8. Help for Heroes (2020).

9. RBL (2017).

10. Nevin, R, L (2015b).

11. Gov.UK (2019).

12. FDA (2020).

13. The Guardian (2014).

14. The Times (2015).

15. The Times (2018).

16. Limitation Act (1980).

17. 3PB (2018).


**Chapter 12**


1. Bathie, P (2020).

2. Hale, A, S (1896).

3. Clauswitz, C von ([1832] 1997).

4. NMA (2020).

5. National Archives (2015).

6. War Office (1922).

7. Quinism Foundation (2020)

8. Lloyd George, D ([1929] 1918).

9. Mefloquine: The anti-malarial drug investigation (2017).

10. Hansard, Commonwealth of Australia (2018).

11. House of Commons, Chambre Des Communes, Canada (2019).

12. Hansard, Commonwealth of Australia (2018).

13. Open Arms (2020).

14. Hansard, Commonwealth of Australia (2018).

# Bibliography

Achan, J., Talisuna, A. O., Erhart, A., Yeka, A., Tibenderana, J. K., Baliraine, F. N., Rosenthal, P. J. and D'Alessandro, U. (2011) 'Quinine, an old anti-malarial drug in a modern world: role in the treatment of malaria', *Malaria Journal,* 10 (144).

Adshead, S. (2014) The adverse effects of mefloquine in deployed military personnel. Journal of the Royal Navy Medical Services, 2014. 100(3) 232-7.

Andersson H., Askling H. H., Falck B. and Rombo L. (2008) 'Well-Tolerated Chemoprophylaxis Uniformly Prevented Swedish soldiers from *Plasmodium falciparum* Malaria in Liberia, 2004-2006', *Military Medicine*, 173(12) 1194-8.

Andrews, J. M. (1963) 'Chapter V. North Africa, Italy, and the Islands of the Mediterranean', in E C Hoff (ed) *Preventive Medicine in World War II, Vol 6. Communicable Diseases. Malaria.* US Army Medical Department.

Baatz, S. (2008) 'Leopold and Loeb's Criminal Minds. In defence of murderers Leopold and Loeb, attorney Clarence Darrow thwarted a nations call for vengeance', *Smithsonian Magazine,* August 2008
https://www.smithsonianmag.com/history/leopold-and-loebs-criminal-minds-996498/ Page accessed 27 May 2020.

Bathie, P. (2020) 'Military Safety: A Systems Perspective on Lariam', *The RUSI Journal*, DOI: 10.1080/03071847.2020.1755107.

Behrens, R. H. (1998) British Medical Journal, Letters. Mefloquine to prevent malaria. Interpretation of study was not based on evidence. BMJ 316, 1980. 27 June 1998.
BMJ (2015) This Week. Lansley takes role with Roche https://www.bmj.com/bmj/section-pdf/909535?path=/bmj/351/8034/This_Week.full.pdf Page accessed 7 August 2020.

Braidwood, A. (2015) A note on mefloquine (Lariam) CDP medical adviser, 21 September 2015.

CDC (2002) Fax Distribution, Richard Steketee, Chief, malaria Epidemiology Branch, Parasitic Diseases, CDC, Expert Mtg. On Malaria Chemoprophylaxis, 1/29-30/03, dated December 11 2002.

CDC (2018) Centres for Disease Control and Prevention 'Malaria, Biology, Lifecycle' https://www.cdc.gov/malaria/about/biology/index.html#:~:te xt=The%20malaria%20parasite%20life%20cycle,(Of%20no te%2C%20in%20P. Page accessed 7 July 2020.

Chatham House (2020) Chatham House Rule https://www.chathamhouse.org/chatham-house-rule?gclid=EAIaIQobChMIguCxqonh6wIVjbLVCh263w1b EAAYASAAEgKDWvD_BwE Page accessed 11 September 2020.

Clauswitz, von C. (1997) On War. (Abridged and edited by L Willmot.) Ware: Wordsworth Editions Ltd.

Clyde D. F., McCarthy V. C., Miller R. M. and Hornick R. B. (1976) 'Suppressive activity of mefloquine in sporozoite-induced human malaria', *Antimicrobial Agents Chemother* 9:384–6

Cochrane (2020) Cochrane. About Us. https://www.cochrane.org/about-us Page accessed 29 September 2020.

Combat Stress (2017) *Annual Report and Accounts, 2017.*

Combat Stress (2020) Combat Stress. For Veterans' Mental Health. https://www.combatstress.org.uk/ Page accessed 30 September 2020.

Comfort, N. (2009) 'The prisoner as model organism: malaria research at Stateville Penitentiary', *Studies in History and Philosophy of Biological and Biomedical Sciences,* 40, 190-203.

Croft, A. M. (2007) 'A lesson learnt: the rise and fall of Lariam and Haflan', *Journal of the Royal Society of Medicine,* 100, 170-174.

Croft, A. M. (2016) 'Opportunities missed to review mefloquine use in the UK military', *The Pharmaceutical Journal,* 297, No 7894, online DOI: 10.1211/PJ.2016.20201729.

Croft, A. and Nevin, R. (2016) Joint scientific response to oral evidence from the Ministry of Defence, given on 12th January 2016. 8 February 2016.

Danchev, A. and Todman, D. (2001) *War Diaries 1939-1945. Field Marshal Lord Alanbrooke.* London: Weidenfeld and Nicolson.

Dannatt, R. (2010) *Leading from the Front. The Autobiography.* London: Bantam Press.

Defence Committee (2015a) House of Commons Defence Committee. Oral evidence: An acceptable risk? The use of Lariam for military personnel, HC 567. Tuesday 8 December 2015.

Defence Committee (2015b) House of Commons Defence Committee. Oral evidence: An acceptable risk? The use of Lariam for military personnel, HC 567. Tuesday 10 November 2015.

Defence Committee (2016) House of Commons Defence Committee. Oral evidence: An acceptable risk? The use of Lariam for military personnel, HC 567. Tuesday 12 January 2016.

Defence Committee (2018) House of Commons Defence Committee. Oral evidence: Armed Forces and veteran's mental health, HC 813. Tuesday 27 March 2018.

Defence Medical Services (2004) Surgeon General's Policy Letter 10/04. Preventing Malaria in Military Populations. DMSD/370/2, 13 May 2004.

Denbeaux, M., Camoni, S., Beroth, B., Chrisner, M., Loyer, C., Stout, K. and Taylor, S. (2011) *Drug Abuse. An exploration of the government's use of mefloquine at Guantanamo.* Seton Hall University School of Law, Center for Policy & Research. Paper No 2010-33.

Duncan, E. (2015) Written Evidence to the Defence Committee submitted by Mrs Ellen Duncan, wife of Major General A D A Duncan, CBE, DSO, 30 November 2015.

Eastwell, I. C. (2006) Letter Directorate of Safety and Claims Ministry of Defence D/DS&C/12/2/l (Z) dated 29 August 2006.

Ellis, C. J. (2004) Letter CJE/LMB/1118636 dated 7 April 2004, C J Ellis, Consultant Physician, Department of Infection and Tropical Medicine, Birmingham Heartlands Hospital.

Elsea, J. K. and Else, D. H. (2017) Naval Station Guantanamo Bay: History and Legal Issues Regarding Its Lease Agreements. Congressional Research Service.

EMA (2014) European Medicines Agency. Updated PRAC rapporteur assessment report on the signal of permanent neurologic (vestibular) disorders with mefloquine. EMA/63963/2014. 31 January 2014.

Encyclopaedia Britannica (2019) *Leopold and Loeb. American Murderers.* https://www.britannica.com/biography/Leopold-and-Loeb#ref632975 Page accessed 27 May 2020.

EPA (2019) United States Environmental Protection Agency. Volkswagen Violations. https://www.epa.gov/vw/learn-about-volkswagen-violations Page accessed 4 November 2020.

FDA (2003) Form FDA 483 Inspectional Observations (Brown, Kelahan and Isbill), date issued 1/9/03. (9 Jan 2003).

FDA (2020) US Food & Drug Administration 'Frances Oldham Kelsey: Medical reviewer famous for averting a public health tragedy' https://www.fda.gov/about-fda/virtual-exhibits-fda-history/frances-oldham-kelsey-medical-reviewer-famous-averting-public-health-tragedy Page accessed 2 October 2020.

Fallon, M. (2015) Letter to William Haig D/S of S/MF MCSOS2015/01346e dated 25 February 2015.

Foucault, M. (1991) *Discipline and Punish. The Birth of the Prison (Translated by A Sheridan).* London: Penguin Books.

Fox, L. (2010) Letter to William Haig D/S of S/LF MC03944/2010 dated 13 October 2010.

Fraser, N. (2000) 'Been there, done that...' *Journal of the Royal Army Medical Corps,* 146, 254-255.

Galbraith, S. N. (2000a) 'Medico-Legal Issues Surrounding Medical Countermeasures Used in the Gulf War— Part 1', *Journal of the Royal Army Medical Corps,* 146, 33-36.

Galbraith, S. N. (2000b) 'Medico-Legal Issues Surrounding Medical Countermeasures Used in the Gulf War— Part 2', *Journal of the Royal Army Medical Corps,* 146, 104-109.

Galbraith, S. N. (2006) Letter 539025 QUINN C J M (DECEASED) D/AMD/Med Leg/16575(R) dated 3 July 2006.

Ghooi, R. B. (2011) 'The Nuremberg Code—A Critique', *Perspectives in Clinical Research,* 2 (2), 72-76.

GMC (2016) email Fitness to Practice. RB/1-1509443633, 28 November 2016, 9.42.

Goslett, M. (2018) *An Inconvenient Death. How the Establishment Covered Up the David Kelly Affair.* London: Head of Zeus.

Gov.UK (2019) Guidance. Mefloquine information signposting service for former and serving personnel. https://www.gov.uk/government/publications/mefloquine-advice-service-for-former-and-serving-personnel/mefloquine-advice-service-for-former-and-serving-personnel#what-should-i-do-if-i-have-concerns-

about-my-experience-of-mefloquine    Page    accessed    30
September 2020.

Gov.UK (2020) Parliamentary Under Secretary of State
(Minister for Defence People and Veterans) Johnny Mercer
MP, Biography.
https://www.gov.uk/government/people/johnny-mercer Page
accessed 26 August 2020.

Grabowski, P. and Behrens, R. H. (1996) Provision of health
information by British travel agents. *Tropical Medicine and
International Health,* 1 (5), 730-732.

Green, A. R. (2006) Letter DMSD/13/1/1 dated 28 November
2006.

Green, A. R. (2007) Letter DMSD/13/1/ dated 26 March
2007.

Haig, W. (2010) Letter, House of Commons, dated 15 January
2010.

Haig, W. (2014) Letter, House of Commons, dated 2014.

Hale, L. A. (1896) *The Fog of War.* London: Edward
Stanford.

Hansard (1996) Gulf War Illness. The Minister of State for
the Armed Forces (Mr Nicholas Soames)
https://hansard.parliament.uk/commons/1996-12-
10/debates/a17ea838-252d-4e5b-b305-

2b73e256dd9f/GulfWarIllness#132 Page accessed 7 August 2020.

Hansard (1997) HC Debate 12 March vol 292 cc 471-8. Ms Jean Cortson (Bristol East).
https://api.parliament.uk/historic-hansard/commons/1997/mar/12/lariam Paged accessed 20 July 2020.

Hansard (2012) Debate. Mental Health. 14 June 2012. Volume 546. https://hansard.parliament.uk/commons/2012-06 14/debates/12061445000002/MentalHealth Page accessed 13 August 2020.

Hansard, Commonwealth of Australia (2018) FOREIGN AFFAIRS, DEFENCE AND TRADE REFERENCES COMMITTEE. Use of the quinoline antimalarial drugs mefloquine and tafenoquine in the Australian Defence Force. Monday 5 November 2018.

Harcourt, B. E. (2011) 'Making Willing Bodies: The University of Chicago Malaria Experiments on Prisoners at Stateville Penitentiary', *Working Paper Series, The Department of Political Science, the University of Chicago,* 1, 1-24.

Harris, P. (2015) 'America's Other Guantanamo: British Foreign Policy and the US Base on Diego Garcia', *The Political Quarterly,* 86 (4), 507-514.

Help for Heroes (2020) Help for Heroes. The Leading Charity for the Armed Forces Community. https://www.helpforheroes.org.uk/ Page accessed 30 September 2020.

Hickman, J. (2016) *Murder at Camp Delta. A Staff Sergeant's Pursuit of the Truth About Guantanamo Bay.* London: Simon and Schuster.

Hodgetts, T. (2016) email MTG MOD & ROCHE IN PREPARATION FOR HCDC. SG-DMed-MedD-D (Hodgetts, Timothy Brig) 05 January 2016 12:03.

House of Commons (2001) Select Committee on Defence First Special Report. Appendix 20. Memorandum from the Ministry of Defence concerning medical preparedness for deployments to Sierra Leone (25 July 2000). https://publications.parliament.uk/pa/cm200001/cmselect/cm dfence/177/17769.htm Page accessed 27 July 2020.

House of Commons (2014) Early Day Motion, Mefloquine Hydrochloride. EDM 257. Tabled 14 July 2014. https://edm.parliament.uk/early-day-motion/47090/mefloquine-hydrochloride Page accessed 26 August 2020.

House of Commons (2016) Defence Committee. An acceptable risk? The use of Lariam for military personnel. Fourth Report of Session 2015-16. 10 May 2016.

House of Commons, Chambre Des Communes, Canada (2019) EFFECTS OF MEFLOQUINE USE AMONG CANADIAN VETERANS, Report of the Standing Committee on Veterans Affairs. June 2019 42nd Parliament, 1st Session.

HSCIC (2015) Health and Social Care Information Centre FOI Request. NIC-351837-KOJOR dated 18 June 2015.

Humer, F. B. (2007) Minutes of the 89th Annual General Meeting of the Shareholders of ROCHE HOLDING LTD, Basel Held at 10.30 a.m. on 5 March 2007 at the Convention Centre, Basel Trade Fair Complex, Basel.

Hutton Report (2004) *Report of the Inquiry into the Circumstances Surrounding the Death of Dr David Kelly C.M.G. by Lord Hutton.* Ordered by the House of Commons to printed 28th January 2004. HC 247.

Information Commissioner (2010) Case Reference Number FS50294261 dated 22 March 2010.
Iraq Inquiry (2016) The Report of the Iraq Inquiry. Executive Summary. Report of a Committee of Privy Counsellors. Ordered by the House of Commons to be printed on 6 July 2016. HC 264.

Irish Medicines Board (2013) Letter, Irish medicines Board FOI 13.02/002 dated 25 April 2013.

Jones, K. (2009) Letter D/Min(Veterans)/KJ MC04583/2009 dated 21 November 2009.

Kamieński, L. (2017) *Shooting Up. A History of Drugs in Warfare.* London: Hurst & Co.

Katznelson, Z. P. (2006) Declaration of Zachary Philip Katznelson, Austin, Texas, dated September 19 2006.

Ketchum, J. S. (2006) *Chemical Warfare. Secrets almost Forgotten. A Personal Story of Medical Testing of Army Volunteers with Incapacitating Chemical Agents During the Cold War (1955-1975).* Santa Rosa: ChemBooks Inc.

Ketchum, J. S. and Salem, H. (2008) 'Incapacitating Agents' in S D Tuorinsky (ed) *Medical Aspects of Chemical Warfare,* 411-439. Borden Institute, Walter Reed Army Medical Center.

Limitation Act (1980) An Act to consolidate the Limitations Acts 1939 to 1980. 13th November 1980.
https://www.legislation.gov.uk/ukpga/1980/58 Page accessed 4 October 2020.

Livingstone, D. (2015) *Transhumanism: The History of a Dangerous Idea.* Sabilillah Publications.

Lloyd George, D. (1929) *Slings and Arrows. Sayings from the Speeches of The Rt Hon David Lloyd George, OM, MP. (Edited by Philip Guedella).* London: Cassell and Company Ltd.
Lobel, H. O., Bernard, K. W., Williams, S. L., Hightower, A. W., Patchen, L. C. and Campbell, C. C. (1991) 'Effectiveness and Tolerance of Long-term Malaria Prophylaxis with

Mefloquine. Need for a Better Dosing Regime.' *Journal of the American Medical Association,* 256, 3.

MacLean, D. S. (2014). *The Answer to the Riddle is Me: A Memoir of Amnesia.* New York: Houghton Mifflin Harcourt.

Marriott, A. G. (2009). Letter, Freedom of Information Inquiry dated 4 August 2009.

Marriott, A. G. (2015) Letter to General Sir Nicholas Houghton, Chief of Defence Staff, 22 April 2015.

Masters, J. (1979) *The Road Past Mandalay.* London: Bantam Books.

MHRA (2010) FOI 10-457/GENQ-00073673 dated 31 December 2010.

MHRA (2017a) FOI 17/069 Lariam/Mefloquine Antimalarials, 15 March 2017.

MHRA (2017b) FOI 17/201 Lariam/Mefloquine Antimalarials, 20 June 2017.

MHRA (2018) Letter, Dr June Raine/Marriott, Director Vigilance and Risk Management, dated 28 February 2018.

Milton Keynes Coroner (2020) Milton Keynes Senior Coroner Regulation 28 Report dated 5 August 2020.

Ministry of Defence (2016a) Freedom of Information FOI12016/08283 dated 3 October 2016.

Ministry of Defence (2016b) Freedom of Information FOI2015/11300 dated 12 January 2016.

Ministry of Defence (2016c) Ad Hoc Statistical Bulletin. Mefloquine Hydrochloride prescribing in the UK Armed Forces, 1 April 2007—31 March 2015. Dated 12 January 2016.

Ministry of Defence (2017) email Meeting 03 August 2017 Richmond House MR02. MoD People-CDP-ExO. Dated 24 August 2017 at 15:04.

Ministry of Justice (2017) Freedom of Information Act (FOIA) Request—113992 dated 11 September 2017.

Ministry of Justice (2018) Coroner's Reports. Letter MoJ ref: MC54582 dated 22 March 2018.

Monckton Chambers (2015) Medicines Regulator's Inspection of Roche was lawful, says Court of Appeal. https://www.monckton.com/medicines-regulators-inspection-of-roche-was-lawful-says-court-of-appeal/ Page accessed 28 February 2020.


National Archives (2015) Courts Martial.

http://www.nationalarchives.gov.uk/pathways/firstworldwar/ service_records/courts_martial.htm Page accessed 20 May 2015.

National Museum, United States Army (2020). The Other Foe: The US Army's Fight against malaria in the Pacific Theatre, 1942-45.
https://armyhistory.org/about-the-museum/ Page accessed 8 July 2020.

Nevin, R. L. (2012a) 'Mass administration of the antimalarial drug mefloquine to Guantanamo detainees: a critical analysis', *Tropical Medicine and International Health,* 17 (10) 1281-1288.

Nevin, R. L. (2012b) 'Limbic encephalopathy and central vestibulopathy caused by mefloquine: A case report', *Travel Medicine and Infectious Disease,* (2012), doi:10.1016/j.tmaid.2012.03.006.

Nevin, R. L. (2015a) 'Rational Risk-Benefit Decision-Making in the Setting of Military Mefloquine Policy', *Journal of Parasitology Research*, Volume 2015, Article ID 260106, 8 pages http://dx.doi.org/10.1155/2015/260106.

Nevin, R. L. (2015b) 'Mefloquine and posttraumatic stress disorder' in E C Ritchie (ed) *Forensic and ethical issues in military behavioural health.* 277-296. Washington: Borden Institute.

Nevin, R. L. (2019) 'Neuropsychiatric Quinism: Chronic Encephalopathy Caused by Poisoning by Mefloquine and Related Quinoline Drugs' in: E Ritchie E and M Llorente (eds) *Veteran Psychiatry in the US.* 317-331. Cham: Springer

NHS UK Malaria Overview (2018) https://www.nhs.uk/conditions/malaria/ Page accessed 18 May 2020.

NMA (2020) The National Arboretum Memorial. Memorials. https://www.thenma.org.uk/related?tag=Remembrance Page accessed 2020.

Noon, G. (2001) 'Military Medicine' in R Holmes (ed) *The Oxford Companion to Military History.* 563-566. Oxford: Oxford University Press.

OED (2011) *Concise Oxford English Dictionary, Twelfth Edition, 2011.* Oxford: Oxford University Press.

Open Arms (2020) Open Arms Veterans and Families Counselling, About. https://www.openarms.gov.au/about Page accessed 3 November 2020.

Overbosch, D., Schilthuis, H., Bienzle, U., Behrens, R. H., Kain, K. C., Clarke, P. D., Toovey, S., Knobloch, J., Nothdurft, H. D., Shaw, D., Roskell, N. S., Chulay, J. D. and the Malarone International Study Team (2001) 'Atovaquone-Proguanil versus Mefloquine for Malaria Prophylaxis in

Nonimmune Travelers: Results from a Randomized, Double-Blind Study', *Clinical Infectious Diseases,* 33, 1015-21.

Owen, J. and Walters, G. (2004) *The Voice of War. The Second World War Told by Those Who Fought It.* London: Viking.

Pages, F., Faulde, N., Orlandi-Pradines, E. and Parola, P. (2010) 'The past and present threat of vector-borne diseases in deployed', *Clinical Microbiology and Infection,* 16 (3), 209-224.

Pappas, M. (2019) General Orde Wingate: Brilliant Eccentric. https://www.warhistoryonline.com/history/general-orde-wingate.html Page accessed 19 May 2020.

Parliament UK (2014a) Armed Forces: Malaria: Written question—215391. Asked 20 November 2014. Answered 26 November 2014.
https://www.parliament.uk/business/publications/written-questions-answers-statements/written-question/Commons/2014-11-20/215391/ Page accessed 1 September 2020.

Parliament UK (2014b) Armed Forces: Mefloquine: Written question HL2901. Asked 18 November 2014. Answered 1 December 2014.
https://www.parliament.uk/business/publications/written-questions-answers-statements/written-question/Lords/2014-11-18/HL2901 Page accessed 1 September 2020.

Pou, S., Winter, R. W., Nilsen, A., Kelly, J. X., Li, Y., Doggett, J. S., Riscoe, E. W., Wegmann, K. W., Hinrichs, D. J. and Riscoe, M. K. (2012) 'Sontochin as a Guide to the Development of Drugs against Chloroquine-Resistant Malaria', *Antimicrob Agents Chemother,* 56 (7), 3475-3480.

Project MKULTRA, The CIA's Program of Research in Behavioral Modification (1977): Joint Hearing Before the Select Committee on Intelligence and the Subcommittee on Health and Scientific Research 95th Cong. August 3, 1977.

Public Health England (2014) *Guidelines for malaria prevention in travellers from the UK 2014.*

Public Health England (2017) Public Health England Letter (FOI Act) 27/04/lh/056 dated 26 May 2017.

Quinism Foundation (2020) The Quinism Foundation. https://quinism.org/ Page accessed 22 October 2020.

Quinn, J. (2006) Letter to General Sir Richard Dannatt KCB CBE MC dated 14 November 2006.
R v Ministry of Defence, ex parte Murray 1997. Queen's Bench Division. Judgement 1 Hooper J, Judgement 2 Lord Bingham C J.

RBL (2017) Royal British Legion, Public Affairs and Campaigns. Email Wed, 15 Feb 2017 10:04.

RBL (2020) Royal British Legion

https://www.britishlegion.org.uk/ Page accessed 30 September 2020.

Rénia, L., Howland, S. W., Claser, C., Gruner, A. C., Suwanurusk, R., Teo, T-H., Russell, B. and Ng, L. F. P. (2012) 'Cerebral malaria. Mysteries at the blood-brain barrier', *Virulence,* 3(2), 193-201.

Roche UK (1991) Application to Vary Licence, Lariam Tablets PL 0031/0236, Introduction to Variation Being Submitted.

Roche UK (2003) *Lariam. Summary of product Information.* May 2003.

Roche UK (2005) *Lariam. Summary of product Information.* Sep 2005.

Roche UK (2012) *Patient Product Information. Lariam.*

Roche UK (2013) *Summary of Product Characteristics.* Updated 13 February 2013.

Roche UK (2014) *Summary of Product Characteristics.* Revised 16 May 2014.

Roche UK (2015) Memorandum submitted by Roche Products Ltd. November 2015.

Roche UK (2016) Letter to Surgeon General, Defence Medical Services. Dr F Nichol, dated 7 October 2016.

Roche US (2002) Roche Laboratories Inc, New Jersey. Letter 'Dear Doctor'. September 2002.

Roche US (2003) Roche Laboratories Inc, New Jersey. Lariam brand of mefloquine hydrochloride Tablets. HLR 15 Aug2003.

Rooney, D. (2000) *Wingate and the Chindits: Redressing the Balance.* London: Cassell Military Paperbacks.

Slim, W. (2009) *Defeat into Victory.* London: Pan Books.

SPVA (2009) Services Personnel & Veterans Agency Letter BT185500D dated 17 April 2009.

Stateville Correctional Center (2020) https://prisoninsight.com/correctional-facilities/state/illinois/stateville-correctional-center/     Page accessed 27 May 2020.

Surgeon General (2009) Letter Surgeon General's Department, D Holdridge, Ref 01-09-2009-172334-004 dated 8 Oct 09.

Surgeon General (2010) Letter Surgeon General's Department, D Holdridge, Ref 23-03-2010-172334-004 dated 27 Apr 10.

Terrell, A. G., Forde, M. E., Firth, R. and Ross, D. A. (2015) 'Malaria Chemoprophylaxis and Self-Reported Impact on

Ability to Work: Mefloquine Versus Doxycycline', *Journal of Travel Medicine,* 22 (6): 383-388.

Thames Valley Police (2017) FOI Response HQ/PA/001035/17 dated 5 May 2017.

The Coroners (Investigations) Regulations (2013) Part 7. Action to prevent other deaths.
https://www.legislation.gov.uk/uksi/2013/1629/part/7/made
Page accessed 21 Sep 2020.

The Royal Irish Rangers, 27th (Inniskilling), 83rd & 87[th,] Regimental Association 'The Royal Irish Regiment and Sierra Leone 2000 Operation Barras',
https://www.royalirishrangers.co.uk/sierraleone.htm
Page accessed 3 July 2020.

They Work For You (2020) They Work For You. UK Parliament—House of Lords. Questions: The Countess of Mar.
theyworkforyou.com/search/?=mefloquine&pid=12904#n4
Accessed 6 August 2020.

Trenholme G. N., Williams R. L., Desjardins R. E., Frischer, H., Carson, P. E., Rieckmann, K. H. and Canfield, C. J. (1975) 'Mefloquine (WR 142,490) in the treatment of human malaria', *Science*, 190:792–4.

UNESCO (2005) Universal Declaration on Bioethics and Human Rights, 19 October 2005.

http://portal.unesco.org/en/ev.php-URL_ID=31058&URL_DO=DO_TOPIC&URL_SECTION=201.html Page accessed 1 July 2020.

US Africa Command (2011) United States Africa Command Notice, Health and Medical, Change to ACM 4200.03, Force Health Protection Procedures for Deployment and Travel, JOO-SG ACH 4200.02, dated 20 September 2011.

USA v Edward Mezvinsky (2002) US District Court for the Eastern District of Pennsylvania. Transcript of Proceedings, 15 March 2002.

USAMMDA (2020) US Army Medical Materiel Development Activity https://www.usammda.army.mil/ Page accessed 26 June 2020.

US Army (1945) HQ 2655th Malaria Control Detachment (OVHD) Office of the Malariologist, MTOUSA APO 512, U.S. Army. THGA/rlk. 30 September 1945.

US Food & Drug Administration (2020) About FDA. Learn about FDA, its mission, history, how it's organized, and more. https://www.fda.gov/about-fda Page accessed 9 July 2020.

Wallace, J. (2004) *Digging the Dirt. The Archaeological Imagination.* London: Duckworth.

War Office (1922) Statistics of the Military Effort of the British Empire During the Great War. 1914-1920. London: HMSO.

Winkenwerder, W. (2002) Letter, The Assistant Secretary of Defence, September 13, 2002.

Weina, P. A. (1998) 'From Atabrine in World War II to Mefloquine in Somalia: The Role of Education in Preventive Medicine, *Military Medicine,* 163, 635-639.

World Health Organisation (1983) 'Development of mefloquine as an antimalarial drug', *Bulletin of the World Health Organisation,* 62 (2), 169-178.

World Health Organisation (2001) 'World Medical Association Declaration of Helsinki. Ethical Principles for Medical Research Involving Human Subjects', *Bulletin of the World Health Organisation,* 79 (4), 373-374.

World Health Organisation (2019a) The "World malaria report 2019" at a glance.
https://www.who.int/news-room/feature-stories/detail/world-malaria-report-2019 Page accessed 24 June 2020.

World Health Organisation (2019b) International Classification of Diseases (ICD 11) 7B01.2 Nightmare Disorder
https://icd.who.int/browse11/l-m/en#/http://id.who.int/icd/entity/1900730309 Page accessed 4 June 2020.

WPA (2009) War Pensions and Armed Forces Compensation (105) Assessment Appeal. NINO: BT 185500D, Further Contents.

WRAIR (2018) Records of the Army Medical Research Program on Malaria, 1963-1979. Walter Reed Army Institute of Research Archives, Gorgas Memorial Library.

WRAIR (2020) Walter Reed Army Institute of Research. Soldier Health. World Health. https://www.wrair.army.mil/ Pages accessed 17-19 May 2020.

3PB (2018) 3PB In Proposed Proceedings Between Lt Col (Retd) Andrew Marriott and The Ministry of Defence (1) and Roche Products Ltd (2). Advice. 3PB November 8th 2018.

Media:
Andrew Marr Show (2011) Transcript of Liam Fox Interview, 29 May 2011. News,
https://news.bbc.co.uk/1/hi/programmes/andrew_marr_show/9500001.stm Page accessed 26 July 2020.

BBC News (2003) UK soldier contracts Lassa fever.
http://news.bbc.co.uk/1/hi/health/2746015.stm Page accessed 24 April 2020.

BBC News (2011) Dr David Kelly: Controversial death examined.
https://www.bbc.co.uk/news/uk-13716127 Page accessed 2 August 2020.

BBC News (2015) Call for army to stop using malaria drug mefloquine. Sima Kotecha, Today Programme
https://www.bbc.co.uk/news/uk-33943282 Page accessed 12 August 2020.

BBC News (2017a) Who are the Guantanamo Brits? By Steve Swann. bbc.co.uk/news/uk-39115761 Page accessed 9 June 2020.

BBC News (2017b) Sir Michael Fallon resigns, saying his conduct 'fell short' https://www.bbc.co.uk/news/uk-politics-41838682 Page accessed 26 August 2020.

BBC News (2020) Volkswagen loses landmark 'dieselgate' case. https://www.bbc.co.uk/news/business-52795376 25 May 2020. Page accessed 4 November 2020.

CBS Baltimore (2014) Notoriously Dangerous Md. House of Correction In Jessup Being Demolished. baltimore.cbslocal.com/2014/01/17/md-house-of-correction-in Jessup-being-destroyed/ Page accessed 24 May 2020.
Eastern Daily Press (2010) Former head of the British Army, General Sir Richard Dannatt, is set to sleep rough on the streets of Norwich—after he was made president of YMCA Norfolk https://www.edp24.co.uk/edp-property/former-army-head-to-sleep-rough-in-norwich-1-684467 Page accessed 23 July 2020.

Forces Net (2016) Royal Navy Nurse Found Dead At Her Home. https://www.forces.net/services/navy/royal-navy-nurse-found-dead-her-home Page accessed 22 Sep 2020.

Guantanamo Bay: World's most controversial prison. Free Doc Bites. Free Documentary. 30 Oct 2019.

youtube.com/watch?v=SHctHcGCdlM

Gov.UK (2015) Defence in the Media: 25 September 2015. Lariam. https://modmedia.blog.gov.uk/2015/09/25/defence-in-the-media-25-september-2015/ Page accessed 14 July 2020.

Mercer, J. (2015) Video, Johnny Mercer, Lariam, 27 Aug 2015. https://www.youtube.com/watch?v=M3-5C4ceWg8 Viewed 28 August 2015.

Johnny Mercer (2019) Johnny Mercer Live, 15 Nov 2019. https://www.facebook.com/JohnnyForPlymouth/videos/4102 19136535853/ Page accessed 23 Sep 2020.

Mefloquine: The anti-malarial drug investigation (2017). Produced and directed by Cailean Watt. Vimeo.com.

RTÉ (2013) RTÉ Prime Time Broadcast 23 May 2013 https://www.rte.ie/news/player/prime-time-web/2013/0523/

Rhyl Journal (2015) Tributes paid to loving Rhyl mum and former soldier. https://www.rhyljournal.co.uk/news/15722458.tributes-paid-to-loving-rhyl-mum-and-former-soldier/ Page accessed 19 Sep 2020.

Rhyl Journal (2018) Former Prestatyn soldier killed herself after battle against depression.

https://www.rhyljournal.co.uk/news/15825742.former-prestatyn-soldier-killed-battle-depression/ Page accessed 19 Sep 2020.

The Daily Mail (2015) Former female soldier with PTSD found hanged 18 months after leaving the Army. https://www.dailymail.co.uk/news/article-3356940/Former-female-soldier-PTSD-hanged-18-months-leaving-Army.html Page accessed 19 Sep 2020.

The Daily Post (2020) Ex-Royal Marine and bodyguard to the stars battled PTSD before his death, inquest hears. https://www.dailypost.co.uk/news/north-wales-news/ex-royal-marine-bodyguard-stars-19022900 Page accessed 30 Sep 2020.

The Daily Telegraph (2019) Cambridge student leapt to her death from plane after fighting off friend. Friday 2 August 2019.

The Guardian (2014) Thalidomide: how men who blighted lives of thousands evaded justice. Fri 14 Nov 2014. https://www.theguardian.com/society/2014/nov/14/-sp-thalidomide-pill-how-evaded-justice Page accessed 25 September 2020.

The Guardian (2017) Body of Iraq WMD dossier scientist David Kelly exhumed. https://www.theguardian.com/politics/2017/oct/29/body-of-wmd-dossier-scientist-david-kelly-exhumed Page accessed 2 August 2020.

The Independent (1997) Soames linked to manufacturer of Gulf War drug. https://www.independent.co.uk/news/soames-linked-to-manufacturer-of-gulf-war-drug-1234292.html Page accessed 13 April 2016.

The Independent (2013) The Lariam Scandal: Former head of army calls for ban on malaria drug. 27 September 2013.

The Independent (2017) Why was 'compensation' paid to British Guantanamo detainees—and why are Blair and Blunkett now distancing themselves from the money? Independent.co.uk/voices/Guantanamo-bay-gitmo-british-detainee-jamal-al-harif-suicide-attack-blair-blunkett-a7596041.html Page accessed 9 June 2020.

The Lake County Star (2020) Stateville prison reopens F-House to hold COVID-19 inmates. https://www.lakecountystar.com/news/article/Stateville-prison-reopens-F-House-to-hold-15272639.php Page accessed 27 may 2020.

The Lariam Legacy (2015). BBC Radio 4. A Whistledown production produced by Deborah Dudgeon.

The New York Times (1974) Prison Official in Illinois Halts Malaria Research on Inmates. https://www.nytimes.com/1974/04/28/archives/prison-official-in-illinois-halts-malaria-research-on-inmates.html Page accessed 25 May 2020.

The New York Times (2006) 3 Prisoners Commit Suicide at
Guantánamo.
https://www.nytimes.com/2006/06/11/us/11gitmo.html Page
accessed 9 July 2020.

The New York Times (2020) The F.D.A. Is in Trouble. Here's
How to Fix It.
https://www.nytimes.com/2020/01/11/opinion/sunday/fda-
commissioner-stephen-hahn.html Page accessed 9 July 2020.

The New Yorker (2012) Operation Delirium.
new.yorker.com/magazine/2012/12/17/operation-delirium.
Page accessed 12 June 2012.

The Northern Echo (2017a) Michael Fallon—a creature of a
different age? 3 November 2017.
https://www.thenorthernecho.co.uk/news/15638189.michael
-fallon---creature-different-age/ Page accessed 26 August
2020.

The Northern Echo (2017b) Ex-Armed Forces chef, 44, died
facing long-term debts—inquest told.
https://www.thenorthernecho.co.uk/news/15114218.ex-
armed-forces-chef-44-died-facing-long-term-debts---
inquest-hears/Page accessed 23 Feb 2017.

The Observer (2000) British troops risk brain damage from
malaria pill. Special report: Sierra Leone. Paul Harris. 10
September 2000.

The Sunday Telegraph (2009) Sunday Telegraph Magazine.
The insect above can kill you. The pill below will protect you.

But what if that pill ruins your life? Rose George. 8 March 2009.

The Sunday Telegraph (2019) Student summoned 'incredible strength' to open plane door/Did Lariam send Alana to her death. 4 August 2019.

The Sunday Times (2018) MOD cash for soldier hit by Lariam drug seizures.
https://www.thetimes.co.uk/article/mod-cash-for-soldier-hit-by-lariam-drug-seizures-kz79mdn28 Page accessed 7 August 2020.

The Times (2015) First pay out over drug blamed for soldier's suicides.
https://www.thetimes.co.uk/article/first-pay-out-over-drug-blamed-for-soliders-suicides-rkv7lc7pt6t Page accessed 2 October 2020.

The Times (2018) MoD cash for soldier hit by Lariam drug seizures.
https://www.thetimes.co.uk/article/mod-cash-for-soldier-hit-by-lariam-drug-seizures-kz79mdn28#:~:text=The%20Ministry%20of%20Defence%20has,before%20an%20expected%20court%20case. Page accessed 2 October 2020.

The Times (2019) Student paranoid before plane death, say family. Friday August 2 2019.

The Washington Post (1979) Not the only solider hit by Patton. J Couch.

Time (2013) A Smoking Pillbox: Evidence that Sgt Bales May Have Been on Lariam. By Elspeth Cameron Ritichie June 20, 2013. file:///G:/Lariam/A%20Smoking%20Pillbox_%20Evidence %20that%20Sgt.%20Bales%20May%20Have%20Been%20 on%20Lariam%20_%20TIME.com.html Page accessed 7 July 2020.

Victoria Derbyshire BBC Two (2016). Joanna Gosling interview with General Lord Dannatt, 31 August 2016.

Voice of America (2001) VOA News. Carolyn Weaver Now Science Segment (4:00) MAY 17, 2001.

# Appendix-1

## MINISTRY OF DEFENCE

**ARMY**

*Army Medical Directorate (Medico-Legal)*
*The Former Army Staff College, Slim Road*
*Camberley, Surrey, GU15 4NP*

Telephone: 01276 41 2705 (Administrator)
Telephone: 01276 41 2727 (Personal)
Facsimile: 01276 41 2715 (Fax) Camberley Military 2715
Email : medleg@amd.mod.uk

| | |
|---|---|
| **Personal for:** | Your Reference: SE06000515 |
| Crown Office & Procurator Fiscal Service | |
| Procurator Fiscal's Office | Our Reference: D/AMD/Med Leg/16575(R) |
| Sheriff Court | |
| SELKIRK | |
| TD7 4LE | Date: 3 July 2006 |

### 539025 QUINN C J M (DECEASED)

Thank you for your letter of 22 June 2006 which has been passed to this Directorate. I note your general query concerning prescribing of chemoprophylaxis for Kenya deployments in 2002. The Ministry of Defence's policy on Prevention of Malaria is and remains that the use of drugs to prevent malaria is based on the guidelines issued by the Advisory Committee on Malaria Prevention of the Public Health Laboratory Service. Chemoprophylaxis is, of course, only one pillar of the prevention of malaria the others being education, bite avoidance and mosquito vector control.

The above explains that in general terms the Ministry of Defence follows medical practice as laid down by the Public Health Laboratory Service, now called the Health Protection Agency. The Ministry has a Defence Consultant in Communicable Disease Control who works from the Defence Medical Services Department (previously called the Surgeon General's Department) leading on such policies.

If you require me to comment specifically on the individual case I could obtain Mr Quinn's Service medical records and, with consent of the next of kin, provide specific advice from those records.

The Army provides full Primary Medical Care to its servicemen and uses Secondary Medical Care partly through the NHS and partly through Ministry of Defence resources. If a serviceman has a problem with a particular drug or any other medical problem he should consult his Service doctor in the normal way. I am unaware of the concept of "Lariam days". It is likely that I would be aware of them as I was closely involved advising in a group action against the Ministry of Defence brought by servicemen deploying to Sierra Leone who had been prescribed Lariam in 2000. You should be aware that the cases were discontinued against the Ministry of Defence as the Ministry was able to show it had followed expert advice on malaria prevention in a logical and rigorous way.

I do hope that the above is of some help to you although I appreciate it may not be quite what Mrs Quinn wishes to hear.

*Yours sincerely*

SP

# Appendix-2

*'Horseshoe Cottage', Main Street, West Linton, Peeblesshire EH46 7EA*
*Tel: 01986 660261*

General Sir Richard Dannatt KCB CBE MC
Chief of the General Staff
Main Building
Ministry of Defence
Whitehall
London SW1A 2HB

14th November 2006

Dear General Dannatt,

### Re: Lariam (mefloquine)

I am writing to urge you to order an investigation into the continued prescribing of Lariam, also known as mefloquine, in the British Army. My concerns have arisen out of my own devastating experience, as a former Army wife.

On 11th March 2006 my much-loved husband and devoted father of our children, the late Major Cameron JM Quinn (1 Highlanders, retired), took his own life. This happened in our bedroom at home, whilst I and my two daughters, then aged 8 and 5, were in the room below him.

The sequence of tragic events which led up to my husband's terrible death is as follows.

In 2001 my husband was prescribed Lariam for a battalion exercise to Kenya, after which he developed severe suicidal depression. Before this time he had no previous history of any mental disorder whatsoever. Unwilling to seek advice from his MO due to the nature of his symptoms, my husband simply stopped taking Lariam before the end of the treatment course, and for a time his mood returned to normal. In the following years however he suffered relapses which took the form of mood swings, episodes of loss of self-worth and frightening dreams which he referred to as 'Lariam dreams'.

On the morning of my husband's death, he told me he had experienced 'Lariam dreams' during the night. As I am not a health professional myself, I was not equipped with the specialist knowledge to identify that my husband's state of mind was any worse that day than on the many previous occasions when he had mentioned such dreams. I could not therefore intervene to prevent my husband's suicide (for example, by keeping him closely in my sight at all times).

I believe, as do our wider families and also my husband's many friends both civilian and military, that the anti-malarial drug Lariam played a pivotal role in his decision to take his own life. In addition, the Procurator Fiscal for Lothian & Borders, who is investigating my husband's death has strongly expressed the same view and has written to the Ministry of Defence, to seek clarification about their use of Lariam. Prescribing Lariam to soldiers is after all very different situation to prescribing anti-malarials for the average tourist, who is able to make a personal decision as to whether they visit a high-risk malaria zone or not, and what drugs they may or may not choose to take whilst doing this.

Prior to and even more so in the months following my husband's death I became aware that there are many other soldiers who have suffered similar psychological reactions to Lariam. While soldiers are reluctant to report vague physical or mental symptoms which, rightly or wrongly, might have a negative impact on their future careers, they nevertheless freely discuss between themselves the effects of this particular drug.

Since my husband's death, I have been party to the stories of other serving and retired officers who have told me of the varied and sometimes bizarre psychological side effects that they, their colleagues or their soldiers experienced after taking Lariam during their Army service. As was also the case with my husband, some of these side effects I have been told about continued for many years after Lariam was taken, and in some cases are still continuing.

It causes me great concern that a drug that can so effectively alter the normal thought processes of an individual, and which has been shown to cause long term brain damage (recent scientific evidence shows this), is still being given to serving soldiers. There also appears to be no rigorous follow-up process in the Army to identify individuals, such as my husband, who have suffered side effects while taking this drug.

The manufacturers of Lariam now state 'suicide and suicidal tendencies' as a recognised side-effect of this drug and there have been cases of violent suicide reported in connection with Lariam in the United States. I am therefore concerned that my husband's death may not be the only one to have occurred in the British Army, as a direct result of this drug.

My husband took Lariam on his first exercise in Kenya but refused it for his second exercise, a year later. He told me that he stated the reasons why he was unhappy about taking Lariam again, but I have a copy of his medical record and it appears that these concerns were never documented, or else the record of the consultation has gone missing from his medical folder.

My husband had had a serious adverse reaction to Lariam but in the absence of any documentation it is difficult to know whether this was ignored, or whether the significance of his symptoms was not realised. Although my husband was not 'killed in action', his life ended as prematurely and as violently as if he were.

The overriding reason for this letter to you, General, is to ask you to investigate my concerns and, if Lariam does predispose soldiers to developing severe mental reactions, then take action to ensure that another Army wife and family does not suffer these same catastrophic consequences.

It is with the greatest respect that I ask for your intervention in this very important matter.

Yours sincerely,


Mrs Jane Quinn

# Appendix-3

**ARMY**

GS/1/4/3 (CGS)

General Sir Richard Dannatt KCB CBE MC ADC Gen
Chief of the General Staff
5th Floor, Zone M,
Main Building, Whitehall, London, SW1A 2HB

| | | | |
|---|---|---|---|
| Telephone | 020 7218 7114 | Military | (9621) 87114 |
| Switchboard | 020 7218 9000 | Switchboard | (9621) 89000 |
| Fax | 020 7218 2474 | Fax | (9621) 82474 |

Dr Jane Quinn
'Horseshoe Cottage'
Main Street
West Linton
Peeblesshire
EH46 7EA

21st January 2007

Dear Dr Quinn,

I am writing further to my letter of 22nd November having also received a copy of your letter of 15th December.

Wing Commander Green, Defence Consultant Adviser in Communicable Diseases, has set out in his very comprehensive letter dated 28th November the medical basis for the continued use of Lariam (using its generic name of Mefloquine). In accordance with national and international guidelines, I can confirm that it is the Army's policy to continue to prescribe Lariam on the basis that it is an extremely effective drug at preventing malaria in parts of the world where British troops deploy. Wing Commander Green has set out why it is preferred to other available alternatives. In addition, the benefit of its use in preventing a life-threatening infection has been balanced against the risk of adverse consequences arising from its use. I should add that I have some personal experience of this drug but, on balance, am content to go with the formal advice.

Soldiers are told by the chain of command of the need to seek medical advice if they experience significant or worrying side-effects from their use of anti-malarial drugs given the importance of continuing to take these drugs in malaria-endemic areas. Where the medical system is made aware of symptoms which may be linked to the use of anti-malarial drugs, these side-effects will be managed in accordance with clinical need. This may include referral to a mental health professional and in extreme cases the Army has a set of very rigorous guidelines for managing soldiers believed to be vulnerable to suicide.

Finally, I have enquired into medical practice for recording the concerns of those suffering side-effects from the use of anti-malarial drugs. It is normal practice to record not only side-effects but also an individual's concerns following use. I do not know whether your husband made any specific comments about his concerns from using Lariam but it appears there is nothing to suggest any recorded comments have been removed. It continues to be the case that servicemen are offered alternative drugs when they are unwilling or unable to take specific medication.

May I reassure you that the continued prescription of Lariam to soldiers will be kept under review and in line with national and international best practice. I sympathise deeply with your truly heartbreaking circumstances and thank you for raising your concerns with me.

Please do not hesitate to get in touch, if I can help further.

Yours sincerely,

Richard Benyon

# Appendix 4

| | |
|---|---|
| **Thames Valley Police**<br>Chief Constable Francis Habgood QPM | Headquarters<br>Oxford Road<br>Kidlington<br>Oxfordshire<br>OX5 2NX |

Mr Josh Hastings

Telephone: 101
Direct dial: 01865 542051
Email: publicaccess@thamesvalley.pnn.police.uk

**Our ref:**     HQ/PA/001035/17

05 May 2017

Dear Mr Hastings

I write in response to the above-referenced Freedom of Information Act (FOIA) request submitted on 04 April 2017. Thames Valley Police has now considered this request, which for clarity, has been repeated below:

| Request | Response |
|---|---|
| Dear Thames Valley Police, | This request is being refused under **Section 12(2)** of the FOIA. |
| Under the Freedom of Information Act 2000 I have some queries about the investigation in to the death of Dr David Kelly: | Section 12 of the FOIA allows that public authorities do not have to comply with section 1(1) of the Act if the cost of complying would exceed the appropriate limit. In accordance with the Freedom of Information Act, this letter represents a Refusal Notice for this request. |
| 1. (a) At what time was Thames Valley's chief constable alerted about the discovery of the body of Dr Kelly ? | |
| 2. (a) Why did DC Graham Coe, one of the first on the scene, not tell the Hutton inquiry that there was a third 'suited' man with him and his partner DC Colin Shields when the body was discovered, as some eyewitnesses had claimed?<br>(b) Why did he subsequently admitted this to be the case after saying otherwise?<br>(c) Why does he still refuse to name him this man publicly?<br>(d) Does Thames Valley Police know who this man was/is?<br>(e) If so, who was he working for? | This information is not held in an easily retrievable format and would require a manual search of the full file. It is estimated that this would exceed the appropriate 18 hour time and £450 cost limit.<br><br>**Section 16:- Further advice & assistance**<br>Under the provisions of the FOIA legislation, Thames Valley Police are obliged to disclose recorded information and not necessarily answer questions or confirm/deny |

www.thamesvalley.police.uk

**Thames Valley Police**
Chief Constable Francis Habgood QPM

3. (a) Former MP Robert Jackson said Dr Kelly's GP, Dr Malcolm Warner told him he saw the Dr Kelly's body immediately after its discovery. Why was that fact not disclosed to the Hutton inquiry at the time?

4. (a) How did Dr Kelly cut his left wrist if, as those who knew him said, his right arm was damaged to such a degree that he struggled cutting steak?
(b) Why was the ulnar artery severed rather than the radial, which is how the cut would naturally have been made, from left to right, with the right hand?
(c) Could this suggest the wound was made by a third party?

5. (a) Why were there no fingerprints on the knife when Dr Kelly was not wearing gloves or on the bottle from which he supposedly drank to swallow the tablets?
(b) Why was that fact not disclosed to the Hutton inquiry at the time?

6. (a) Why did a helicopter which passed over the scene with heat-seeking equipment not detect the body so soon after Dr Kelly likely died?
(b) Why was that fact not disclosed to the Hutton inquiry at the time?

7. (a) What explains the discrepancy between the account of the position of the body given by the person(s) who discovered it and the paramedics when they arrived?
(b) Did someone or something move the body and/or destroy evidence?
(c) Did Dr Kelly die where his body was found?
(d) Why did the head of the investigation into Dr Kelly's death, Superintendent Alan Young of Thames Valley Police, not

statements. Under Section 8, the majority of the elements of your request are questions and therefore, not deemed to be valid under the provisions of the Act.

give evidence to the Hutton inquiry at the time?

8. (a) Why did Operation Mason, the police code-name for the search for Dr Kelly, officially start before his family had reported him missing?
(b) did Who authorised the opening of documentation on the operation and at precisely what time? and for what reason?
(c) Did the Thames Valley Police and/or others remove wallpaper in Dr Kelly's home?
(d) Some have claimed that Dr Kelly was writing/had written a book. Did Thames Valley Police take any writings such as a manuscript (digital or on paper) as evidence during the investigation?
(e) Where are his belongings and any other evidence on the case now?
(f) Has any belongings/evidence been returned to Dr Kelly's family?

9. (a) Whose fingerprints where on Dr Kelly's dental records file that went missing for 24 hours from his surgery on the day of his death?. (Information confirming the existence of the fingerprints was released under an FOI request on 23 May 2011.)
(b) Why was contradicting evidence about this given to the Hutton inquiry at the time?

10. (a) Why was Dr Kelly's death certificate only completed on August 18th 2003, a whole three weeks into the Hutton inquiry?

11. (a) Does Thames Valley police know why Lord Hutton placed a 70 year embargo on release of the post-mortem documents?
(b) Did Lord Hutton provide a written (e.g

**Thames Valley Police**
Chief Constable Francis Habgood QPM

| | |
|---|---|
| an email or letter) explanation for this to Thames Valley Police?<br>(c) If so can I see a copy of this document/correspondence?<br><br>12. (a) There where reports at the time of a helicopter landing a the scene after Dr Kelly's body was discovered, did this helicopter belong to Thames Valley Police?<br>(b) If not,to what organisation or individual did it belong?<br>(c) Who was on board the helicopter at the time?<br>(d) Why was this helicopter at the scene?<br>(d) What was the registration number of the helicopter?<br>(e) Can I see the helicopter's flight log for that day?<br><br>13. (a) Did Thames Valley police erect a large communications mast outside Dr Kelly's house immediately after he was declared missing?<br>(b) If so, under whose instruction?<br><br>I appreciate it could take some time to answer these questions, please tell if that is the case and roughly when I can expect a reply.<br><br>Many thanks,<br>Josh Hastings | |

**Complaint Rights**

If you are dissatisfied with the handling procedures or the decision made by Thames Valley Police, you can lodge a complaint with the force to have the decision reviewed within two months of the date of this response. Complaints should be made in writing to the FOI inbox; publicaccess@thamesvalley.pnn.police.uk.

If, after lodging a complaint with Thames Valley Police, you are still unhappy with the outcome, you may make application to the Information Commissioner at the

**Thames Valley Police**
Chief Constable Francis Habgood QPM

Information Commissioner's Office, Wycliffe House, Water Lane, Wilmslow, Cheshire, SK9 5AF.

If you require any further assistance, please do not hesitate to contact this office.

Yours sincerely

Jonathan Hands
Public Access
Joint Information Management Unit